KANTIAN COURAGE

just ideas

transformative ideals of justice in ethical and political thought

series editors

Drucilla Cornell

Roger Berkowitz

Kenneth Michael Panfilio

KANTIAN COURAGE

ADVANCING THE ENLIGHTENMENT IN
CONTEMPORARY POLITICAL THEORY

Nicholas Tampio

FORDHAM UNIVERSITY PRESS

NEW YORK   2012

Library of Congress Cataloging-in-Publication Data is available from the publisher.

Printed in the United States of America

14 13 12 5 4 3 2 1

First edition

Contents

Preface

The Enlightenment was an intellectual and political movement committed to charting a new course for Europe and North America after the religious wars of the seventeenth century. The Enlightenment continues to shape academia and progressive politics by supplying ideas, conceptual toolkits, and an ethos celebrating the construction of timely political theories. How is it possible to continue the Enlightenment, though, after Darwin shifted the conversation about human nature in the nineteenth century, the Holocaust displayed barbarity at the historical center of the Enlightenment, and the 9/11 attacks showed the need to modify both the ideals and the strategies of the Enlightenment? This book considers how several of the most important political theorists of our time—including the American liberal John Rawls, the French poststructuralist Gilles Deleuze, and the Muslim political reformer Tariq Ramadan—take up the legacy of perhaps the key figure in contemporary debates about the Enlightenment, Immanuel Kant. Drawing upon Michel Foucault's late writings on the Enlightenment, I contend that political progressives should embody Kantian courage—a critical and creative disposition to invent new political theories to address the problems of the age—rather than take up any particular idea or system of ideas, such as the categorical imperative or the metaphysics of morals. In this preface, I explain why scholars of the Enlightenment, political theorists and political philosophers, and a general audience concerned about the future of the relationship between Islam and the West may find this book interesting.

The initial aim of this book is to provide a map of contemporary political theory as well as an in-depth investigation of several of its most important figures. Rawls, Deleuze, and Ramadan draw profoundly upon the Kantian ethos, Kantian metaethics (such as constructivism), and the critical philosophy as a whole. Discovering the Kantian themes in one of these authors may provide clues for where to find Kantian traces in the others; read in conjunction, these authors indicate what elements of Kant's philosophy are central or peripheral for contemporary intellectual and political life. One purpose of this book, then, is to understand better difficult authors at the peak of Anglo-American, Continental, and Islamic political thought and their common predecessor, Kant. Yet this scholarly exercise is undertaken with the conviction that authors are envelopes of ideas and that we study philosophic giants to gain insight into the big issues that concern us, such as the future of the Enlightenment.

The next aim of this book is to forge a conversation about shared matters of concern across intellectual traditions. Kant is one of the few authors read by most students of Anglo-American and Continental philosophy, and, increasingly, philosophers and theologians around the world. Kant, then, may be a resource for building a *lingua franca* that global citizens may use to discuss common concerns about how to construct new ideas or better honor human dignity. In this book, I employ this Kantian *lingua franca* to show how Rawls, Deleuze, and Ramadan formulate political principles and concepts for deeply pluralistic communities. I argue for and aspire to exemplify a broad-minded style of progressive political theory that moves across disparate national, philosophical, and religious traditions.

Finally, this book envisions the future of the Enlightenment in the face of the global Islamic revival. Kant's philosophy, in its original form, does not contain much guidance for negotiating religious pluralism. Yet Rawls and Deleuze employed Kantian strategies to construct new political theories that could better address the problem of pluralism. Alas, neither Rawls nor Deleuze wrote much on Islamic political thought or Muslim politics, for the understandable reason that there were not many Muslims in Europe or the United States in the mid-twentieth century. Today, however, Islam and Muslims have become a vibrant presence in Europe and the United States. Furthermore, Muslim political reformers—many of whom take up the legacy of the Nahda, the mid–nineteenth- to mid–twentieth-century Arab cultural renaissance—have been rethinking how Muslims may contribute to as well as challenge liberal democratic polities and political cultures. This book aims to respond to one such effort with agonistic respect, appreciative of the need to collaborate with a wide range of peoples on matters of common concern. To prevent the emergence of new religious wars and advance the

Enlightenment into the twenty-first century, we may need to forge a new Enlightenment-Nahda assemblage.

This book reflects decades of thinking about the philosophical foundations of progressive politics. For supporting this ambition in an inquisitive boy and young man, I thank my parents: Charles and Phyllis Tampio and Nancy and Guy McMichael. Guy, in particular, opened new vistas by giving me a copy of Peter Gay's *The Enlightenment*, a model, in a different style, for this book. My brother Jesse has served as a sounding board for many of my ideas and projects. Many other family members and friends have asked me questions, raised points, and shown me love and support at key junctures.

Outstanding teachers—including Robert Hines in the IB program at Richard Montgomery High School, Eugene Lewis at New College of Florida, Jeffrey C. Isaac at Indiana University, and William E. Connolly, Jane Bennett, and Richard Flathman at Johns Hopkins University—have guided me on my political theory studies. In addition to supervising my dissertation, Bill Connolly has shown me the exhilaration and importance of envisioning a better world. The gambles taken in this book would not have been possible without his support and encouragement.

For creating an environment in which it made perfect sense to debate the relationship between Kant's ethics and politics late at night on rooftops and in living rooms in Baltimore, I thank my friends from graduate school, including Harry Gould, Patrick Peel, Lars Tønder, Andrew Ross, Riccardo Pelizzo, Paulina Ochoa-Espejo, and John O'Doherty. Matt Filner has remained a close friend and advisor since our time together in Bloomington.

Many of the ideas in this book have been presented at conferences and events sponsored by the American Political Science Association, the Western Political Science Association, the Association for Political Theory, Deleuze Studies, the Middle Eastern Middle Eastern American Center, and the American Philosophical Association. Stephen K. White taught me the ropes of academic publishing when I served as his assistant editor at *Political Theory*. Mary Dietz and anonymous reviewers at *Political Theory* gave me valuable advice on how to navigate the terrain between Euro-American and Islamic political thought.

Most of the ideas in this book were originally tested out in classrooms at Johns Hopkins, the University of Virginia, George Mason University, Hamilton College, and Fordham University. I thank my colleagues and students from those institutions, including my first two graduate students at

Fordham: Yulia Golobokova and Bret Nelson. Patrick J. Ryan, S.J. and I discussed Islamic political thought once a week over tea in the fall of 2009. Three Fordham philosophy professors—Allan Hazlett (now at the University of Edinburgh), Jeffrey Flynn, and Samir Haddad—and I met regularly from 2008 to 2010 to talk about the *Critique of Pure Reason* as well as books on Islam and secularism. My Fordham political science colleagues—including Bruce Berg, William Baumgarth, Jeffrey Cohen, Jonathan Crystal, John Entellis, Nicole Fermon, Melissa Labonte, and Robert J. Hume—have shared valuable insights. William Germano has taught me, and a generation of young scholars, how to turn a manuscript into a book.

I thank Helen Tartar at Fordham University Press for her enthusiasm for this project as well as the two external reviewers, Mort Schoolman and Paul Patton, for recommendations on how to improve the manuscript. *Political Theory* has graciously permitted me to reprint sections of my article, "Constructing the Space of Testimony: Tariq Ramadan's Copernican Revolution," vol. 39, no. 5, October 2011. The Fordham Dean's Office and Office of Research provided much appreciated grants to complete this book.

Finally and most importantly, I wish to express my love and gratitude to my wife Gina and our three sons Giuliano, Luca, and Nicola. The final drafts of this book were written in a house filled with laughter, and memorable scenes of our boys discovering the world. Gina is an amazing wife, mother, editor, advisor, and friend: marrying and raising a family with her is the best thing that has ever happened to me.

KANTIAN COURAGE

Introduction:
Advancing the Enlightenment

I've come here to seek a new beginning between the United States and Muslims around the world, one based on mutual interest and mutual respect, and one based upon the truth that America and Islam are not exclusive and need not be in competition. Instead, they overlap, and share common principles—principles of justice and progress; tolerance and the dignity of all human beings.

—BARACK OBAMA, "On a New Beginning"

On January 27, 2009, US President Barack Obama announced that the War on Terror was over. Appearing on the Al Arabiya news network for his first official interview as president, Obama explained, "The language we use matters." The language of war on terror perpetuates a Manichaean dualism between good and evil, the West and Islamic violent extremists.[1] We need new terms of art, according to Obama, to distinguish between those who seek the violent destruction of the United States and those who make thoughtful criticisms of American foreign policy in the Middle East. Obama's new concept for the conflict in Iraq and Afghanistan was "overseas contingency operations."[2] The advantage of this term is that it avoids the inflammatory rhetoric that arguably helped contribute to atrocities in such places as the Abu Ghraib prison in Iraq or the Guantanamo Bay detention camp in Cuba.[3] The disadvantage of this term, however, is that it does not contain much descriptive or normative force.[4] Who are we and what are we fighting for? Obama's impetus is admirable, but he is grappling with a question that consumes many political actors and theorists on the left: How do we find or construct the language we need for contemporary political circumstances?

This book is born of the conviction that the Enlightenment remains a valuable resource for progressive political thinking. Certain aspects of the Enlightenment—such as Kant's views on gender and race—clearly need to be jettisoned or refashioned. But other aspects of the Enlightenment— particularly its critical ethos, or what I call *Kantian courage*—can inspire us to create new concepts to envision the singular opportunities and dangers of our time. To flesh out this argument, I draw upon several of the most important political thinkers of our time—including the Kant scholar Allen W. Wood, the political liberal John Rawls, the French poststructuralist Gilles Deleuze, and the Muslim political reformer Tariq Ramadan—as they take up the legacy of Kant, widely considered to be the most profound and influential Enlightenment philosopher. In this introduction, I provide the historical and sociological context of my argument, analyze Kant's legacy and its components, describe the main participants in the book's Socratic dialogue about the future of the Enlightenment, and offer a map of the book's itinerary. Though the book is a work of scholarship—describing the state of Kantian political theory in the twenty-first century—the book also presents a vision of the Enlightenment as a living tradition.[5]

TWO WARS

Political theorists respond to crises in the world. When historical events sunder traditional ways of thinking, acting, and feeling, theorists have an opportunity to illuminate new paths for human beings to reconstitute their world. By inventing concepts and schemes, theorists may fashion a political cosmos out of political chaos, helping human beings rearrange their affairs in new ways after old ways have disintegrated.[6] One of the most important events in modern European history is the Thirty Years War (1618–48), and its unprecedented scale of religious violence helped call into being the intellectual and political movement known subsequently as the Enlightenment.[7] Below, we consider parallels and divergences between this conflict and recent forms of religious warfare. But first, we review the scale of devastation and the lessons learned by the European Enlightenment thinkers.[8]

The human and material costs of the Thirty Years War were astonishing. Though figures are difficult to calculate precisely, approximately five to eight million people died in the conflict, 20 to 32 percent of the Holy Roman Empire's prewar population. The raw numbers of Europeans killed during major conflicts between 1914–18 (27 million) and 1939–45 (33.8) were much higher, but the percentage of the population was much smaller (5.5 and 6 percent, respectively).[9] The causes of death were manifold—soldiers killed in battle, civilians slaughtered in massacres, everyone decimated by the war's spread of Bubonic plague, typhus, starvation, governmental breakdown, ecological devastation, and forced migration. Losses around Prague reached at least 50 percent, and certain towns in the bishopric of Halberstadt lost between seven- and nine-tenths of their inhabitants.[10] Europe's population levels in 1618 were not reached again for nearly a century.[11] Those who survived the war watched the old world disintegrate before their eyes. Hyperinflation led people to abandon industry and agriculture, despondent about their futures and fearful that soldiers would steal whatever they produced.[12] Ancient structures of authority collapsed, as numerous lordships, abbeys and manors were appropriated and redistributed. Once esteemed families became bankrupt and destroyed, and new men such as the Habsburg general Wallenstein climbed the social ranks.[13] The Catholic Church was left in a fundamentally altered state, as, for instance, the ratio of clergy to parishioners in the Habsburg Sundgau in Alsace fell from 1:345 to 1:1,177.[14] In addition to the concrete cost of lives and objects destroyed, the Thirty Years War had a profound effect on the modern European imaginary. In the 1960s, Germans told public opinion polls that they rated the Thirty Years War as the greatest disaster in the country's history, ahead of the world wars, the Holocaust, and the Black Death.[15] In literature, art, philosophy, and folk wisdom, the Thirty Years War became, in historian Peter H. Wilson's words, "Europe's tragedy," and a touchstone for all subsequent European civil wars.[16]

Why did the Thirty Years War start and then rage so intensely? There were many factors, including common human desires for material goods and property, social status and prestige, and a sense of belonging to a community different than others. Individuals and groups made choices—such as the Defenestration of Prague in 1618 that triggered the Bohemian Revolt and the larger conflagration—that could have turned otherwise.[17] To attribute the conflict solely to religion is to assign the conflict an air of inevitability, as well as to lock in a pattern of "preremembered" incidents that channel all religious differences into future conflict.[18] Yet religion played a decisive role in the Thirty Years War. First, nearly everyone in Europe at the time subscribed to one of three confessional faiths: Catholicism, Lutheranism, or Calvinism. Despite doctrinal differences between them, each confession posited that its version of Christianity provided the sole path to salvation and moral and political rectitude.[19] Religious and political leaders—at various moments such as the Council of Trent in 1545–64—had opportunities to find points of accommodation. And ordinary citizens at the end of the sixteenth century often lived in religiously mixed communities. Yet the underlying assumption that faith could not broker compromise or doubt created a climate in which militants could incubate and flourish. Thus, as soon as a spark was lit—by an event such as the Defenestration of Prague or a subsequent atrocity during the war—militants were able to exercise a power disproportionate to their relatively small numbers. Religious militancy, Wilson explains, "creates a delusional sense in those who rule of being chosen by God for a divine purpose and reward. It encourages the conviction that their norms alone are absolute, their form of government is automatically superior to all others and their faith is the only really true religion."[20] Religious militants often suffer setbacks, as they did in the Thirty Years War, because they do not deign to study their opponents or make tactical concessions. Yet the cost of their belligerence can be steep.

European responses to the Thirty Years War took place on many levels, in many venues, and in many ways. The peace treaties that ended the war in 1648 explicitly stated that they were instruments of a "Christian, general and permanent peace."[21] The parties to the peace treaties were Christian, and the postwar religious settlement granted rights to some communities and not others, such as Orthodox Christians, Jews, or Muslims. Certain patterns of thinking about religion and politics persisted after the war. Other habits, however, were called into question as political leaders sought ways for people of diverse faiths to coexist peacefully and repopulate territories that had been emptied during the war. Though the Westphalian settlement did not secularize politics as such, it did discredit the use of force to advance confessional objectives in the Holy Roman Empire.[22] Politically, the Westphalian settlement configured a balance between respecting religious allegiances and fashioning a worldly settlement to confessional strife.

This balance was tenuous, however, unless reinforced by theological and philosophical arguments. One of the great questions of *the* Enlightenment after the Thirty Years War was how to establish a moral politics on a basis other than a militant Christian sectarian faith.[23] The Enlightenment has coherence as an intellectual-political movement insofar as its participants grapple with this question. This view is compatible with recent scholarship differentiating rival Enlightenments, such as the Spinozist radical Enlightenment, which works to demystify religious orthodoxy and promote radical democratic politics, and the Lockean moderate Enlightenment, which seeks common cause with religious believers and traditional political authorities;[24] or between the Pufendorfian civil Enlightenment, which employs natural law to desacralize politics, and the Leibnizian metaphysical Enlightenment, which aims to resacralize politics in a neo-Platonic manner;[25] between the Humean Scottish Enlightenment, which bases morality on the human sentiments, and the Kantian German Enlightenment, which grounds morality on pure practical reason;[26] or between the British Enlightenment's sociology of virtue, the French Enlightenment's ideology of reason, and the American Enlightenment's politics of liberty.[27] The Enlightenment was a plural tradition—encompassing diverse ideas, authors, movements, and tendencies—but it was united by its common goal of refusing the political-religious model that contributed to the devastation of the Thirty Years War.[28]

Looking out our windows today, we see a political-religious landscape that both resembles and differs from the world of the seventeenth and eighteenth centuries. First, the differences: In the historical Enlightenment, philosophers sought to contain the violence perpetrated by and between Christian sects. Many of the most important texts of the European Enlightenment—including Hobbes's *Leviathan*, Locke's *Two Treatises of Government*, Spinoza's *Theological-Political Treatise*, and Kant's *Religion within the Boundaries of Mere Reason*—straddle political philosophy and biblical exegesis. Though strategies and tonalities differed—Locke and Kant, for instance, display more respect for biblical morality than do Hobbes or Spinoza—the Enlightenment philosophers situated themselves primarily vis-à-vis Judaism and Christianity. Today, political theorists need a broader and more nuanced understanding of global religions. In a world where ideas, products, weapons, armies, ideas, cultures, and people flow faster and more steadily across borders than ever, political theorists need to expand their mental maps of the constituencies discussing a common future of religious peace or strife. All global citizens today, for instance, need to pay attention to the dangers posed by Christian survivalists in the United States, Jewish militants in Israel, Hindu and Sikh partisans in India, Buddhist fighters in Sri Lanka, Islamists in the Middle East, and transnational global jihadists.[29] Furthermore, Euro-American political theorists need to make alliances with people from around the world and this entails shifting numerous perspectives, including our own.[30] Just as the problem of religious warfare has become more complex, so too will any potential solution. The Enlightenment, insofar as it has a future, must open itself to new voices, ideas, practices, conversations, and tendencies—all united by a common concern with stopping sectarian violence.[31]

In addition to drawing a larger and more complex map of political-religious conflict, contemporary political theorists must also acknowledge that one strand of Enlightenment ideology has attained worldly success as well as provoked a global reaction against it. In *Global Rebellion: Religious Challenge to the Secular State, from Christian Militias to al Qaeda*, the sociologist Mark Juergensmeyer presents the point this way. "The Enlightenment ushered in a new way of thinking about religion"—one that differentiated a religious private sphere and a public sphere governed by different codes and mores.[32] The Enlightenment philosophers appropriated a concept that originated in Christianity—the secular—and used it as the basis for a new ideology that would reduce the scope of religious authority in political affairs. In their private lives and free time, citizens could turn to religion to answer great metaphysical questions about why we are born, how we should live, and where we will go when we die. In their public lives, however, citizens were bound by terms developed with no explicit reference to religion—at least, church religion. The Enlightenment philosophers presented a new type of glue that would congeal society into a solid whole: secular nationalism, the notion that "individuals naturally associate with the people and place of their ancestral birth . . . in an economic and political system identified with a secular nation-state."[33] For secular nationalists, the ideological foundation of the nation-state is a secular contract formed, at least tacitly, by citizens inhabiting the same territory. The notion of secular nationalism—which Juergensmeyer attributes primarily to Locke and Rousseau[34]—comes naturally to many Americans and Europeans and has become a popular ideology for political leaders around the globe. Secularism empowers political authorities to rule independently of religious or traditional authorities. Yet the idea that political power may be indifferent to religion strikes many people around the globe as morally corrupt. "From the perspectives of the mullah in Iraq, the rabbi in Jerusalem, and the Lutheran pastor in Maryland, it is secular nationalism, and not religion, that has gone wrong."[35] Secular nationalism has had several centuries or decades to prove its worth—and for many religious activists, it has failed to provide moral or efficacious governance. Juergensmeyer shows that religious activists are often reflective, globally conscious, and politically astute—not the close-minded "fundamentalists" that secularists often portray them as being.[36]

The challenge facing the contemporary Enlightenment is how to address the legitimate complaints registered by religious activists against a movement that has had some worldly success over the past several centuries.

For all of the differences between the eighteenth and twenty-first centuries, however, the problem of religious militancy remains. Juergensmeyer acknowledges that modern warfare has many root causes, including a desire to protect one's homeland from foreign invasion. Political leaders may be thinking rationally—about how to advance secular ends of material prosperity and territorial autonomy—when they use religious rhetoric as a strategy to mobilize a population.[37] Based upon his research on religious activism in Sri Lanka, India, Egypt, Iran, Israel, Palestine, Central Asia, Japan, Iraq, Afghanistan, Indonesia, North Africa, Europe, and the United States, however, Juergensmeyer maintains that one strand of religious thinking has a profound impact on the nature of conflict: the idea of cosmic war.

> The idea of cosmic war is a remarkably consistent feature among all of these cases. It is a powerfully restorative image for social malaise. Those whom we might think of as terrorists often think of themselves as soldiers. They are engaged in attempts to restore their sense of power and control in what they imagine to be sacred battles. Acts of religious terror serve not only as tactics in a political strategy but as symbolically empowering sacred deeds. These are performances of violence, enacted to create a moment of spiritual encounter and personal redemption. Religious violence is especially savage and relentless since its perpetrators see it not merely as part of a worldly political battle but as part of a scenario of divine conflict.[38]

Juergensmeyer describes religion's role in contemporary conflicts in terms that could just as easily apply to the religious wars of early modern Europe. The idea of cosmic war provides an all-encompassing worldview that assigns the individual a meaningful role in a purposeful struggle. It turns ordinary men and women into religious soldiers fighting a battle on an epic scale with a vast time line. It absolutizes conflicts and demonizes opponents, preventing the possibility of reconciliation with satanic forces. Most important, the idea of cosmic war provides a justification for violence against all others that do not bear witness to the same version of confessional truth.[39] The idea of cosmic war is not a monopoly held by religious activists. The US War on Terror between 2001 and 2008, for instance, often used Manichean imagery to prosecute a war that was not—explicitly at least—between Christians and Muslims.[40] Though the combatants and context of religious warfare have changed in the twenty-first century, the problem that provoked the rise of the historical Enlightenment remains with us: how to convert religious or secular strife into acceptable alternatives.

We need a new Enlightenment for the twenty-first century. There is no way that we can go back to the philosophers of the European Enlightenment and expect direct guidance for our contemporary dilemmas and opportunities. Too much has changed in the past two or three hundred years for the concepts and principles of an earlier epoch to solve our current quandaries. Yet the Enlightenment also provides a fund of resources to launch our current reflections, and we gain strength from tapping into the Enlightenment as a moral and intellectual source. To confront the religious wars of the twenty-first century, we need to learn from our forbearers and also have the confidence to walk without the "leading strings" (*Leitbande*) of earlier authors, books, and ideas. To make explicit the theoretical commitments of this project, I now turn to a particularly rich set of reflections on the contemporary relevance of the Enlightenment: Michel Foucault's late writings on Kant and the Enlightenment.

FOUCAULT'S CALL

In the late 1970s and early 1980s, Foucault wrote several essays on Kant and the Enlightenment.[41] As several scholars have detailed, Foucault's entire corpus can be read as a prolonged engagement with the Kantian tradition— from his *thèse complémentaire* on Kant's *Anthropology from a Pragmatic Point of View* to his epistemological investigations in *The Order of Things*. In Amy Allen's words, Foucault, like his ostensible nemesis Jürgen Habermas, practices "a continuation-through-transformation of the Kantian critical project."[42] Fewer scholars, though, have noted that Foucault's late writings on the Enlightenment are as much a prescription for future political theorists as a description of where he himself has gone. In other words, Foucault polemicizes on behalf of a certain vision of the Enlightenment—one that arises, in part, as a response to the emerging presence of Islam on the global stage.[43] This book takes up Foucault's project, and, thus, it is worth elaborating how he envisions contemporary political theorists situating themselves towards the controversial notion of the Enlightenment.

Foucault declares that honesty requires us—presumably Euro-American liberal-left political theorists and actors—to acknowledge an Enlightenment inheritance. "Even if it is relatively and necessarily vague, the Enlightenment period is certainly designated as a formative stage of modern humanity."[44] The Enlightenment is a "period without fixed dates" and "multiple points of entry."[45] It is a process that began fitfully and unevenly and has manifested itself in various ways. Foucault—who in an earlier stage of his work deplores "the metahistorical deployment of ideal significations" in favor of "gray, meticulous, and patiently documentary" genealogy[46]—acknowledges that the Enlightenment as a concept cannot do justice to all that has happened in the modern West. In the past several centuries, Europe has experienced the birth of capitalism, the fall of feudalism, the rise of the bourgeoisie, the formation of nation-states, scientific and technological developments, and political revolutions and counterrevolutions. No one, or two, or three concepts can possibly capture all or even most of the momentous changes that have transformed human life in Europe since the Middle Ages. In this instance, though, Foucault is willing to deploy a singular concept—Enlightenment—to describe three developments that have had a profound influence on who we are, what we do, and how we think.

First, the Enlightenment has shaped the modern institutions—including schools, prisons, hospitals, asylums, cultural practices, and political arrangements—that encompass many aspects of our lives. Foucault's earlier books, including *The History of Madness* and *Discipline and Punish*, are often read as condemnations of modern power-knowledge relations and the institutions that create docile and utile bodies. Below I'll demonstrate how this reading is only partly right. For now, though, I shall note that Foucault thinks that the formation of bodies and souls differs in the modern West than it does in earlier times and other places. As historical, embodied beings, we are profoundly influenced by the technological, political, cultural, economic, and social developments that transpired during the Enlightenment. Many of Foucault's critics note that his early books appeal tacitly to Enlightenment values that this work overtly eschews. That is, Foucault's *exposé* of the modern prison in *Discipline and Punish*, for instance, shocks us because we believe in the values of human dignity and autonomy, but Foucault shows that such normative criteria were used by the founders of prisons—implying that they were, and we are, hypocrites.[47] In his late essays on the Enlightenment, however, Foucault overtly appeals to normative terms such as liberty, freedom, and autonomy to criticize the unenlightened practices of prisons, asylums, and so on. Christina Hendricks observes that Foucault's critiques of Enlightenment institutions "must make sense and operate as a catalyst for transformative efforts by those who are already enmeshed to some degree in current discourses."[48] The second legacy of the Enlightenment, then, is a set of terms and frameworks that still permeate normative discourses. Our bodies, souls, and normative frameworks, in sum, are historically conditioned by the complex event that has become known as the Enlightenment.

The third legacy of the Enlightenment, however, is the most important for determining how we should take this movement into the future. For Foucault, the greatest legacy of the Enlightenment is a certain style of thinking that has lost none of its relevance since Kant displayed it memorably in his 1784 essay, "What is Enlightenment?": "The thread which may connect us with the Enlightenment is not faithfulness to doctrinal elements but, rather, the permanent reactivation of an attitude—that is, of a philosophical ethos that could be described as a permanent critique of our historical era."[49] Foucault's appeal to an Enlightenment ethos is surprising, given that Kant himself avoided sensual (*sinnliche*) concepts to describe philosophical or practical dispositions. One explanation may be simply that Foucault imports a concept from his research on Greek and Roman antiquity in late work such as *The History of Sexuality* to describe his continual fascination with Kant. This explanation partly suffices if one notes that Foucault has a reason for describing the Enlightenment manner of philosophizing as an ethos. Stephen K. White expresses Foucault's conviction as such: "To think in terms of an ethos, or 'manner of being,' implies skepticism of both universalizing neo-Kantian reason and the idea that a substantive political position can be derived merely from the application of that reason to a given historical situation."[50] For Kant, reason is a faculty within human beings to transcend the sensible world and think and act freely. For Kant, reason manifests itself in history, but history does not reverberate back on reason.[51] For many Kantians, the universal-and-necessary quality of Kantian ethics is a strong point in its favor. For Foucault, however, we need to detach the critical ethos from certain Platonic assumptions that linger in Kant's philosophy. The critical ethos, as a dynamic and evolving cast of mind, empowers us to treat the Enlightenment as a living tradition that may and must adjust with the times.

Both employing and redefining Kantian terminology, Foucault describes the critical ethos as an expression of negative freedom. In his late essays—and particularly "What is Critique?"—Foucault situates Kant's argument about the Enlightenment in a broader historical context. The medieval Christian Church developed the idea of the pastoral in which each individual had to be governed "by someone to whom he was bound by a total, meticulous, detailed relationship of obedience."[52] The pastoral idea maintained that the church possessed the truth, that the church's prerogatives included an intimate awareness of each individual's life, and that the church could assign techniques for the individual to attune her body and soul with God. Through what the Greek Church called *technè technôn* and the Latin Roman Church called *ars artium*, Christianity had developed an art of governing men and directing consciences. The critical attitude arose as a rejection of the church's right to craft bodies and souls. At its core, the critical attitude states that we do not want to be governed *like that* or *so much*. The critical attitude is not necessarily anarchistic, but it does rebel against the total coercion implied by the Christian pastoral.[53] Foucault identifies this impulse in Kant's essay when Kant criticizes religious guardians for trying to lead (*leiten*) people into a state of immaturity by assigning books, foods, and spiritual mentors. For Kant, the Enlightenment is an *Ausgang*, a "way out" from religious tyranny. Foucault does not endorse Kant's metaphysics of freedom and his own reflections on how to transcend one's historical milieu are tentative.[54] Bracketing these philosophical questions, though, Foucault thinks that Kant expresses a critical ethos of "voluntary insubordination" and "reflected intractability."[55] One side of the critical ethos, then, refuses to accept the necessity of current political, social, economic, cultural, or spiritual relationships.

Foucault also thinks that the critical ethos expresses a sense of positive freedom, though here Foucault departs more radically from Kant's lead. For Kant, positive freedom means assigning oneself the law of pure practical reason. Lawless freedom, for Kant, is an absurdity, and the only law that expresses our rational nature is the supreme principle of morality that he identifies in the *Groundwork for the Metaphysics of Morals*. For Foucault, the critical ethos spares nothing, not even Kant's ostensible "formal structures with universal value."[56] Still, for Foucault, the critical ethos inspires us to construct concepts and principles to aid theoretical, practical, and aesthetic judgment. Foucault's advice in his essay on Enlightenment is two-fold. *Research our limits*: perform empirical research into the precise events that have contributed to the constitution of our identities, thoughts, habits, and actions. This research is archaeological, in that it investigates the conditions of real (rather than possible) experience, and genealogical, in that it serves to remove the veneer of necessity that attends so much of experience. Then, *experiment with our limits*. Rather than try to formulate practical rules that apply always and everywhere, thoughtfully and carefully test out new ideas and practices. After the horrors of the twentieth century, we ought to recognize the dangers of any system that claims, "to escape from the system of contemporary reality so as to produce the overall programs of another society."[57] Foucault, then, makes no mention of Kant's idea of the realm of ends as the correlate to the formula of autonomy in the *Groundwork*. But Foucault does think that the idea of autonomy can be preserved if we think of ourselves as contingent beings capable of self- and other-transformation. Thus Foucault's conception of autonomy prizes "a permanent creation of ourselves" and an acknowledgement that "we are always in the position of beginning again."[58]

From the perspective of traditional Kant scholarship, Foucault takes liberties by ascribing to Kant a conception of reason open to historical vicissitudes. In contrast with Kant's other historical writings that posit a *telos* that arrives regardless of whether human beings, here and now, recognize it,[59] the essay on Enlightenment views humanity inhabiting a present with multiple layers of possibility to pursue: "In the text on *Aufklärung*, he deals with the question of contemporary reality alone. He is not seeking to understand the present on the basis of a totality or of a future achievement. He is looking for a difference: What difference does today introduce with respect to yesterday?"[60] In his lecture "What is Critique?" Foucault chides an audience of philosophers for thinking, along Kantian lines, that they can ignore the historical dimension of philosophy. For Foucault, human reason is embedded in a historical-linguistic milieu, and thus philosophers need to recognize themselves as belonging to this "instant of humanity which is subjected to the power of truth in general and truths in particular."[61] For Foucault, human beings are deeply affected—though, importantly, not determined—by their environment. Foucault's conception of practical reason is thus *impure* without being fatalistic.[62] Yet why does Foucault stretch Kant's text to say something that will be much more overt among post-Kantians as diverse as Hegel, Marx, Nietzsche, and Habermas? Why does Foucault contravene traditional histories of philosophy to have Kant defend the singularity of the present rather than the universality of human reason?

The reason is that Foucault wants to differentiate two sides of Kant's legacy, one worth embracing, and the other that may be assigned to the history books. Kant's analytic of truth—the search for universal conditions of justified theoretical, practical, and aesthetic judgments—fits within the historical epoch of the Enlightenment. This may be worth studying to understand the modern *episteme* that still filters how we in the modern West understand certain things, but it is not a living project (in Foucault's eyes). This Enlightenment is a "singular event inaugurating European modernity," but insofar as it represents a static body of doctrines then it cannot help us think perceptively and creatively about *today*.[63] A Kantian ontology of the present, on the other hand, renews the spirit that motivated Kant in his 1784 essay on Enlightenment. For Foucault, Kant's *Walspruch*, or heraldic motto of the Enlightenment—"have the courage, the audacity, to know"—inspires us to investigate our time and determine points of positive change.[64] For Foucault, the critical ethos, rather than any of Kant's specific doctrines, is what remains vital in the Enlightenment tradition.

Foucault's invocation of the Enlightenment, then, is less a locutionary act—describing a tradition that already exists—then a perlocutionary one—mobilizing the formation of a new *us* to advance a certain type of political and philosophical practice.[65] The first task for the new partisans of the Enlightenment, then, is to criticize aspects of the historical Enlightenment. This can take the form of Foucault's early work—the "history of the present"—that documents how the growth of capabilities manifested in modern schools, prisons, and factories actually diminishes human autonomy. Foucault's critique of governmentality—the ensemble of modern "institutions, procedures, analyses and reflections" that shape, rather than merely control, populations[66]—is thus consistent with a certain interpretation of Enlightenment values. As his critics such as Habermas, Nancy Fraser, and Thomas McCarthy have noted, Foucault's deconstruction of Enlightenment accomplishments *is* motivated by a love for freedom and autonomy. Furthermore, Foucault thinks that the contemporary Enlightenment must cut the link to many Enlightenment doctrines. "Let us leave in their piety those who want to keep the *Aufklärung* living and intact. Such piety is of course the most touching of treasons."[67] Foucault's polemics against Enlightenment piety must be taken with a grain of salt; early Foucault did, after all, translate Kant's *Anthropology from a Pragmatic Point of View* into French, and he expressed a desire, after the Iranian revolution, to write a sympathetic history of liberalism.[68] His point, though, is that the critical ethos of voluntary insubordination must apply to even the most sacrosanct of Enlightenment doctrines. Foucault's writings on Kant and the Enlightenment are as noticeable for what they leave out—for example, all mention of categorical imperatives—as for what they highlight. For Foucault, spiritual maturity means thinking without the "walkers" (*Gängelwagen*) of our Enlightenment predecessors.

Criticism does not mean abandonment, however, and the second task of Enlightenment partisans is to take up its banner. An interesting fact of the eighteenth century, Foucault notes, is that the "*Aufklärung* calls itself *Aufklärung*. It is certainly a very singular cultural process that became aware of itself by naming itself, by situating itself in relation to its past and future, and by designating the operations that it must carry out within its own present."[69] The Enlightenment called itself the Enlightenment and fabricated its own understanding of its history, its mission, and its future. The same dynamic is at work today. "In this historical-philosophical practice, one has to *make one's own history*."[70] The Enlightenment only thrives as a tradition if we make it our own, drawing selective sustenance from certain authors and practices and embodying its spirit in contemporary circumstances. Foucault's orientation to the Enlightenment, I believe, can be well phrased in the terms of Charles Taylor's *Sources of the Self*. For Foucault, the Enlightenment is a moral source—a tradition that helps constitute who we are and provides an at least provisional structure for thinking about theoretical, practical, and aesthetic questions. "Doing without frameworks is utterly impossible for us"—Taylor explains, and Foucault concurs.[71] Foucault's naturalistic sources differ from Taylor's theistic ones, and Foucault thinks that sources are more plastic than Taylor does. But Foucault agrees with Taylor that we can draw strength—intellectually and practically—by situating ourselves in a larger movement. Foucault exhorts *us*—an us that does not yet exist in full and that is not confined to any one space on the globe—to create a twenty-first century Enlightenment.

Foucault, Paul Rabinow observes, did not intend his reflections on the Enlightenment to be his late work.[72] When Foucault was writing his "history of the present," he thought that the task of thinkers was to raise problems rather than to propose solutions. By the late 1970s, though, Foucault became uneasy with that position and started to mine Hellenistic philosophy for concepts and terms (salvation, care of the self, equipment, and so on) that could be recast for contemporary purposes. Though Foucault thought that Habermas overstated the differences between them, Foucault agreed that he needed to go farther in fleshing out his vision of the Enlightenment. And then time ran out. For Rabinow, Foucault's untimely death does not diminish his contribution to contemporary theorizing: "The questions that Foucault posed and reposed during the 1980s remain challenging: what difference does today make with respect to yesterday? How to find an exit towards maturity? How to give form to our impatience for liberty?"[73] Had Foucault lived longer, we would have benefited from his thoughts. But for those inspired by Foucault's call for a new Enlightenment, there is plenty of work to do.[74]

The aim of this book is to think about the future of the Enlightenment. The book proceeds by situating itself in ongoing debates about Kant's legacy—a singularly powerful thread that connects us to the Enlightenment. In the following two sections, I describe Kant's place in contemporary political theory, the diverse components of his legacy, and several figures who contribute to fashioning a twenty-first–century Enlightenment. In the remainder of the book, I say more about what shape the critical ethos takes in contemporary political theory and how contemporary thinkers preserve and transform the Enlightenment inheritance. At the end of the book, I provide a concrete example of why we should view the Enlightenment's primary legacy as an ethos rather than a doctrine, namely, that it empowers us to construct theories to envision a way out of the looming religious wars of the twenty-first century.

KANT'S LEGACY: ETHOS, METAETHICS, DOCTRINES

Why Kant? Why, in other words, do contemporary political theorists who wish to understand the future of the Enlightenment look backwards to this figure above nearly all others?[75] Kant's importance to contemporary political theory may be attributed to several factors. First, his framing of the history of philosophy profoundly influences how we read authors such as Plato, Aristotle, the medieval scholastics, and Kant's main competitors for leading thinker of the Enlightenment: Descartes, Hobbes, Locke, Spinoza, Hume, and Leibniz. Even for present-day thinkers who wish to dethrone Kant's version of the Enlightenment acknowledge that, for the time being, political theorists must pass through Kant rather than around him.[76] Second, Kant is a point of orientation for many subsequent philosophical movements, including Hegelianism, Marxism, pragmatism, liberalism, and other schools of thought in Anglo-American and Continental philosophy. As Tom Rockmore details in *In Kant's Wake*, "consciously or more often unconsciously, the main thinkers in the twentieth century are in dialogue with each other on the basis of a shared Kantian tradition, which they understand in different ways, often markedly so."[77] We could simply add that Kantian terminology serves as a *lingua franca* for philosophical discussions at the end of the eighteenth, throughout the nineteenth, and into the twenty-first century as well. In this section, I propose to articulate three components of Kant's legacy that enable us to see what, precisely, philosophers find compelling in his work: ethos, metaethics, and doctrines. We will then be able to differentiate post-Kantian philosophies by how they mix these ingredients.

Foucault notes that Kant's 1784 call for courage took place in a newspaper article, which makes the piece both a philosophical argument as well as something like "a sermon."[78] In fact, Kant distributes popular exhortations for philosophical courage throughout many of his political essays—that likewise often first appeared in the *Berlinische Monatsschrift*—as well as in parts of the three *Critiques*, particularly the preface to the 1787 edition of the *Critique of Pure Reason*, in which Kant presents what is often called his Copernican revolution in philosophy. The substance of much of Kant's metaphysics would remain the same even if these polemical or inspirational passages were removed from Kant's corpus. Yet Kant's appeal to a wide reading public transforms his work into *political* philosophy, the subject of which (in Hannah Arendt's words) is the "relation between philosophy and politics."[79] All philosophers have created ideas and theories. Yet Kant was among the first to announce forthrightly that that was what he was doing.[80] In his popular exhortations, Kant invites most people to partake in what, for Plato, was the purview of the few. Even if Kant's philosophy is abstract and difficult, it is still democratic insofar as it invites everyone to exercise the courage of his or her own understanding. Philosophers differ on how best to conceptualize the Kantian ethos, or spirit—for how one describes this ethos affects how one views one's own task as a philosopher. But more so than perhaps for any other philosopher, the adjective *Kantian* implies that one has undertaken an ongoing assignment to exercise negative freedom (to break away from old ways of thinking) and positive freedom (to inaugurate a new way to think).

One of the more remarkable features of Kant's philosophy is that he keeps his readers informed as to the status of his enterprise. Rather than simply develop or present his ideas, Kant reflects upon *how* philosophers can go about creating ideas—like a master architect teaching others how to design and build their own edifices. The classic example of this is the *Groundwork for the Metaphysics of Morals*—an instruction manual for the conceptual structure that he subsequently builds in the *Metaphysics of Morals* proper. In each section, Kant explains the nature of the transitions he is enacting and thereby giving future Kantians clues about how they too can replicate and update those transitions, namely, the engagement with common sense in Section I, the search for moral concepts and principles in Section II, and the establishment of those concepts and principles in Section III.[81] In contemporary political theory, Kant is if not the first, then one of the most powerful advocates of what has come to be known as constructivism—the notion that philosophers make theoretical lenses rather than discover them.[82] For self-described constructivists such as Rawls and Deleuze, Kantian metaethics are a resource for the production of theories that refine or transform Kant's.

The bulk of Kant's writings, naturally, exposit the doctrines—the categories, ideas, methodologies, axioms, deductions, postulates, and so forth—that compose the bricks and mortar, as it were, of Kant's philosophy. For contemporary political theorists, there has been a renaissance of interest in Kant's political writings—including the articles published in the *Berlinische Monatsschrift* (such as "On the Common Saying: This May Be True in Theory, but It Does Not Hold in Practice"), the *Rechtslehre* (the Doctrine of Right, the first part of the *Metaphysics of Morals*), the *Conflict of the Faculties* (particularly Part 2 on the possibility of human progress), and the forthcoming translation of Feyerabend's transcription of Kant's lectures on natural right.[83] For many contemporary political theorists—as diverse as Foucault, Habermas, Jacques Derrida, Jean-Francois Lyotard, Christine Korsgaard, and Onora O'Neill—Kant scholarship has served as a training ground for learning how to philosophize.[84] A great question among contemporary Kantians is how much of Kant's corpus to preserve in its original form and how to change the remainder.[85]

Kant is one of the most cited figures from the historical Enlightenment in contemporary political theory.[86] This is due partly to the power of his own thought, but also because Kantian terminology is a resource for so many other theorists in diverse schools of thought. To present a case for *the* Enlightenment, one needs to enlist Kant. This book interprets Kant's writings, then, as a symbolically and intellectually powerful source for the contemporary Enlightenment.

KANT'S HEIRS: WOOD, RAWLS, DELEUZE, RAMADAN

The thread that connects us to the Enlightenment is an ethos rather than a doctrine. I observed above that Foucault's *us* is partly a description of current philosophical practice and partly a prescription for how philosophers should proceed in the future. This book shares Foucault's sense that the contemporary Enlightenment—facing a historical crisis that bears imperfect parallels with the religious wars of early modernity—needs to think and act courageously. To substantiate this argument, I build upon the work of four philosophers who advance the Kantian legacy in important but disparate ways. Thinking with and against these authors, we see both the diversity the contemporary Enlightenment may encompass and the power of viewing the Enlightenment as a living tradition. I focus on these authors because they both draw profoundly on Kant and represent leading movements within contemporary political theory. Here, then, are synopses of the four major authors who participate in this book's Socratic dialogue about the future of the Enlightenment.

Allen W. Wood is a leading scholar and advocate of Kantian ethics. He co-edits, with Paul Guyer, *The Cambridge Edition of the Works of Immanuel Kant*, has translated or introduced several popular English editions of Kant's *Groundwork*, and has written influential books on *Kant's Ethical Thought* and *Kantian Ethics*. Wood is arguably the one Kant scholar who all Anglo-American Kant readers must address. Wood believes that Kant's ethical thought "exercises such a strong and continuing influence on us that replacing commonly accepted ideas about it with more accurate . . . ones might help to transform our conception of our history and of ourselves as heirs of the Enlightenment."[87] Wood unabashedly defends Kant's doctrines properly understood. In this book's narrative, Wood presents an argument against Foucault's thesis that we should cut the link to Enlightenment doctrines such as Kant's.[88] Wood displays a profound understanding of how Kant's philosophy fits together into a coherent whole. Wood also takes seriously arguments made against Kant's philosophy in its original form, as attested to by his scholarship on Fichte, Hegel, Marx, and other figures in the history of philosophy. Wood concedes that contemporary Kantians may discard many of Kant's peripheral doctrines and judgments. Yet Wood thinks that Kant's core concepts and principles remain a most powerful expression of Enlightenment ideals and that our task is to actualize Kant's vision. Though I ultimately disagree with Wood's assessment of Enlightenment fidelity, I appreciate his concern for passing on Kant's legacy in its original form to future generations.

John Rawls placed Kant at the center of contemporary Anglo-American political theory with the publication of his 1971 book, *A Theory of Justice*.

In that book, Rawls presented a Kantian interpretation of his conception of justice—justice as fairness—and elaborated on its Kantian roots in a series of essays throughout the 1970s. In the mid-1980s, however, Rawls began to distance himself from Kant's moral doctrine, arguing that Rawls's theory of justice could be endorsed from an overlapping consensus of reasonable moral, philosophical, and religious viewpoints. In a letter to his editor written in 1998, Rawls explains that he wants to further remove Kantian elements from *Political Liberalism* (originally published in 1993) lest he be seen as alienating constituencies that do not endorse Kant's version of individual moral autonomy.[89] Yet Rawls lectured and wrote on Kant throughout his life and over the course of his career he trained several generations of prominent Kant scholars, including Samuel Freeman, Paul Guyer, Thomas E. Hill Jr., Christine Korsgaard, Onora O'Neill, and Andrew Reath. For Rawls, "all the main conceptions in the tradition of moral philosophy must be continually renewed"—which means, for Kantians, that they must listen to criticisms of Kant's philosophy and incorporate contending insights if that makes the Kantian tradition stronger.[90] Thus Rawls's philosophy contains elements that may properly be called Humean, or Hegelian, or Deweyan, more than Kantian. For Rawls, however, this approach is perfectly consistent with the Kantian imperative to think for ourselves. Rawls, then, embodies Kantian courage, freely employs and modifies Kantian metaethics (or constructivism), and appropriates and adapts elements of Kant's practical philosophy. Though Rawls and Foucault differ on many substantive issues, they concur that the Enlightenment must renew itself to remain vibrant and timely.

Gilles Deleuze, co-author of *A Thousand Plateaus*, is arguably the most important Continental political theorist of his generation.[91] Deleuze grappled with Kant's legacy from his earliest monographs on Hume, Kant, Nietzsche, Spinoza, and Bergson, through his first major work in his own voice, *Difference and Repetition*, up to his late reflections on philosophical constructivism in *What Is Philosophy?* Deleuze challenges many aspects of the Kantian inheritance, particularly the moral philosophy that demands adherence to laws that cannot be fully understood or obeyed. In the essay "On Four Poetic Formulas that Might Summarize the Kantian Philosophy," Deleuze takes up Nietzsche's charge that Kant's moral philosophy reeks of cruelty. Yet Deleuze, like his friend Foucault, thinks that Kant's moral doctrines compose only a part of his legacy. How Deleuze constructs his political theory is deeply Kantian, and Deleuze appropriates many terms and strategies from Kant's critical philosophy for his own.[92] Deleuze shares Rawls's general approach to the Kantian legacy: that the most prized part is the critical ethos, the next most important element is the metaethics of constructivism, and the least valuable (but still interesting) component is the system itself. Yet whereas Rawls situates his project at the heart of the moderate Enlightenment, seeking a position that may appeal to citizens of faith, Deleuze aligns himself with members of the radical Enlightenment who more deeply question the presuppositions that have guided Western political, philosophical, and theological thinking.[93] Deleuze stretches, in other words, the range of voices and issues that most contemporary partisans of the Enlightenment have been willing to countenance.

I place myself in this dialogue by affirming and contesting elements from each of these thinkers. I agree with Wood that Kantians should strive for accuracy and comprehension when surveying Kant's legacy, but I draw upon Rawls and Deleuze to argue that the Enlightenment tradition should be open to political and philosophical developments since the eighteenth century. Enlightenment ideals such as liberty, equality, and community form part of our common political vocabulary—particularly for those on the left[94]—but we should still be willing to rethink or redefine them to better serve our purposes. Rawls best displays the power of the Enlightenment to move forward as a political force that can exercise authority and legislate timely principles. Though Rawls emphasizes that political liberalism is not Enlightenment liberalism—meaning that people can endorse the former without subscribing to the Kantian or Humean morality of the latter—he still powerfully advocates for a political conception of justice that respects many ways of life. Whereas Wood, at his worst, has a militant conception of the Enlightenment that can slide into secular dogmatism, Rawls consistently defends a conception of reasonable pluralism that diminishes the drive for ideological strife. Yet Rawls's conception of the reasonable, by minimizing public discussion of controversial metaphysical questions, can foster close-mindedness. I thus draw upon Deleuze to argue that the Enlightenment should house a wide array of political-philosophical positions. Deleuze's controversial writings jolt thinking and keep the Enlightenment alert to developments that might pass notice if we rest content with our current ideological lenses. On my account of the Enlightenment, we need to combine respect for our eighteenth-century forbearers, a willingness to articulate and actualize Enlightenment ideals, and a restless desire to imagine how things could be otherwise.

Near the end of the book, I discuss a fourth philosopher who has a complex relationship to the historical Enlightenment: Tariq Ramadan. Partly as a result of the controversy that banned him from the United States from 2004 to 2010, partly as a result of his books such as *The Quest for Meaning: Developing a Philosophy of Pluralism*, *What I Believe*, and *Radical Reform: Islamic Ethics and Liberation*, Ramadan has become one of the leading Muslim figures in Euro-American debates about political and religious pluralism. On the one hand, Ramadan espouses Muslim ideas and arguments that depart, sometimes radically, from Enlightenment ideals as interpreted by liberal hawks.[95] On the other, Ramadan calls upon Muslims to cultivate a creative political-intellectual mindset: "Our sources help us in this if we can only try hard to reappropriate for ourselves the universality of the message of Islam, along with its vast horizon. This reappropriation should be of a depth that will enable it to produce a true 'intellectual revolution' in the sense intended by Kant when he spoke of the 'Copernican revolution.'"[96] May we speak of Ramadan as a Muslim Immanuel Kant?[97] Well, no, if we mean to imply that Ramadan seeks to secularize Islam in the same way that Kant purportedly secularizes Christianity. Nor may we say that Ramadan builds his political theory upon pure practical reason, advocates a rationalistic metaphysics of morals, or embraces any particular doctrine employed by Kant scholars to determine who is in or out of the Kantian tradition. Yet Ramadan thinks "scholars have always imported and exported ideas . . . that promote the cross-fertilization of civilizations," and that Muslim scholars may import Kant's idea of a Copernican revolution to envision the political and philosophical task before them.[98] Furthermore, Ramadan's political theory as a whole amalgamates (among other sources) Arabic concepts—such as *ijtihad*, *tajdid*, and *islah*—and ones associated with Kant's philosophy, such as autonomy, critique, and universal morality.[99] Ramadan begins *The Quest for Meaning*, for example, by addressing Kant's three great questions in the *Critique of Pure Reason* (What can I know? What should I do? What may I hope?), and he appeals to Kant's *Groundwork for the Metaphysics of Morals* and the *Critique of Practical Reason* to develop an idea of the "ethics of liberation."[100] Ramadan, to be sure, does not advocate Kant's practical philosophy. But Ramadan seems to agree with Judith Butler that the Kantian legacy may contribute to a critique of religious and secular presumptions.[101] To the charge that his rhetoric differs, but his message is identical to that of, say, his grandfather Hassan al-Banna (the founder of the

Muslim Brotherhood) or Jamal al-Din al-Afghani (the theorist of modern pan-Islamism), Ramadan replies, "languages convey and transmit sensibilities; they have and *are* particular sensibilities."[102] By expressing a critical sensibility, Ramadan both situates himself within and stretches the borders of *a* Kantian tradition. In the contemporary world, welcoming hybrid thinkers such as Ramadan into the Enlightenment might be a key to its survival.

I wish to note that because any manageable conversation limits the number of participants, this book does not discuss in depth many worthy voices in the contemporary debate about Kant's legacy or the future of the Enlightenment, including those of Anglophone and Continental Kant scholars such as Christine Korsgaard and Otfried Höffe; the Frankfurt School critical theorists Max Horkheimer and Theodore Adorno; the towering figure of post-war Kantian political theory, Jürgen Habermas; or the Chinese philosophers discussed in Wei Zhang's book, *What is Enlightenment?: Can China Answer Kant's Question*. My hope is that other scholars as well as myself continue to use Kant as a common resource to build bridges across different intellectual and political traditions.[103]

THE ITINERARY

To envision the future of the Enlightenment, I enter a conversation with several of the most profound and influential political thinkers of our time through a shared Kantian vocabulary. Initially, I consider the shape that the critical ethos, or Kantian courage, takes in late-modernity (Chapter 1). Then, I examine the distinct problems of our day (Chapter 2) and how Kantian metaethics helps us construct ideas and principles to address them, particularly the need to articulate political terms of justice that can be shared by a wide array of democratic constituencies (Chapter 3). I then put this argument to the test by showing how Kantian courage empowers Rawls, Deleuze, and Ramadan to construct new terms of interreligious dialogue and cooperation (Chapter 4). I conclude by arguing that the contemporary Enlightenment should view autonomy as an ongoing assignment for temporal, embodied beings who are also capable of thinking.

What follows is a more detailed map of the itinerary.

Chapter 1 presents an interpretation of Kantian courage and its implications for contemporary political thinking. In his 1784 essay on the Enlightenment, Kant famously enjoins his readers, "*Sapere aude!* Have the courage to use your *own* understanding!" For over two hundred years, Kant's heirs have been inspired and perplexed by this command or invitation. On the one hand, Kant spurs us to think for ourselves about personal, religious, political, and cultural questions. This thinking is both combative—as we refuse to accept on trust inherited beliefs or practices—and creative—as we propose new ideas to confront our problems. In this essay, Kant seems to accept, indeed welcome, revisions to his critical philosophy. On the other, Kant defines courage in the *Metaphysics of Morals* as moral strength in the face of opposing inclinations. Here, courage means following resolutely the letter of Kant's doctrines, *not* thinking for oneself about moral principles. Kant's conflicting views on courage, I contend, reverberate in contemporary debates about how best to take up Kant's legacy.

I then elaborate how Kantian courage has been inflected in contemporary political theory. For Wood, Kantian courage means apologizing for Kant's doctrines in the same way that Plato apologized for Socratic philosophy. Wood does not embrace all of Kant's judgments (about, say, animals, women, or non-European peoples), but Wood does believe that Kant presents the best available account of true moral convictions. For Wood, Kantian courage means fighting for Kant's idea in the world and combating misreadings of Kant in the academy. For Rawls, on the contrary, Kantian courage means perfecting, rather than preserving, Kant's philosophy in the light of alternate insights or historical developments. Rawls's model of Kantian courage is the Supreme Court: a body that constructs the highest law of the land in a way respectful of precedent but still aware of the tides of history. Deleuze, at his most polemical, opposes the apologetic or reconstructive appropriation of the Kantian legacy. Instead, Deleuze takes up Nietzsche's project of pushing the Kantian idea of critique as far as possible—to the point where one constantly seeks to transgress limits placed by traditional moral or political values. Deleuze's model critic, at least in his early work, aims to destroy established modes of evaluation. At the end of the chapter, I contend that all three inflections of Kantian courage—as apology, legislation, and transgression—contribute to strengthening the Enlightenment as a coherent, powerful, and vibrant tradition.

In Chapter 2 I consider the problems that confront the Enlightenment today. In the *Groundwork for the Metaphysics of Morals*, Kant sets himself the project of formulating a pure moral philosophy to clarify healthy common sense and encompass both virtue and right. There are several reasons why contemporary Kantians hesitate to frame their problems this way. The rise of philosophic naturalism—often associated with Darwinism—has made appeals to pure reason emblematic of a medieval, rather than modern, worldview. The Holocaust—perpetuated by "ordinary" Europeans in Kant's homeland—throws a dark shadow over his account of common sense. And the events of September 11, 2001, suggest that the most pressing practical task today is to fashion a political vocabulary that may be shared by citizens of diverse faiths, not to insist that everybody endorse a rationalist conception of morality. In this chapter, I build upon Rawls's and Deleuze's efforts to recast Kant's problems for contemporary political life.

The contemporary Enlightenment, I maintain, confronts several major tasks. The first is to naturalize Kant's account of practical reason, that is, to explain our faculty of normativity within a post-Darwinian account of human nature. Interestingly, both Rawls and Deleuze pursue this project by drawing upon David Hume, one of Kant's great rivals in the eighteenth-century Enlightenment. The next task for contemporary Kantians is to engage common sense. Here, Rawls and Deleuze part company in how they take up Kant's legacy. Rawls thinks that philosophy should clarify and defend healthy democratic common sense, whereas Deleuze thinks that philosophy *qua* philosophy challenges conventional ways of thinking, acting, and feeling. Rawls, in other words, largely participates in the Pythagoras story that holds that people already know on a fundamental level what they ought to do, while Deleuze largely agrees with Nietzsche that philosophy must constantly criticize common sense from an untimely perspective. Here, I argue that the contemporary Enlightenment benefits from maintaining a charge between its moderate and radical poles—in this instance, between those who respect, and those who challenge, democratic common sense. The final task is to envision how diverse religious, moral, and philosophical constituencies can coexist peacefully on the same terrain. Rather than seek a comprehensive practical doctrine such as Kant's metaphysics of morals, Rawls and Deleuze exercise Kantian courage to invent concepts—such as a "political conception of justice" and "rhizome"—that help us grasp how democratic citizens can form political coalitions to address public problems. Rawls and Deleuze want strict Kantians to have a voice in contemporary political debates, just not be *the* voice.

At the end of the chapter, I consider how the debate over Kant's legacy parallels a debate over the future of the Left. My point of departure is the fact that liberty and freedom—twin ideals of the Left—originally had opposite meanings. Liberty, from the Greek word *eleutheria*, suggests a condition of being independent, separate, and distinct; freedom, from the Indo-European root *priya* (dear or beloved), means participating in an autonomous tribe or family. The challenge for the Left, then, is to balance the competing goods of individual liberty and collective self-governance. Both Rawls and Deleuze situate themselves on the left, but Rawls is more concerned with building a free society, and Deleuze is more adamant about the politics of difference. The Enlightenment, I contend, should pitch a tent big enough to encompass both sides of the liberty-freedom continuum.

In Chapter 3 I present a case for how the contemporary Enlightenment can construct theories to address the problems of our day. The idea of constructivism expresses Kant's insight that human beings make, rather than discover, the principles that regulate scientific knowledge and constitute practical norms. To its defenders, constructivism empowers each generation to write the laws that govern practical affairs. To its critics, constructivism relinquishes one of the defining features of Kant's philosophy, namely, the promise of a pure moral philosophy cleansed of empirical or historical elements. Rawls and Deleuze refuse to accept the choice between moral realism and moral nihilism. The interesting question for them is how to construct principles to navigate a fluctuating political realm as best we can. Rawls and Deleuze thus appropriate and modify Kantian constructivism, in a pragmatic spirit, to create political concepts and principles for the twenty-first century.

In the heart of the chapter, I show how Rawls and Deleuze identify and enact the activities of constructivism. The first and most important step is to posit a conception of the person (in Rawls's terms) or a conceptual persona (in Deleuze's). A conception of the person is the agent of thinking in our minds, a mental figure who poses questions, follows lines of arguments, raises objections, and ultimately chooses a course of action. In *Political Liberalism*, Rawls elicits the conception of a citizen who is reasonable, rational, free, and equal with her fellow citizens. In *A Thousand Plateaus*, Deleuze invents the conceptual persona of a Body without Organs (BwO) that shares certain structural features with a democratic citizen (including fairly stable commitments to individual and collective identity) and has a side that expresses dissatisfaction with conventional ways of thinking, feeling, and acting. Despite the differences between their language games, but both philosophers recognize that a conception of the person is the foundation of any post-Kantian political theory. Rawls and Deleuze also think that democratic citizens are often pulled between reasonable political behavior and a desire to chart a new life course. However, Rawls's conception of the person is more accommodating to democratic social norms than Deleuze's; Deleuze's conceptual persona is less keen to subject her desires to the collective will.

The next stage of constructivism is to lay out a plane, or a mental landscape, on which the conception of the person thinks, moves, and decides. Rawls places the citizen in the original position, behind a veil of ignorance, to determine the principles of justice to govern the basic structure of society. Deleuze lodges the BwO on a social stratum in which she must choose, for herself and with others, how to balance society's need for order with the potential rewards of experimentation. Rawls and Deleuze concur that capitalism is a defining feature of our age, and that liberal democratic discourse has attained partial hegemony in Europe and the United States. Rawls's and Deleuze's planes resemble the current world order, at the same time that they render possible a perspective to envision alternate futures.

The third step of constructivism is to think through what principles the person would endorse for the plane. In *A Theory of Justice*, the citizen in the original position selects principles that protect each citizen's basic rights and liberties, guarantee citizens fair equality of opportunity to occupy privileged positions in the basic structure of society, and ensure that public policy benefits the least-advantaged members of society. In *Political Liberalism* and *The Law of Peoples*, however, Rawls thinks that other citizens, domestically and globally, may choose different principles that could still be worthy of respect and allegiance. In *A Thousand Plateaus*, Deleuze constructs a normative theory for the individual and society that balances experimentation and caution. The BwO should open her body to new ideas, affects, percepts, and practices to fill herself with joy; at the same time, she must protect enough of her identity to survive as a coherent entity. Both Rawls and Deleuze assemble their constructivist procedures employing historical and linguistic elements, and thus neither Rawls's or Deleuze's principles are pure, in a Kantian sense. Yet Rawls and Deleuze show how the contemporary Enlightenment can produce principles to help steer the future of progressive politics in a world that differs dramatically from eighteenth-century Europe.

The final stage of constructivism is to evaluate principles, that is, to determine the worth of the principles constructed. Neither Rawls nor Deleuze think that it is possible to deduce practical principles (as Kant attempts in the *Groundwork*) or justify them by invoking a fact of reason (as Kant tries in the *Critique of Practical Reason*). Instead, Rawls and Deleuze evaluate their theories by appealing to diverse faculties. Rawls posits the idea of reflective equilibrium to test whether a theory accommodates our philosophic principles (which are more cognitive) and our considered convictions (which are more affective). Deleuze employs aesthetic criteria—such as love, beauty, and intensity—to invite people to adopt his principles, but the mental energy required to interpret his writings demands reflection. Both Rawls and Deleuze, in other words, maintain that we evaluate theories on several different layers, including the intellectual, affective, and intersubjective. Yet Rawls and Deleuze express different philosophical tastes: Rawls thinks that philosophy should foster social harmony, while Deleuze thinks that philosophy should induce discomfort with established values.

At the end of the chapter, I consider the prospects of renewing constructivism for the twenty-first century. Rawls and Deleuze display the power of constructivism to create timely political theories. Yet how are we to understand the differences between their constructivisms? Rawls, I contend, participates in the tradition of the moderate Enlightenment that promotes reasonableness and tolerance but still admires Christian ethical norms. For Rawls, it is imperative that his constructed principles be acceptable to reasonable Christians. Deleuze, on the contrary, embraces the atheism of the radical Enlightenment often associated with Spinoza. Deleuze's political theory hovers between respecting Christianity as a potential partner in left-political coalitions and disputing Christianity on a fundamental level. I do not think that it is possible or desirable to reconcile—in the Hegelian sense of *aufheben*—the moderate and radical Enlightenment traditions. The history of the European Enlightenment teaches us, however, that the radical Enlightenment generates philosophical, artistic, scientific, and political ideas that become concrete by being implemented by the moderate Enlightenment. The Enlightenment should stand firm in the project of constructivism against dogmatists who claim access to political truth; and the moderate and radical branches of the Enlightenment should propose constructivisms that do not marginalize the other tradition. In political terms, the Left has room for those who exercise authority (as presidents, legislators, or judges) and those who challenge authority (as protestors, social critics, or poets). Constructivism is a malleable procedure that can evolve over time to help the Enlightenment create political theories for changing circumstances.

In Chapter 4 I offer a concrete example of how Kantian courage advances the twenty-first–century Enlightenment by showing how it empowers contemporary political theorists to create new terms of political-religious discourse. After the Battle of Vienna in 1683, few Muslims lived in northern or western Europe until after World War II, when Muslim immigrants helped rebuild the postwar landscape. Today, Muslims constitute a large and growing minority in Europe and North America. How should global citizens conceive of political relationships between Muslims and non-Muslims? Militants propose familiar terms of enmity: Islam and the West, or *dar al-Islam* ("abode of Islam") and *dar al-harb* ("abode of war"). At the end of the eighteenth century, Kant proposed the concept of the ethical community to describe how diverse ecclesiastical faiths could coalesce on a pure rational faith. Though Kant sought unity between Catholics and Protestants, his vision of pluralism pointedly excludes Muslims and Jews. Fortunately, Kantian courage empowers contemporary theorists to create concepts that are more nuanced and inclusive.

The chapter then shows how Rawls and Deleuze propose new terms to conceptualize political-religious pluralism. Rawls invents the notion of the overlapping consensus to describe how diverse peoples—including Muslims in the imaginary republic of Kazanistan—can coalesce on global issues related to the environment, security, and human rights. For Rawls, Western liberals should confidently and modestly reach out to other global constituencies in terms that the latter could endorse from within their own universes of reference. Deleuze shares and radicalizes Rawls's sense that the Enlightenment needs to rethink its political-religious imaginary. Deleuze invents the concept of the assemblage to describe political bodies that are provisional, multilayered, and receptive to the claims of minorities. The concept of the overlapping consensus illuminates the role of global institutions such as the United Nations, while the concept of the assemblage displays the flows—of ideas, images, people, products, cultures, weapons, viruses, and so forth—that shape the prospects of global religious pluralism. By inventing these concepts, Rawls and Deleuze extend the Enlightenment tradition in admirable ways—rejecting outdated concepts and creating new ones that honor the rights and claims of emerging constituencies.

Today, certain Muslim political theorists seek to join a conversation with Western political thinkers working in the Enlightenment tradition. According to Tariq Ramadan, Muslims may and should appropriate certain Enlightenment notions, reject others, and contribute new ones to the tradition. For Ramadan, the critical ethos, more than any specific doctrine, defines the Enlightenment—a position that resonates with those of the other major figures in this study. To exhibit how the Enlightenment is redefining itself in a positive way today, I show how Ramadan, in a Kantian spirit, invents the concept of *dar al-shahada* ("space of testimony") to describe Western societies in which Muslims may freely practice their religion, participate in politics, and present the message of Islam to their fellow citizens. For contemporary secularists such as Paul Berman and Caroline Fourest, Ramadan represents a threat to the epochal achievements of the Enlightenment. I argue, to the contrary, that Ramadan's exercise of Kantian courage opens up the prospects of respectful and contentious interreligious dialogue and cooperation. The Enlightenment changes with the addition of new constituencies. Yet Kantian courage demands that we reconceptualize political discourse to reflect the new religious diversity on the ground. Like the great European philosophers of the historical Enlightenment, contemporary political theorists are constructing new ideas and frameworks to prevent a recurrence of the religious wars that wracked early modern Europe.

In the conclusion, I restate my case for advancing the Enlightenment by entering a debate about the meaning of autonomy. Kant's earliest critics—such as Friedrich Heinrich Jacobi—accused Kant of fostering moral nihilism by arguing that human beings give themselves the moral law. Many Kantians up to the present try to counter this charge by arguing that Kant provides a true account of morality for imperfectly rational beings such as humans. The problem with this approach is that it freezes Kantianism—and the Enlightenment—in its original eighteenth-century form. In contrast, this book argues that we need to heed Kant's call for us to think for ourselves about the problems of our day. This approach enables us to strengthen Kant's philosophy by modifying it in light of later philosophical developments and to think creatively about how to welcome new religious constituencies into the twenty-first–century Enlightenment.

1

Kantian Courage

In 1932, shortly before the Nazis exiled him from Germany, Ernst Cassirer defended the Enlightenment against its opponents. "Instead of assuming a derogatory air, we must take courage and measure our powers against those of the age of the Enlightenment."[1] Cassirer's call for courage resonates today when the Enlightenment is again under attack from several angles. There is, firstly, a war of maneuver in which religious activists employ violence against symbolic targets of the "Enlightened" world. The 9/11 attacks against the heart of the United States' financial, military, and political power were one example. But so were the November 26, 2008, attacks in Mumbai that targeted the Taj Mahal Hotel and other symbols of global pluralism. Many religious activists around the world have declared war on what we—arrogantly, from their perspective[2]—call an age of Enlightenment. At the same time, there is an ongoing war of position in which intellectuals and scholars attack the very idea of the Enlightenment. Clearly, the diversity of thinkers, movements, schools, traditions, and countries involved in the long eighteenth century render any appeal to a singular set of ideas or values problematic.

There is also the fact that the Enlightenment did foster certain ideas—such as capitalism and secularism—that have helped decimate the natural environment and admirable religious and cultural traditions. The enlightened world may not radiate disaster triumphant—as Horkheimer and Adorno notoriously declared[3]—but the Enlightenment deserves critique even from its admirers. Partisans of the Enlightenment, then, need courage to face its enemies. But what kind exactly? How can we conceptualize and exercise courage without descending into thoughtlessness—a perennial complaint against this ancient virtue?[4]

This chapter aims to unpack the contemporary relevance of Kant's famous exhortation to exercise the courage of our *own* intellect.[5] Initially, I describe how Kant offers several, partially conflicting definitions of courage, including a morally neutral quality of temperament, an admirable disposition to question and contribute to political discourse, and a strength of mind to combat radical evil within oneself. I then show how contemporary political theorists inflect Kantian courage in different ways, as apology (Wood), jurisprudence (Rawls), and critique (Deleuze). In the conclusion, I argue that Kantian courage should maintain a productive tension between its faithful, reformist, and revolutionary moments. In a word, Kantian courage demands that we confront the singular problems of our day and then construct new solutions, selectively drawing upon the resources of the historical Enlightenment—a case that I develop in the remainder of the book.

KANT ON COURAGE

Kant's reflections on courage are rich and complex. They are rich because, in a few condensed passages, Kant explains how his moral philosophy differs from Aristotle's—and, by extension, how the moderns differ from the ancients. They are complex because Kant's reflections on courage take at least three forms—each of which influences contemporary appropriations of Kant's legacy. In this section, I show how Kant conceptualizes courage as a morally neutral, or potentially corrupting, character trait in the *Groundwork for the Metaphysics of Morals* and the *Critique of Practical Reason*; then, how Kant redefines courage as intellectual disquietude and creativity in "What is Enlightenment?"; and, finally, how Kant extols courage as an embattled comportment of mind in *Anthropology from a Pragmatic Point of View* and the *Metaphysics of Morals*. Taken individually, each conception of courage contains a blind spot—as do many appropriations of the quintessentially militaristic virtue of courage. Together, however, they provide a promising way to think about courage in late modernity.

Like many Enlightenment philosophers, Kant treats Aristotle as both a valuable teacher and the authority to dethrone.[6] Kant's famous description of courage in the *Groundwork*—a quality of temperament that is only of relative value compared to the unqualified goodness of the good will[7]—implicitly references and contests Aristotle's account of courage in the *Nicomachean Ethics*. Here, it is worth saying a few words about Aristotle so that we may better understand the novelty of Kant's thinking. "The courageous person," Aristotle explains, "will stand his ground for the sake of what is noble (since this is the end of virtue) in the right way and as reason requires."[8] Aristotle's conception of courage contains several planks. First, courage, as a virtue of character, is a product of habituation. Nature provides us with the raw material for the virtues, but habituation develops and polishes the virtues.[9] Courage, then, is a type of refined sensibility—a mean between fear and confidence.[10] Second, courage only becomes manifest when an individual confronts a dangerous, or evil, situation. As a virtue, courage is exceptional—one only needs it when one feels pain or the potential for pain.[11] Third, courage requires practical reason, or the capacity to survey the situation at hand and determine the best course of action. Brutes are not courageous because they race from a dangerous situation to an apparently safe one without reflection; but human beings have the faculty of practical reason (*phronesis*) that turns spiritedness into courage. Fourth, courage can only be exercised for noble ends or motives. Courage expresses a desire for honor from one's community or, alternately, the desire to avoid shame at failing to live up to one's civically defined ideals. For the ancient Greeks, courage was a way to separate oneself from the crowd, which is why it was the "political virtue par excellence."[12] Finally, courage finds its preeminent display in combat. The courageous man wants to test his mettle in the most dangerous, and thereby most noble, circumstances. "So it is the person who does not fear a noble death, or the risk of immediate death, that should really be described as courageous; and risks in battle are most of all like this."[13] Aristotelian courage, in sum, is a rare and noble disposition to face dangerous situations, particularly warfare, with practical judgment, spiritedness, and self-control.

In the *Groundwork* and the *Critique of Practical Reason*, Kant attempts a systematic refutation of Aristotelian ethics. One way that he does this is by criticizing each component of Aristotle's account of courage. Kant seems to banish courage from the canon of modern ethics. First, qualities of temperament—such as courage, resolution, and perseverance—are only as good as the will that employs them. Surely we want to develop these qualities—for we could not universalize our maxim *not* to cultivate these qualities in situations where they serve our morally permissible ends—but in themselves they deserve no respect. From Kant's perspective in the *Groundwork*, courage is a natural gift—albeit one we can and should refine—for which we deserve no moral praise or blame. Second, morality imbues our life at all moments. Kant's famous models of moral decision making in the *Groundwork*—such as the shopkeeper deciding whether to charge a consistent price, or the child reflecting upon the rectitude of lying[14]—are not trying to be courageous. By offering banal examples, and silently dropping all references to heroes or acts of heroism, Kant contributes to the modern project of affirming everyday life.[15] Third, Kantian morality must be based on *pure* practical reason. Kant, here, challenges Aristotle's valorization of the properly cultivated habits or inclinations to focus on the comportment of mind (*Gesinnung*) that follows its own moral compass. Kant, to be sure, retains a place for *phronesis*, or empirical practical reason, to advance our ends by formulating rules of skill or maxims of prudence. Yet Kant insists that morality emanates from our thinking, noumenal natures and not our corporeal, phenomenal ones. In addition to providing a pure moral philosophy, Kant articulates an egalitarian one, that is, one that does not hinge on one's physical or intellectual capabilities. Fourth, and along these lines, Kant rejects all socially conditioned conceptions of nobility. Kant grants that the moral law, or its ideal as the realm of ends, may be considered noble.[16] Yet Kant, as a rule, rejects the idea of describing people or actions as noble. "By exhortation to actions as noble, sublime, and magnanimous, minds are attuned to nothing but moral enthusiasm and exaggerated self-conceit."[17] For Kant, morality must be grounded on principles, not a desire to emulate somebody else. Merit, or personal excellence, confuses matters; we need to place the concept of duty—honoring the commands of our own legislative reason—center stage. For Kant, appeals to nobility are more likely than not to foment the worst kinds of moral willing and action, including a desire to participate in senseless combat such as dueling.[18] In his foundational works of moral philosophy, then, Kant contributes to the modern attack on courage as a militaristic, masculine virtue that needs to be transformed, or sublimated, for civilized society.[19]

One of the defining features of Kant's thinking, however, is a desire to incorporate the insights of his adversaries. As Lewis White Beck notes in his study of the *Critique of Practical Reason*, Kant accompanies his critique of heteronomous philosophers such as Epicurus and Hutcheson with a systematic reappropriation of their key doctrines, such as a duty to pursue happiness and cultivate moral feelings.[20] Kant's thinking is that his predecessors have captured an element of our moral experience that has had some traction with people. Therefore, the "one true system of philosophy" must be able to offer an explanation and a role in an architectonic system for each of these elements.[21] The ideal of courage, then, spoke to the citizens of the ancient Greek city-states, as it did to the Prussians of the eighteenth century (including the "Soldier-King" Frederick William I), and as it continues to do for many political actors today. In his essay on the Enlightenment, Kant redefines this ancient virtue as a quality of the mind rather than a quality of the heart. For Kant, courage makes possible a genuine reform in thinking (*wahre Reform der Denkungsart*).[22] Here, I propose to isolate several aspects of Kant's account of courage in his essay on Enlightenment that persist in much contemporary Kantian political theorizing.

Courage, first, entails saying no to what has been handed down to one on trust. As commentators have noted, Kant vacillates in this essay on the source of immaturity (*Unmündigkeit*) that prevents people from exercising their own understanding.[23] On the one hand, Kant suggests that the free exercise of reason—a right protected by the king and instantiated through the formation of a concrete public sphere—by itself will be enough to enable people how to think for themselves. On the other, Kant states that immaturity is self-incurred (*selbstverschuldet*) when people do not have the resolve (*Entschließung*) and courage (*Mut*) to think without the reassurance of a guardian's approval. Kant vacillates, then, on whether immaturity persists because of social conditions or individual mental characteristics. Yet Kant thinks the first step out of societal intellectual timidity requires a courageous mental disposition of the individual. For Kant, unenlightened human beings have grown accustomed to the leading strings (*Leitbande*) and walkers (*Gängelwagen*) that steer their growth and movement.[24] Societal guardians, or authority figures, at one point may have been responsible for creating and imposing these leading strings and walkers, but now, these devices, or ossified mental habits, have become second nature for many people. Courage, then, demands that one throw aside these patterns of thinking, or rather, of not thinking. It is important to see that Kant's preeminent example of courage in this essay is refusing religious orthodoxy. Kant addresses the political question of whether a "society of clergymen" may propose a religious constitution that prohibits amendments or revisions.

> Such a contract, which is concluded in order to prevent for eternity all future enlightenment for the human race is quite simply null and void, even if it were to be confirmed by the most supreme authority. . . . One generation cannot form an alliance and conspire to put a subsequent generation in such a position in which it would be impossible for the latter to expand its knowledge (particularly where such knowledge is so vital), to rid this knowledge of errors, and, more generally, to proceed along the path of enlightenment.[25]

Kant, here, battles against religious orthodoxy that wants to protect itself from criticism. The sixteenth- and seventeenth-century religious wars demonstrated the dangers of enforcing a doctrinal creed. In addition to destroying life and property, the religious wars put a clamp on freethinking. For Kant, as for many of the other leading figures of the historical Enlightenment, the major political problem was how to prevent a descent back into religious warfare.[26] The polemical tone of Kant's 1784 essay expresses his exasperation at religious authorities—and the complicit publics that support them—that wish to reinforce intellectual laziness and cowardice. Kant does not deny religious believers the right to believe what they want to believe. Nor does Kant think that violent revolution will accomplish a substantive transformation in mentalities. Only gradual transformation, facilitated by the exchange of ideas in the public sphere, will bring about the proper conditions for individual and collective autonomy. Yet Kant insists that enlightenment can only transpire if individuals exercise the courage to challenge entrenched dogmatic ways of thinking.

Like the term *critique*, however, courage has a positive as well as a negative sense.[27] Courage entails battling intellectual complacency, but it also demands that one propose new ideas and arguments. In his essay, Kant offers three examples of intellectual courage: the military officer who publicly questions the justness of a war or its proper handling; the citizen who publicly denies the propriety of a government's tax code and, by extension, its policies; and the clergyman who publicly suggests an improvement of a church and its interpretation of religion. We must immediately note that Kant's conception of publicity only applies to scholars (*Gelehrten*) addressing a reading public.[28] For Kant, courage does *not* mean taking up arms against the military, the government, or the church. Yet courage does mean standing up to intellectual prejudices and proposing new ways to think about international relations, domestic politics, and religion. "As a scholar," Kant says of the clergyman, "he enjoys full freedom and is even *called upon* to communicate to the public all of his own carefully examined and well-intentioned thoughts."[29] Kant attributes to Frederick the Great the motto: "*argue* as much as you like and about whatever you like, but *obey!*"[30] Kant, in turn, reverses the emphasis: obey (to guarantee the functioning of the civil machinery and to preserve the peaceful conditions that make possible intellectual growth), but argue! In this way, Kant's essay on the Enlightenment politicizes the Copernican Revolution of the *Critique of Pure Reason*. In the first *Critique*, Kant maintains that human beings construct the mental framework that makes possible experience.[31] In other words, we legislate our basic metaphysical categories. In his essay on Enlightenment, Kant contends that this prerogative extends to practical matters—even, and especially, the most controversial ones touching upon religion. Kantian courage calls upon us to contribute our own thoughts to public dialogues about the future of our collective life.

Kantian courage does not permit the reflective human agent much rest. Intellectual courage, for Plato, may have meant standing up to the Athenian demos and sacrificing one's life for a truth that one did not doubt.[32] In its own way, though, this approach permitted Plato—or Plato's Socrates—a way to *stop* thinking once he had reached a certain comfort with his own conclusions. For Kant, on the contrary, "statutes and formulae"—intellectual rules that do not bend to human reflection or historical experience— "are the shackles of a perpetual state of immaturity."[33] Kant does not assert that we can reach the end of history or conclusively solve all of humanity's deepest riddles. A remarkable feature of Kant's 1784 essay is that it protests those moments when any philosopher, including Kant, falls into the habit of intellectual dogmatism. Consider, for example, Kant's 1799 public declaration on Fichte's *Wissenschaftslehre* that professed to take Kant's spirit in a direction opposed to Kant's letter: "The critical philosophy must remain confident of its irresistible propensity to satisfy the theoretical as well as the moral, practical purposes of reason, confident that no change of opinions, no touch up or reconstruction into some other form, is in store for it; the system of the *Critique* rests on a fully secured foundation, established forever; it will prove to be indispensable too for the noblest ends of mankind in all future ages."[34] This is precisely the type of statement that Kant, in his 1784 essay, would have viewed with skepticism and derision. To "agree to a permanent religious constitution"—or to assert the permanence of any moral or political philosophy—would "destroy, and render vain a span of time in humankind's progress toward improvement."[35] In a genuine age of criticism, Kant explains in the *Critique of Pure Reason*, everything must submit to free and public examination.[36] Courage, then, means having the intellectual and spiritual fortitude to listen to one's viewpoints criticized in a public forum. Courage also calls upon us to challenge any dogmatism that presents itself as immune from critique and to venture new ideas into public conversations. Kantian critique is a task that calls us to think with and against our time. Kant's 1784 essay inspires a dissatisfied and experimental mental disposition, one that views thinking as both permeated by and resistant to historical or sensual elements.

Kant's 1784 essay on Enlightenment retains an Aristotelian component even as it displaces others. Courage does not manifest itself only or primarily in physically dangerous or fearful situations. The model of Kantian courage is the brave scholar willing to critique dogma—even one widely shared in a religious, political, or cultural community—not the soldier fighting on behalf of shared communal values. Kant either eliminates or drastically redefines nobility as a curious and innovative way of thinking rather than as a propensity to keep levelheaded in physical combat. For Aristotle, courage requires *phronesis*, practical reason or judgment, whereas for Kant courage requires thinking (*denken*), or the exercise of reflective judgment, to produce concepts for situations where old ones do not suffice. Yet Kant's 1784 conception of courage still retains an Aristotelian flavor insofar as courage combines cognitive and affective elements. Kantian courage is receptive to ongoing events—in Kant's case, the age of Frederick—as it determines the need for or shape of philosophical concepts. This element of his thinking is reinforced by English translators who render key Kantian terms—such as *Gesinnung*, *Denkungsart*, and *Haltung*—into sensualist terms, such as, respectively, mental attitude, sentiment, or disposition.[37] Perhaps to recapture the philosophical line of flight of his earlier essay, Kant subsequently emphasizes that courage can only be exercised in the pursuit of Kantian moral principles. Kant retains the concept of courage, then, but purges the elements that could be used to turn it against him or his work.

Courage, Kant explains in the *Anthropology from a Pragmatic Point of View*, is the composure of mind to "take on fear with reflection."[38] Several features of this definition are worth noting. First, the source of courage, properly understood, is the mind or the will, even though courage subsequently becomes manifest in the physical body. Kant's new term for courage as a quality of temperament is stout-heartedness (*Herzhaftigkeit*). Like courage (*Mut*) in the *Groundwork*, stout-heartedness is a quality of remaining cool in dangerous situations and is thus morally neutral or even potentially corrupting. Fools or the reckless can be madmen who do not recognize dangers or are indifferent to consequences; the stouthearted are at least capable of diagnosing a situation accurately and acting prudently. Yet stout-heartedness, as an instrumental virtue, can be used for evil as well as good ends. Courage, on the other hand, "rests on principles and is a virtue."[39] In line with the moral phenomenology of Kant's *Groundwork* and *Metaphysics of Morals*, courage or virtue "signifies a moral strength of will."[40] The source of courage, then, lies deep inside of us, even though—like other moral endowments that Kant identifies in the *Metaphysics of Morals* such as moral feeling, conscience, love of human beings, and respect[41]—these predispositions of the mind become felt by our sensible natures. Thus "courage as affect (consequently belonging in one respect to sensibility) can also be aroused by reason and thus be genuine bravery (strength of virtue)."[42] Affects stimulate the flow of blood, and the person feeling courage recognizes his or her pulse quicken in a dangerous situation.[43] Yet Kant's position in the *Anthropology* and the *Metaphysics of Morals* is that the causality arrow goes one way, from the mind or will to the body. Kant, we may say, has transvalued courage from a Greek to a Christian concept, one that characterizes the nature of the will rather than a quality of the embodied mind.

Along those lines, Kant transfers the realm of courage from the battlefield to the domain of everyday affairs. The true enemy of courage is not physical threats to our wellbeing, but, in Rousseau's terms, *amour-propre*, our propensity to value ourselves and our actions through the eyes of others. In the *Anthropology*, the greatest threat to courage is not the sword of a combatant, but rather the demeaning word of a peer: "If, in doing something worthy of honor, we do not allow ourselves to be intimidated by taunts and derisive ridicule of it, which is all the more dangerous when sharpened by wit, but instead pursue our own course steadfastly, we display a moral courage which many who show themselves as brave figures on the battlefield or in a duel do not possess."[44] For Kant, being courageous is doing something worthy of honor, not something necessarily honored in present-day circumstances. Honor, in the sense of social esteem, can move us to overcome "cruder self-interest and vulgar sensuality" to act for the common weal (*gemeinnützig*).[45]

We should work to promote a high regard for virtuous acts; the feeling for honor can still serve as a "simulacrum of virtue" to remove obstacles to the growth of the real thing.[46] Yet, of course, people may always promote lying or murder or other evil acts, in which case we ought to hold fast to the supreme principle of morality. For Kant, in other words, true courage means willful resolve to adhere to the categorical imperative even in the face of social ridicule.

In 1784, as I have shown, Kantian courage displayed itself by thinking with others in the public sphere. By the time of the *Metaphysics of Morals* (1797) and *Religion within the Boundaries of Mere Reason* (1793), however, Kant has dehistoricized and depoliticized the notion. Here, Kant's moral philosophy merges with his philosophy of religion, particularly the discussion of radical evil in the first part of *Religion within the Boundaries of Mere Reason*. We may reconstruct Kant's argument as follows. The human being is a *homo duplex*. That is to say, human nature is divided between its noumenal, or rational, self, which legislates and obeys the moral law, and its phenomenal, or sensible, nature, which has its own desires that sometimes align, but often resist, the imperatives of duty. "Now the capacity and considered resolve to withstand a strong but unjust opponent is *fortitude* (*fortitudo*) and, with respect to what opposes the moral disposition *within us*, virtue," or courage.[47] One might think that Kant endorses a type of moral Manichaeanism in which the good soul exercises courage to combat the evil body, but, in fact, Kant's argument retains an Augustinian moral psychology.[48] In other words, the source of temptation resides within the will itself. Radical evil is "the propensity of the power of choice to maxims that subordinate the incentives of the moral law to others (not moral ones)."[49] There is a perverse germ in the will that strives to make moral compliance depend on happiness, and not the reverse. In Kant's late writings, moral courage means fighting a battle within oneself that one cannot reasonably expect to win in this lifetime, which is why, in the *Critique of Practical Reason*, Kant says that we must postulate the immortality of the soul, and in the *Religion within the Boundaries of Mere Reason*, Kant tarries with the idea of grace. For our purposes, I only wish to note that Kant's late conception of courage does not express itself in history or with others. As J. B. Schneewind observes of Kant's conception of radical evil: "What is essential is individual moral improvement. Political action cannot improve matters."[50] By locating courage in the will, in our noumenal selves, Kant fully purifies the Aristotelian aspects of his thinking at the cost of eliminating courage as a political virtue.

In a moment, we consider how contemporary political theorists appropriate elements of Kant's conceptions of courage. Here, though, we may
anticipate the conclusion of the argument and summarize the strengths and
weaknesses of each one. Kant's description of courage as a quality of temperament in the *Groundwork* rightly leads us to be suspicious of appeals to
courage. As history repeatedly demonstrates, demagogic leaders often start
unjust wars by labeling their enemies or critics as cowards. For moderns,
we need to elevate peaceful virtues—such as tolerance, curiosity, or sympathy—and demote others—such as courage—that serve to inflame passions
and warfare. Yet courage has too much of a hold on the popular imagination, as Kant subsequently realized, to simply remove it from the core of
practical philosophy. So the Enlightenment needs to rethink rather than
ignore the virtue. In "What is Enlightenment?" Kant redefines courage as
the ability to think for oneself. Courage, in this instance, means confronting the problems of one's historical milieu and constructing concepts and
principles to address them. This conception of courage infuses the parts
of the critical philosophy that appeal to philosophers as diverse as Arendt,
Deleuze, Foucault, Habermas, Rawls, and Ramadan. My view, which I substantiate in the remainder of the book, is that embodying this conception
of Kantian courage is the best way to advance the Enlightenment in the
twenty-first century, particularly as we face different problems than the ones
that confronted Kant in the eighteenth century. Yet Kant's late conception
of courage reminds us that we should not hold our principles too lightly.
For heirs of the Enlightenment, the doctrinal legacy of the *Aufklärung* still
provides a valuable way to think about many important practical matters,
and it is a treasure worth preserving. Ultimately, though, I wish to argue
that we ought to view Enlightenment era philosophies as toolboxes that we
may use for our own purposes. This, I think, is the best way to exercise the
courage of our own understanding.

KANTIAN INFLECTIONS

In this section, I look more closely at how leading political theorists conceptualize and embody Kantian courage in contemporary circumstances.
Wood, Rawls, and Deleuze agree that Kant's philosophy, and the Enlightenment tradition more broadly, continues to inform progressive political
thinking. Each of these thinkers thus dedicates some of their scholarly energy to clarifying Kant's insights and some to revising or applying Kant's

insights to late modern political life. Wood's introductions to the *Cambridge Editions of the Work of Immanuel Kant*, Rawls's *Lectures on the History of Moral Philosophy*, and Deleuze's *Kant's Critical Philosophy: The Doctrine of the Faculties* are, respectively, classics in contemporary mainstream, analytic, and poststructuralist Kant scholarship, while Wood's *Kantian Ethics*, Rawls's *A Theory of Justice* and *Political Liberalism*, and Deleuze's *A Thousand Plateaus* illustrate how Kant's philosophy can infuse contemporary political theorizing. Yet Wood, Rawls, and Deleuze inflect Kant's legacy in different ways. For Wood, Kantian courage means what it does for Kant in the *Anthropology* and *Metaphysics of Morals*: a firm mental resolve to interpret correctly and apply concretely the supreme principle of morality. For Rawls and Deleuze, on the contrary, Kantian courage means what it does for Kant in his 1784 essay on Enlightenment: a disposition to refuse religious, or philosophical, dogmatism and to propose new ideas and principles in their stead, though Rawls is more cautious than Deleuze in how he balances the moments of transgression and legislation. In the following three subsections, I track how Wood, Rawls, and Deleuze conceptualize Kant's legacy and its importance for contemporary political theorizing, focusing particular on their accounts of the role of the social critic as militant, judge, and nomad, respectively.[51] In the conclusion to this chapter, I argue that Kantians today should appreciate the tension between these three contending strands of the Enlightenment tradition.

Kantian Courage as Apology

Wood is an unabashed apologist for the Enlightenment. In an essay entitled "Philosophy: Enlightenment Apology, Enlightenment Critique," Wood puts his cards on the table and states how we should take up the Enlightenment legacy and not merely study it. The historical Enlightenment "thought of itself as a philosophical age, and its best and most forward-looking thinkers proudly assumed the title of *philosophe*."[52] The *philosophe*s assigned reason the ultimate responsibility to evaluate systems of thinking and ways of life. The French Revolution extolled the ideals of *liberté, égalité, fraternité*, and the Enlightenment philosophers provided a consistent framework in which to think of these ideals.[53] Yet, many historians point out, the Enlightenment was an extremely complex movement that contained much diversity and disagreement. Wood's reply is that "*we* ought to see ourselves as heirs of the Enlightenment," and, of our ancestors, so to speak, the most important is Kant.[54] To advance the Enlightenment into the future, we progressives need to apologize for Kant in the same way that Plato apologized for Socrates: that is, honor his philosophy as the finest expression of our deepest thoughts and aspirations for humanity. Here, then, is how Wood apologizes for Kantian ethics today.

Of all modern moral theorists, Wood declares, "Kant did the best job of identifying what lies at the heart of our moral values and principles."[55] At the same time, "nobody today actually subscribes to every aspect of Kant's thought about morality."[56] The intellectual task facing contemporary Kantians is to separate the rational kernel of Kantian ethics from its inessential husk. That is to say, Kantians must distinguish what is living in Kantian ethics—namely, the core ideas of the *Groundwork*—from what is dead—including Kant's particular judgments about women, race, suicide, the death penalty, and other topics that seem to reflect more Kant's eighteenth-century Prussian prejudices than his metaphysical principles. For Wood, the process of self-critique is entirely consistent with Kant's philosophy. After all, the *Critique of Pure Reason* assigns human reason to police itself: "We rely on reason to criticize feelings, desires, inspirations, revelations, and even reason itself, not because it is infallible but rather because it is only through reason that we have the capacity to criticize or correct anything at all."[57] Wood is open- and broad-minded. He recognizes that Kantians must take up the Kantian spirit even if it opposes the Kantian letter. Wood also does an admirable job of directly confronting criticisms of Kant in their strongest form. Yet Wood thinks that Kant's doctrines ultimately emerge unscathed from the criticisms that have been leveled at them. For Wood, Kant's doctrines must remain the foundation of any contemporary progressive political movement.

Within Kant scholarship, one of Wood's great contributions has been to examine the interconnectedness of Kant's various formulations of the supreme principle of morality in the *Groundwork*. The most famous formulation is the first: "Act only in accordance with that maxim through which you at the same time can will that it become a universal law" (FUL). Kant's idea that the categorical imperative serves as a universalizability test has become a standard trope in introductory ethics courses. More surprisingly, the FUL remains the focus of scholarly attention largely through Rawls's and Onora O'Neill's interpretation of Kant's "CI-procedure" that forms, generalizes, and tests maxims for their universalizability. According to Wood, however, the FUL is vulnerable to many valid criticisms as an account of the supreme principle of morality. The FUL cannot generate a positive moral rule or duty—all it can do is show that certain maxims cannot be universalized. The FUL also issues in false negatives—whereby innocuous maxims such as holding the door open for other people are forbidden—and false positives—immoral actions that are logically universalizable. Wood accepts Hegel's charge that the FUL is empty without more determinate content.[58] Yet Wood thinks that a comprehensive view of Kant's ethical thought reveals that the FUL is just the initial step in a longer journey. The formula of humanity (FH)—"So act that you use humanity, as much in your own person as in the person of every other, always at the same time as an end and never merely as a means"—provides the ethical value that FUL lacks. The ground, the fundamental value, of Kantian ethics is the respect for human beings as dignified and equal ends in themselves. Attention to FH illuminates Kant's own writings—for Kant appeals to this value throughout the *Metaphysics of Morals*, where testing maxims by their universalizability is relatively rare. More importantly, FH provides the philosophical basis for a progressive politics that respects each person's—man or woman, rich or poor, in the racial or religious majority or minority—equal dignity. To apologize for Kantian ethics means to correct mistaken or incomplete readings of Kant's philosophy.

Yet the Enlightenment was not just or primarily an academic movement. According to Wood, Kant and other great eighteenth-century *philosophes* originated a movement of self-reflective political practice that was taken up by Bentham, Hegel, Marx, and Freud. Kant's claim that practical reason has precedent over theoretical reason planted the seed for Marx's thesis that philosophy's task is not to interpret the world, but to change it. "Reason is a capacity to know the world, but chiefly it is a capacity to act in it, and because reason is also oriented toward society, its vocation above all is to transform the social order—actualizing the Enlightenment ideals of liberty, equality, and fraternity."[59] The instantiation of Enlightenment principles has changed throughout history. In the eighteenth century, the Enlightenment combated feudalism, aristocracy, and religious superstition. In the nineteenth and twentieth centuries, the Enlightenment has protested economic, racial, cultural, and gender inequalities. The future Enlightenment might fight for Kant's principles on other terrains. Yet the social dynamic remains the same today and for the foreseeable future as it did in Kant's time. The problems of civilized life are social in nature: human goodness has become corrupt through restless competitiveness with each other. The solution to these problems is digging deep into human reason to discover the moral compass that can reorient us in the right direction. To realize reason's end, we need to actualize these principles in social life. To complete our apology of Kantian ethics, then, we need to fight in the real world using Kant's practical philosophy as a battle plan.

Are post-Kantians friends or enemies? That is, should true and proper Kantians view post-Kantians as allies or opponents in the contemporary Enlightenment? Wood's position is that philosophers *qua* philosophers need to listen to reasoned objections to their positions. Drawing upon the essay "Philosophe" in the French *Encyclopedia*, Wood argues that a philosopher differs from ordinary people because of her capacity for reflection. External forces and internal drives buffet other people, whereas the philosopher moves only according to principles and grounds that she has chosen through reason. To exercise reason, the philosopher must listen to and evaluate arguments other than her own. Overweening authority and the systematic spirit both hinder philosophical reflection: "A philosopher is not so attached to a system as to be unable to understand the strength of the objections that can be raised against it."[60] Wood, then, is a philosopher, not a wise man: he thinks that we still must tolerate, even encourage, discussion of fundamental principles. He titles his book *Kantian Ethics* because he thinks that Kantians may criticize and modify Kant's practical philosophy. Yet, he maintains, "I do not think the most defensible version of Kantian ethics needs to depart as far from what Kant thought and wrote as most recent practitioners of Kantian ethics do."[61] In his essay on Enlightenment apology, Wood puts the point more belligerently: "The enemies of Enlightenment, in the twentieth century as well as the eighteenth, often include not only its natural enemies—political tyranny and religious superstition—but also some of its own offspring."[62] There are limits to respectful debate. In the face of a conservative Counter-Enlightenment, we need to get everybody on the same page. Wood's militancy becomes clear when he discusses Anglo-American and Continental Kantians who stray too far from the pack.

The main intellectual target of *Kantian Ethics* is Rawls and his students, including Kantian constructivists such as Onora O'Neill and Christine Korsgaard. Wood acknowledges a debt to Rawls and Rawlsians for bringing Kant and Kantian ethical theory to the center of moral and political philosophical debates.[63] Wood also recognizes that many of them have become insightful readers of Kant. Yet Wood thinks that Rawlsians are threatening to derail the Enlightenment. Rawls's great mistake is to build a moral epistemology upon intuitions. Rawls's main justificatory strategy is premised upon forging harmony between our judgments and our principles. Rawls's starting point of ethical reflection is considered convictions—intuitive judgments and principles that we feel reasonably confident about upon reflection. Rawls's idea of "reflective equilibrium" presses philosophers to forge frameworks that achieve consilience of intuitions. "This way of understanding Kantian ethics," Wood decries, "could hardly get Kant's conception of ethical theory more wrong if it tried."[64] For Kant, the supreme principle of morality is metaphysical, which means that it may and must be formulated independently of experience (*a priori*). Kant's conclusive derivation of the categorical imperative, in Section II of the *Groundwork*, performs a philosophical analysis of rational willing as such. There are no empirical elements—intuitions or convictions—in Kant's argumentation. Wood criticizes Rawls's model of ethical theory for the same reason that Kant criticized heteronomous or empiricist moral doctrines throughout his practical philosophy: they are utterly unreliable as moral guideposts. By presenting his political theory as political, not metaphysical, "Rawls too seems to be saying that he was attempting no more than to make coherent and systematic the moral and political consensus of modern liberal Enlightenment culture. But this misses the main point of the Enlightenment, which was to subject everything—including religious beliefs, political institutions, and common moral opinions—to the judgment of reason."[65] Rawls's empiricism threatens us with moral relativism, the belief that different people may reasonably disagree about the fundamental principle of morality. For Wood, political liberalism betrays the heart of the Enlightenment. Given his repeated belittling remarks (for instance, the Rawlsian reading "could hardly get Kant's ethical theory more wrong if it tried"), we may speculate that Wood aims to marginalize Rawlsians within Kant scholarship and, as much as possible, political liberals within the progressive Left.

Wood has less to say about Continental appropriations of Kant's legacy by thinkers such as Deleuze, Derrida, Foucault, or Lyotard. He prefers to give them the silent treatment—which, in academia, can also be a form of attack. But Wood does dedicate a few words to Foucault's essay on the Enlightenment. Wood commends Foucault for drawing attention to the Enlightenment ethos. Wood questions, though, Foucault's position that this ethos means "*seeking* the mature adulthood of enlightenment."[66] Foucault implies that once individuals have discovered Kantian ethics that they are not yet adults, whereas Foucault, Wood asserts, plays the role of a petulant child who does not want to admit that his parents are right. Foucault is right to show that the world does not yet practice Enlightenment ideals, as he is also correct to seek new political agents and practices to advance the Enlightenment. Yet Foucault's critique of the Enlightenment implicitly draws upon Enlightenment values even as it explicitly attacks them. This "lightheartedly nihilistic attitude toward Enlightenment principles" simply provides ammunition to the Enlightenment's traditional enemies.[67] Postmodernists "have no clear idea of what they are seeking, nor will they ever get any as long as they sink themselves in skepticism, aestheticism, and self-subversion."[68] Wood, then, banishes Foucault and his ilk from the Enlightenment as well.

Wood, in sum, embraces Kant's account of moral virtue as an embattled comportment of mind. We all know, upon philosophic reflection, that the supreme principle of morality is the categorical imperative. Yet other civilized human beings, as well as our innate propensity to radical evil, encourage us to quibble away our duties. According to Wood, this is a huge mistake, a failure of our responsibilities as beings endowed with reason. In academia, we have a duty to present and understand Kant's principles correctly, even if we do not have to agree with how he applied them using the empirical evidence at his disposal. We also have a duty to actualize those principles in a world that fails to honor the Enlightenment ideals of autonomy, equality, and community.

Wood presents himself, then, as a militant. Like the Kantian figure in the *Anthropology*, Wood stands up for Kant's principles even in the face of ridicule. Rawls and other constructivists offer the "standard or dominant conception of ethical theory today," whereas Wood's more philosophical and rigorous Kantian ethics now appears "decidedly reactionary."[69] Yet Wood thinks that the future of the Enlightenment depends upon having the mental fortitude to hold on to Kant's principles in the face of moral and political corruption. "In an *un*philosophical century such as ours, the defense of philosophy can consist only in the reassertion of the most radical aims of the Enlightenment in a spirit of patient perseverance and (if need be) of stubborn impenitence."[70] Wood does not apologize for being a doctrinal Kantian. Or rather, Wood polemicizes for Kant's principles rightly understood. Below, I will demonstrate that Wood's position has a commendable aspect—it motivates him to distribute Kant's ideas widely—but it also has a chilling effect on Enlightenment debates about principles. This book, however, advocates a different conception of Kantian courage, which can be fleshed out by turning to Rawls.

Kantian Courage as Jurisprudence

Rawls has a complex relationship to the Kantian tradition. In *Political Liberalism*, Rawls emphasizes that he does *not* take up the so-called Enlightenment project of formulating a secular comprehensive moral doctrine to replace the discredited faith of the Christian ages.[71] Rawls renounces *this* interpretation of the Enlightenment, for in many ways it replicates the dogmatism of religious militancy, simply replacing secular for theological grounds. And in a 1998 letter to his editor, Rawls proposes to eliminate most Kantian phrases for a revised edition of *Political Liberalism*.[72] Rawls, here, seeks to complete the turn he began in the 1980s by envisioning his political theory as political and not metaphysical. For Rawls, Kant's metaphysics of morals is not a viable option to form the constitutional charter, so to speak, for liberal democracies or the global community. Rawls, then, is not a doctrinal Kantian. At the same time, one cannot reach a profound understanding of Rawls's philosophy without seeing how it is imbricated through and through with Kantian ideas, themes, strategies, and inspiration. In this section, I consider the Rawlsian case for treating Kantian courage as the ethos of a Supreme Court judge, one who both respects precedent and is receptive to philosophical arguments and historical developments.

In the *Lectures on the History of Moral Philosophy*, Rawls explains how he orients himself by the history of philosophy, particularly by the era of modern European philosophy often called the Enlightenment. In his lectures, Rawls immerses himself in the ideas of such thinkers as Locke, Rousseau, Kant, or John Stuart Mill. Rawls seeks to enter their thought and understand their problems as well as their attempts to solve them. Rawls, here, exhibits humility as he encourages his students to surpass him in sensitivity to aspects of the texts as well as the sense of the whole.[73] Rawls endorses the truism that historians of philosophy must get the facts right, both by seeing how the pieces of the philosopher's arguments fit together as well as how they relate to the broader intellectual and political context. Why, though, go through this effort besides the pleasure of solving puzzles? The reason is that apprenticing with masters is the best way to learn how to become a thinker oneself. Rawls makes clear in his *Lectures* that he does not study the history of philosophy to discover ideas that we can neatly insert into our time and place. We don't study the classics "in the hope of finding some philosophical argument, some analytic idea that will be directly useful for our present-day philosophical questions in the way they arise for us."[74] Rather, we study the history of philosophy because it provokes us to look afresh at our contemporary circumstances. The study of earlier forms of philosophical thought "prompts us to consider by contrast our own scheme of thought, perhaps still implicit and not articulated, from within which we now ask *our* questions."[75] Rawls's account of the history of philosophy shows how each generation of philosophers departed from their predecessors. Greek philosophers such as Plato and Aristotle plumbed the resources of human reason to replace the fading ideals of Greek civil religion. Medieval philosophers sought to accommodate Christian theology and Greek philosophy. Modern philosophers such as Hume, Kant, and Leibniz attempted in different ways to reconcile Christian ethics and Newtonian physics. Our problem, which differs from the one facing the Enlightenment thinkers, is how to forge civil alliances between citizens who endorse widely disparate faiths. The problems of philosophers in the future, presumably, will differ from ours. For Rawls, philosophy is the pursuit of wisdom and, as such, does not reach definitive answers to timeless problems.

How, then, to explain Rawls's relationship to Kant—clearly the pivotal figure in his account of the history of philosophy? From the perspective of traditional Kant scholarship, Rawls's interpretation of Kant's practical philosophy is rife with mistakes. Consider, for example, Rawls's claim that the original position offers "a procedural interpretation of Kant's conception of autonomy and the categorical imperative within the framework of an empirical theory."[76] Rawls's goal in *A Theory of Justice* is to modify Kant's thought process in Section II of the *Groundwork* in which Kant deduces several formulations of the supreme principle of morality. Rawls uses the device of the original position to formulate, in analogous fashion, the principles of justice as fairness. On its own, philosophers can accept or reject Rawls's argument in Part I of *Theory*. The problem for many Kant scholars, though, is that Rawls presents a Kantian interpretation of justice as fairness in paragraph 40 of *Theory* that seems to give a Kantian imprimatur to his theory of justice. Yet Kant vehemently rejected the idea that human beings could formulate principles in "the framework of an empirical theory." Kant offered his metaphysics of morals in Section II of the *Groundwork* precisely to serve as an antidote to the popular moral philosophers who offered up a mishmash of rational and empiricist concepts. Rawls's interpretation of Kant's practical philosophy—for example, his identification of a four-step Categorical Imperative procedure that resembles Rawls's Original Position procedure—has struck many Kantians as misguided. For Kantians such as Allen Wood, Rawls's project is beyond repair: it must simply be opposed as a heteronomous doctrine that betrays the hopes of the Enlightenment. Other Kantians, however, try a different tack and argue that Rawls's political theory must be "reconstructed" to salvage the Kantian moral insights at its heart.[77]

Political liberals, as a rule, try to avoid unnecessary controversies about how to interpret comprehensive moral doctrines such as Kant's. Yet Rawls often notes that Kantians who cling to the letter of his doctrines miss an essential part of his message. In a reminiscence that serves as the foreword to the *Lectures on the History of Moral Philosophy*, Rawls explains how he approached the history of philosophy in a Kantian spirit:

> I followed what Kant says in the *Critique of Pure Reason* at B866, namely that philosophy is a mere idea of a possible science and nowhere exists *in concreto*: "[W]e cannot learn philosophy; for where it is, who is in possession of it, and how shall we recognize it? We can only learn to philosophize, that is, to exercise the talent of reason, in accordance with its universal principles, on certain actually existing attempts at philosophy, always, however, reserving the right of reason to investigate, to confirm, or to reject these principles in their very sources." Thus we learn moral and political philosophy . . . by studying the exemplars, those noted figures who have made cherished attempts at philosophy; and if we are lucky, we find a way to go beyond them.[78]

For Rawls, being a Kantian philosopher does not simply mean mastering Kant's ideas. In Architectonic of Pure Reason, from where this quote is taken, Kant distinguishes historical cognition from the self-development of reason. The first approach takes the form of imitation, which renders the individual a "plaster cast of a living human being."[79] The second approach renders the philosopher's ideas his or her own. There are passages throughout Kant's writings in which thinking for oneself means thinking along the path of pure reason that Kant discovered. Kant may mean, in the quote that Rawls cites, that we study "actually existing attempts at philosophy" merely to sharpen our mental faculties so that we may ultimately arrive at the Kantian system. For Rawls, however, Kant's warnings about imitation may justly apply to Kant scholars, and Kant's admonition to philosophize—to keep plumbing reason to pose questions to the given—work against Kant's and Kantian attempts to dogmatize. Like Foucault, then, Rawls thinks that the

Kantian ethos demands that we sometimes cut the doctrinal cord that connects us to the Enlightenment.

In "The Independence of Moral Theory" (1975), Rawls explains why he experiments with the Kantian frame: "All the main conceptions in the tradition of moral philosophy must be continually renewed: we must try to strengthen their formulation by noting the criticisms that are exchanged and by incorporating in each the advances of the others, so far as this is possible. In this endeavor the aim of those most attracted to a particular view should be not to confute but to perfect."[80] Kantians who fail to renew their tradition risk becoming scholastics, mastering the intricacies of Kant's system for its own sake. Kant scholars, in other words, can fiddle while the Enlightenment tradition comes under sustained—and often thoughtful—attack. More seriously, Kantians risk becoming dogmatic if they treat Kantian courage as an embattled moral comportment of mind that refuses to listen to reasonable criticisms or adjust to global realities. Consider, for example, Robert S. Taylor's call for a universalistic Kantian liberalism to intervene in a global environment that harbors illiberal theocratic, authoritarian, and totalitarian regimes.[81] Rawls would surely say that universalistic Kantian liberals ought to have a voice in domestic and international affairs. Numerous Rawls scholars take it for granted that in his nonpublic life Rawls believed in and practiced a form of Kantian ethics.[82] Yet Rawls thinks that it is unreasonable to demand that citizens of faith in domestic societies, or decent but nonliberal peoples around the world, embrace universalistic liberalisms. Such an approach refuses to listen to the often-reflective comments of others; it also is highly unlikely to convince citizens of faith who accept liberal democratic societies, for their own reasons, without wishing to have the ideal of moral autonomy imposed upon them. A far better approach, for Rawls, is to keep Kantianism a living tradition by reconstructing it using new historical and philosophical materials—even if certain cherished ideals must be left by the wayside. A few examples may illustrate this point.

In his *Lectures on the History of Moral Philosophy*, Rawls spells out several interlaced criticisms Hegel makes of Kant's practical philosophy—as well as how a Kantian political theory can address them. First, Hegel criticizes Kant's view of human nature that posits a sharp divide between our noumenal, thinking selves and our phenomenal, embodied selves. Kant's account of transcendental freedom posits that the free will rises above the contingencies of its inclinations, needs, social arrangements, or historical background. Though Kant's writings on history, politics, and anthropology complicate this assessment, in the *Groundwork* Kant focuses moral philosophy's attention strictly on the individual will. According to Hegel, Kant misses how persons are "rooted in and fashioned by the system of political and social institutions under which they live."[83] Hegel values freedom, but he sees it as a collective, historical achievement that cannot be premised on the individual comportment of mind. For Hegel, human beings inhabit an ethical life (*Sittlichkeit*) of a community that encompasses the family, civil society, and the state and that shapes what they can do, think, perceive, feel, and will. Rawls departs from Hegel's account of human nature in important ways, but he accepts the outlines of what is often called the communitarian critique of liberalism: that human beings are not atomistic individuals but are rather deeply permeated and shaped by *Sittlichkeit*.[84] Second, and related, Rawls agrees with Hegel that practical philosophy cannot be sharply divided between its moral and political sides—as Kant attempts, for instance, by distinguishing the Doctrine of Virtue and the Doctrine of Right as two branches of the Metaphysics of Morals. Rawls agrees with Hegel that it is "only within a rational (reasonable) social world, one that by the structure of its institutions guarantees our freedom, that we can lead lives that are fully rational and good."[85] By directing attention to individual decisions in the *Groundwork*, Kant displaces attention from the structure of the economy that deeply impacts our choices. It makes a difference, for example, whether or not the economy compels people to steal to feed their families. That is why even late Rawls insists that a political conception of justice also has a moral component. To facilitate the conditions of individual and collective freedom, one has to insure that the basic structure of society distributes benefits and burdens fairly, that is, is just. The focus of Rawls's political theory is thus Hegelian rather than Kantian.[86] Finally, Rawls thinks that political philosophy must try to reconcile us to our social world rather than merely criticize it. Part of political philosophy's purpose, for Hegel and Rawls, is "to calm our frustration and rage against our society and its history by showing us the way in which its institutions, when properly understood, from a philosophical point of view, are rational."[87] In *A Theory of Justice*, Rawls reconciles his readers to the need for civil liberties, affirmative action, and a property-owning democracy; and in *Political Liberalism*, Rawls reconciles liberals to reasonable pluralism that may water down liberal ambitions, for instance, to prohibit religious speech in the public sphere. For Rawls, a Kantian ethics can direct our attention to other worlds rather than the world before our eyes. In this third respect, then, Rawls sides with Hegel's account of *Sittlichkeit* (what is) rather than Kant's morality of *Sollen* (what should be). For Rawls, Kantians may perfect Kant's practical philosophy by appropriating Hegel's valid criticisms of it.

At the same time, Rawls is no more a doctrinal Hegelian than he is a doctrinal Kantian. In the *Lectures on the History of Moral Philosophy*, Rawls describes the metaphysical background of Hegel's political philosophy. For Hegel, *Geist*—spirit or mind—becomes increasingly self-consciousness as the master-slave dialectic plays itself out in history. There is a logic to this course of events—encompassing politics, art, religion, and philosophy—that cannot be reversed or altered. The task of philosophy is to capture this development in thought so that we may understand and reconcile ourselves to it. "A true metaphysician, [Hegel] believes that *reality is fully intelligible . . .* and so it *must* answer to the ideas and concepts of a reasonable and coherent categorial system."[88] Rawls seems to find Hegel's metaphysics as incredible as Kant's, and, in "Kantian Constructivism in Moral Theory," Rawls admits that he finds Dewey naturalized Hegelian idealism more to his taste.[89] Yet Rawls makes a poignant observation about Hegel's system: "Hegel often speaks of the fate and suffering of individuals in a way that cannot but strike us as callous and indifferent."[90] For Rawls, criticizing metaphysical dogmatism constitutes its own moral act. Courage—for secular and theological metaphysicians alike—often means blocking out criticisms of one's dogma. For Rawls, on the contrary, courage means keeping open one's eyes, ears, and hearts to other perspectives.

This is as true of historical developments as it is of philosophical ones. To build a Kantian political theory on an empiricist framework, as Rawls does, means forging a dialectical relationship with one's historical milieu. "As far as possible, the knowledge and ways of reasoning that ground our affirming the principles of justice and their application to constitutional essentials and basic justice are to rest on the plain truths now widely accepted, or available, to citizens generally."[91] Rawls's point in *Political Liberalism* is Rousseauian, or Kantian, insofar as Rawls seeks an egalitarian foundation for political legitimacy. Yet Rawls differs from Kant, at least, by focusing on how democratic citizens—rather than rational beings as such—interpret their shared historical experience. For Rawls, many of the "plain truths" held by late modern liberal democratic citizens concerns the relationship between religion and politics. Consider, for example, the lessons learned by early modern philosophers after the Reformation. The Reformation "fragmented the religious unity of the Middle Ages and led to religious pluralism. . . . This in turn fostered pluralisms of other kinds, which were a basic and permanent feature of contemporary life by the end of the eighteenth century."[92] Modern philosophers responded to European pluralism in myriad ways, of course, but one widely shared assumption among Enlightenment philosophers was that theologians could no longer write political laws with an unchecked hand. Thomas Hobbes in *Leviathan* promulgated one version of this thesis. All of the main premises in Hobbes's argument for a secular social contract, according to Rawls, could be defined and explicated without reference to religion or theology. After the rudiments of Hobbes's secular moralism were in place, religion could be brought in to buttress the system. The force of Hobbes's philosophy,however, was to place religion on the defensive. A plain truth shared by liberal democratic citizens is that religious oppression is unfair and unreasonable.[93] This is a sociological or historical claim, rather than an *a priori* premise. As such, the sense of the plain truth is liable to shift—as it did, for instance, after the Abolitionist movement in the 1830s used religious arguments to protest slavery in the face of political intransigence. At the time, these religious activists may have seemed unreasonable with their demands for the immediate and uncompensated emancipation of the slaves. In hindsight, though, it is clear that the Abolitionists were advancing the ideals of liberty and equality in ways that could ultimately be justified to nonreligious, but reasonable, fellow citizens. As a result of the Abolitionists—and the latter-day Civil Rights Movement—liberal democratic citizens recognize that Hobbes's assault on religious "superstition" needs to be tempered.[94] Furthermore, our sense of the relationship between religion and politics may change as new constituencies make their voices heard. "Social changes over generations also give rise to new groups with different political problems."[95] Kantian courage, for Rawls, means adapting to the times.

Richard Rorty overstates the case, though, when he argues that Rawls's approach is "thoroughly historicist" and that he is "simply trying to systematize the principles and intuitions typical of American liberals."[96] Rorty's argument contains a grain of truth insofar as Rawls thinks that political theorists must construct their arguments primarily using the material at hand. Political constructivism employs impure practical reason to fashion political principles and thus does not aspire to the status of Kant's metaphysics of morals. Yet Rorty hands Rawls over to his many critics who accuse him of simply capitulating to the mood of the times. Michael Sandel, for instance, argues that political liberals today would surely want to support the

Abolitionists, but in the 1830s they would have lacked the philosophical resources to do so. "The notions of equal citizenship implicit in American political culture of the mid-nineteenth century were arguably hospitable to the institution of slavery." Kantians, of course, could argue that the formula of humanity demands that we treat all people as ends, and not merely as means, and therefore we are morally obligated to free slaves—but this is precisely the type of metaphysical argument that Rawls eschews in *Political Liberalism*.[97] Yet Rawls resists being placed in the historicist box in which Rorty, Sandel, and others wish to place him.[98] Political philosophy, Rawls explains in the *Lectures on the History of Political Philosophy*, probes the limits of practical political possibility. Philosophy must be realistic—to have some purchase in the world—but it must also be utopian—helping us envision worlds that more consistently realize our practical principles. For Kant, political philosophers must perform the role that Kant assigned them in the 1784 essay on Enlightenment: publicly criticizing, debating, and proposing ideas in the public sphere. In this respect, political philosophy is not just philosophy about politics, but it is itself a political activity subject to perpetual contestation.[99]

In *Political Liberalism*, Rawls invites ordinary citizens to think of themselves, in their political roles, as judges. "Public reason sees the office of citizen with its duty of civility as analogous to that of judgeship with its duty of deciding cases."[100] This invitation parallels Kant's proposal, in the preface to the 1781 (A) edition of the *Critique of Pure Reason*, to establish a "court of justice, by which reason may secure its rightful claims while dismissing all its groundless pretensions."[101] Like Kant, Rawls seeks to determine a standard of reasonableness to guide judges in their decisions. Unlike Kant, Rawls does not think that judges can appeal to "eternal and unchangeable" laws given by pure reason, nor that the court of pure reason can govern all the domains—theoretical and practical—where reason is active. For Rawls, the standard of reasonableness changes over time, and the idea of public reason applies strictly to political actors discussing constitutional essentials. Rawls's metaphor of judging, then, highlights affinities and differences between Kant and him. By looking more closely at Rawls's discussion of "The Supreme Court as the Exemplar of Public Reason" in *Political Liberalism*, though, we may gain a sense of how Rawls thinks Kantians should philosophize today.

The task of judges, according to Rawls, is to "develop and express in their reasoned opinions the best interpretation of the constitution they can."[102]

How do judges decide, though, what qualifies as the best interpretation of the constitution? Clearly, judges need to master the constitution and the history of its interpretation in Supreme Court cases. There are boundaries within which Supreme Court justices must work. "The constitution is not what the Court says it is. Rather, it is what the people acting constitutionally through the other branches eventually allow the Court to say it is."[103] One criterion of the best interpretation of the constitution, then, is that it accords with the constitutional text, Supreme Court precedent, and democratic will as manifested through the legislative, executive, and judicial branches. Yet Rawls does not subscribe to the notion that judges simply interpret the law. As a theoretical matter, texts, precedents, and democratic will are open categories that do not lead, as in an arithmetic equation, to a conclusive result. Even the most literally minded Supreme Court judge still has to make a choice about what words or precedents or ideas to emphasize in how he or she interprets the constitution. Furthermore, practically speaking, texts, traditions, or practices can all be unjust or immoral. Up until the US Civil War, for instance, the Constitution, Supreme Court, and Congress all permitted slavery. That is why constitutional interpretation, for Rawls, must combine textual, historical, or political arguments with untimely philosophical ones. The best interpretation of the constitution appeals to the relevant constitutional materials and "justifies it in terms of the public conception of justice or a reasonable variant thereof."[104] As Rawls makes clear in his discussion of political constructivism, democratic citizens do not *find* a public conception of justice. They *make*, or construct, it, with the help of philosophers. Supreme Court justices, then, must think for themselves about how to decide cases, performing a delicate balancing act of respecting tradition but also weighing philosophical arguments and historical developments.

For Rawls, then, judges do not look to the original intent of a constitution's founders, nor do they try to deduce judgments from a higher law. Rather, they believe in a notion of the living law that refines its principles in light of historical developments and ongoing reflections. In *Political Liberalism*, Rawls identifies three instances in US constitutional history to show how political actors and judges shifted their appraisal of the higher law. In the 1780s, the founders recognized that the Articles of Confederation did not provide for a strong enough federal government so they wrote the Constitution stipulating an amendment process. After the Civil War, the Reconstruction amendments expanded the range of who could be considered an equal American citizen. And in the New Deal, the Supreme Court allowed the growth of the so-called welfare state that permitted the government to redistribute wealth. In each case, political actors and judges upheld certain broad values such as liberty and equality. At the same time, these actors and judges rethought the nature of the higher law.[105] Once again, Rawls seeks a path between pure decisionism and pure literalism. Supreme Court judges may not simply invent the law or invoke their own personal morality when deciding cases. "Rather, they must appeal to the political values *they think* belong to the most reasonable understanding of the public conception and its political values of justice."[106] Thinking, for Rawls, is an essential quality of judging. Rawlsian judges are handed a certain body of theoretical materials as well as the facts of the case, but often concepts and facts align uneasily: judges must exercise reflective judgment to render a decision.[107] Rawlsian jurisprudence appreciates the tension between abstractly held principles and the singularities of cases, the need for conceptual consistency over time and receptivity to intellectual and historical transformations. This cast of mind, furthermore, does not belong exclusively to judges: "To check whether we are following public reason we might ask: how would our argument strike us presented in the form of a supreme court opinion?"[108] Rawls, in sum, invites all citizens *as if* they were Supreme Court judges exercising reflective judgment.

In his reminiscence on teaching the history of philosophy, Rawls expresses his admiration for Kant—as well as how he thinks that we should advance the Enlightenment legacy:

> All the great figures . . . lie to some degree beyond us, no matter how
> hard we try to master their thought. With Kant this distance often
> seems to me somehow much greater. Like great composers and
> artists . . . they are beyond envy. It is vital in lecturing to try to exhibit
> to students in one's speech and conduct a sense of this, and why it is
> so. That can only be done by taking the thought of the text seriously, as
> worthy of honor and respect. This may at times be a kind of reverence,
> yet it is sharply distinct from adulation or uncritical acceptance of the
> text or author as authoritative. All true philosophy seeks fair criticism
> and depends on continuing reflective public judgment.[109]

Rawls seeks a profound understanding of Kant's doctrines and expresses "a kind of reverence" for Kant in his writings and lectures. Yet Rawls does not adulate or uncritically accept Kant's ideas. Rawls's metaethics (political constructivism), for instance, draws deeply upon Kant's Copernican revolution in philosophy at the same time as Rawls transforms it for contemporary philosophical and political circumstances. Furthermore, Rawls anticipates—and even encourages—his readers to criticize his work and subject it to "continuing reflective public judgment." For Rawls, then, Kantian courage does not mean an embattled comportment of mind that adheres to Kant's principles in the face of philosophical or political objections. Rather, Rawls invites us to view ourselves in our role as citizens as pragmatic Supreme Court justices who respect the past but are ultimately responsible to the needs of the present.

Kantian Courage as Critique

Deleuze, like Rawls, has a complex relationship to Kant and the Enlightenment more broadly. For each aspect of Kant's legacy that I consider in this book—its doctrines, metaethics, and ethos—Deleuze selects some components and rejects others. Many of the key themes in Deleuze's principal thesis for his doctoral thesis, *Difference in Repetition*, have a Kantian provenance, such as immanence, ideas, faculties, and the transcendental. And yet Deleuze pries these concepts from the Kantian architectonic—particularly its theme of the unity of reason—and transmogrifies them for his own philosophy. As several recent studies have shown, Deleuze participates in a line of post-Kantian philosophers such as Salomon Maimon, Henri Bergson, and Nietzsche whose work both builds upon and departs from Kantian foundations. Likewise, Deleuze states in *What is Philosophy?* that philosophy is a constructivism, yet his understanding of constructivism exemplifies his notorious claim that his Kantian notions are a "monstrous offspring" that no orthodox Kantian would recognize as legitimate.[110] Finally, Deleuze often shares Nietzsche's harsh assessment of Kant as a timid university professor, an underhanded Christian, and a day laborer in philosophy who simply compresses common sense morality into formulae. Yet Deleuze shares Nietzsche's hope for "a radical transformation of Kantianism, a re-invention of the critique which Kant betrayed at the same time as he conceived it, a resumption of the critical project on a new basis and with new concepts."[111] Like Nietzsche and Foucault, Deleuze casts aside the leading strings of one type of Kantian Enlightenment in order to walk freely into a new Enlightenment.[112] In this section, I consider Deleuze's description of critique, Kant's betrayal of it, and how to resume the project of critique today. I conclude this section by noting that both Rawls and Deleuze agree that Kantian courage requires thinking for oneself: yet Rawls's ethos is more conciliatory, and Deleuze's more combative, to established patterns of thought.

In *Nietzsche and Philosophy*, Deleuze speaks for himself and Nietzsche when he extols Kant's contribution to modern philosophy. "Kant's genius, in the *Critique of Pure Reason*, was to conceive of an immanent critique."[113] Critique, from the Greek word *krinein*, means to judge, to discern, or in its most primitive meaning, to weigh.[114] In the *Critique of Pure Reason*, Kant sets out to weigh certain statements that have been the prerogative of metaphysics. Some statements, suitably adjusted, may be preserved—for example, every event has a cause—just as other statements, such as the world having or not having a beginning in time, literally have no sense. Kant's *Critique of Pure Reason* entails a massive restricting of what types of statements that reflective people may understand to be within the purview of human cognition. Yet critique cannot weigh statements to their sense or senselessness without investigating the mental faculties that make those judgments possible. The *Critique of Pure Reason* thus performs a detailed topological survey of the powers and limits of mental faculties such as reason, understanding, imagination, and sensibility.[115] Kant is the first philosopher, Deleuze continues, "who understood critique as having to be total and positive *as* critique."[116] Kant held that in the age of critique, *nothing*—no political, religious, or cultural orthodoxy—could rightfully excuse itself from "free and public examination."[117] By undermining the philosophical foundations of theological doctrines such as the free will, the immortal soul, and the existence of God, Kant played the role—in Mendelssohn's famous words—as the *Alles-Zermalmer*, the "all-destroyer" of medieval metaphysics.[118] Kant's total critique is positive insofar as it clears the ground for the development of new ways of thinking. Destruction and creation are the two sides of critique. What does it mean to say, though, that Kant's critique is *immanent*? The issue is the nature of reason that performs the critique. From Socrates and Plato onwards, rationalists have argued that reason is capable of critique because it mentally transcends the empirical realm. Empiricists such as Epicurus and Hume argue that there is only one world, but the tendency of their philosophies is to console us to living harmoniously within it. Kant's genius is to forge the idea of immanent critique from the critical impulse of rationalism and the one-world metaphysics of empiricism. From a post-Kantian perspective, the idea of immanent critique is an open problem that compels us to constantly reevaluate our mental frameworks using a reason that is both embedded in the material world and capable of ascending or descending its levels to find new perspectives for critique.[119]

At the same time that Kant opens up brilliant prospects for philosophy with the idea of immanent critique, he erects arbitrary barriers that occlude them from view. Consider, for example, Kant's account of the postulate of immortality in the *Critique of Practical Reason*. The categorical imperative is, strictly speaking, empty—it takes the pure form of law that requires material content to be added to it to be given substance. But how do we know that we are following the command to act through duty? We cannot: The moral law "*never acquits us,* neither of our virtues nor of our vices or our faults: at every moment there is only an apparent acquittal, and the moral conscience, far from appeasing itself, is intensified by all our renunciations and pricks us even more strongly."[120] We can never be sure that we are acting on moral maxims because there is always another way to frame our subjective principles of volition: we can literally go mad thinking about the disposition of our will (which we can never perceive) and possible ways to restate our maxims. Rather than dwell upon the problems with this account of morality—as Freud, Kafka, and Nietzsche did, each in his own way—Kant covers them up with an account of the postulate of immortality that posits a realm beyond human experience in which we will forever grapple with the mysteries of an empty moral law. "But this indefinite prolongation, rather than leading us to a paradise above, already installs us in a hell here below."[121] Kant's demands for a pure moral law and a notion of immortality are arbitrary and cruel, an apparent concession to the moral prejudices of his time. Far better, for Deleuze, to subject Kant's practical philosophy itself to critique.

Deleuze, then, participates in the philosophical tradition of *metacritique*. For philosophers as diverse as Hamann, Reinhold, Schelling, Hegel, Marx, and Nietzsche, the great project of modernity is to dig deeper into human reason or human history to discover the foundation for a self-justified critique. The post-Kantians, Christian Kerslake notes, shared two objectives: "to remain faithful to the central claim of Kant's Copernican turn (that 'objects must conform to our cognition')" and a commitment "to eradicating all the presuppositions that hampered the purity of Kantian critique."[122] The post-Kantians diverged on how to complete Kant's Copernican revolution and even to what extent such a venture could succeed. Deleuze himself seemed to shift his expectations and hopes for his own philosophy. At certain times, he presents his philosophy as "the only realized Ontology," at others, he admits that the best a philosopher can do is construct *a* plane of immanence, or a map of the actual and virtual realm, including its political dimensions.[123] In this section, I focus on Deleuze's account of the critical ethos in *Nietzsche and Philosophy*. Though Deleuze tempers his revolutionary rhetoric over time, he never gives up Nietzsche's thesis that philosophy must be untimely, that is, "acting counter to our time and thereby acting on our time and, let us hope, for the benefit of a time to come."[124]

In *Nietzsche and Philosophy*, Deleuze explains how Nietzsche employs the idea of critique to undercut Kant's doctrinal system. In the *Lectures on Logic*, Kant famously states that citizens of the world approach the field of philosophy with four basic questions: What can I know? What ought I to do? What may I hope? What is man? Metaphysics, Kant explains, answer the first question, morality the second, religion the third, and anthropology (broadly conceived) the fourth. Critique is the propaedeutic—or, the preliminary exercise to determine the powers and limits of our mental faculties—upon which Kant builds his metaphysics that systematically answers these philosophical questions.[125] Kant simply takes it for granted that these are the right questions. Thus "Kant merely pushed a very old conception of critique to the limit, a conception which saw critique as a force which should be brought to bear on all claims to knowledge and truth, but not on knowledge and truth themselves; a force which should be brought to bear on all claims to morality, but not on morality itself."[126] According to Deleuze, Nietzsche discovered a way to explain the genesis of our concepts and mental faculties. We cannot assume that all human beings arrive at moral principles or judgments in the same way. Nor can we assume that there are transhistorical mental faculties such as reason, understanding, or imagination. Rather, Nietzsche proposes an "active science" to unearth the sense, value, and origin of mental, physical, and spiritual entities. Initially, this active science is a *symptomology* that interprets phenomena as symptoms of a deeper clash of forces. Then, active science becomes a *typology* that interprets forces by the standpoint of their quality. Active forces express their identity before casting an evaluating glance at other beings or forces, whereas reactive forces emerge from saying no to what they are not. Finally, active science becomes a *genealogy* that evaluates "the origin of forces from the point of view of their nobility or baseness."[127] According to the doctrine of the will to power, every animal, including the philosopher, instinctively strives to "fully release his power and achieve his maximum of power-sensation."[128] By patiently unpeeling the layers of our moral judgments, then, we discover their origin in an affirmative or negative will to power. For Nietzsche, an active science explains why Kant is, ultimately, an "underhanded Christian."[129] Kant's philosophy is a symptom, as well as a contributing factor, to the modern loss of faith of Christian theology. Yet as a type, Kant's philosophy—with its underlying egalitarian drive to honor the humanity of even the basest— preserves the heart of Christian morality. Nietzsche, furthermore, evaluates Christian-modern morality harshly, as an expression of *ressentiment* against nobility as such. Nietzsche writes *On the Genealogy of Morality* precisely as "a polemic," or a critique, of this morality in order to espouse the rise of a newly confident pagan aristocracy.[130]

Deleuze agrees with Nietzsche's attack on Kant's moral doctrine for positing unconditional laws in a world that calls for more nuanced judgments.[131] Deleuze also takes up Nietzsche's philosophy of sense and value that prizes noble forces and an affirmative will to power. Yet Nietzsche's philosophy is not free of prejudices. Though he sometimes qualifies this assessment, in general Nietzsche identifies two types of human beings: masters and slaves, nobles and the common who abhor them. This dichotomous vision imparts a plaintive quality to much of Nietzsche's writings: "The ruin, the destruction of higher people, of strangely constituted souls, is the rule: it is horrible always to have a rule like this in front of your eyes."[132] For many democrats who read Nietzsche, however, his vision is too stark. For the fact of the matter is that "nobles," for most of their lives, compromise with the majority of their peers, even in matters of simply speaking the same language. Conversely, Nietzsche overlooked the possibility that ordinary people could break from dominant codes and innovate—though not necessarily with the grandeur of say Napoleon or Wagner. William E. Connolly expresses the insight behind left-Nietzscheanism this way: "Nietzsche, still dazzled by an aristocratic imaginary he no longer endorses as historically actualizable, could not purge the odor of democratic mediocrity from his aristocratic nose long enough to explore the positive relation of democracy to some possibilities he does admire."[133] In other words, Nietzsche hesitates to criticize his own aristocratic contempt for the modern world.

Part of the lasting fame of *Nietzsche and Philosophy* is that it lays an ontological foundation for left-Nietzschean political thought.[134] One way that it does this is by maintaining that every body is plied by active and reactive forces, an affirmative and a negative will to power.

> Every relationship of forces constitutes a body—whether it is chemical,
> biological, social or political. Any two forces, being unequal, constitute
> a body as soon as they enter into a relationship. . . . Being composed of
> a plurality of irreducible forces the body is a multiple phenomenon, a
> "unity of domination." In a body the superior or dominant forces are
> known as *active* and the inferior or dominated forces are known as *reac-
> tive*. Active and reactive are precisely the original qualities which express
> the relation of force with force.[135]

According to Deleuze, every body has a side that conforms to dominant
codes, states, habits, discursive norms, and so forth, as well as a side that
branches free from those territorializing or normalizing forces. For Deleuze,
noble and slave *traits* permeate every body. It is not that some people are
purely noble and some purely slavish; it is that every body is a "multiple
phenomenon" composed of warring forces, some demanding conformity
to physical or social pressure, others seeking to affirm their difference from
other forces or beings. The political question is how to arrange the active and
reactive forces in a hierarchy, that is, how to compose our political bodies
so that active forces prevail over reactive ones. One Nietzsche scholar howls
at Deleuze's translation of his avowedly elitist political philosophy: "Nietzsche's power relation conception demands that an active hierarchy of relations of force be a *real* hierarchy" and "Nietzsche's unique voice in the canon
must be preserved."[136] In his famous "Letter to a Harsh Critic," Deleuze
acknowledges that his monographs in the history of philosophy silently add,
drop, or rearrange elements.[137] Deleuze forms a "zone of indistinction" with
his subject matters so that one can, with reasonable confidence, quote these
books as evidence of Deleuze's thinking at the time.[138] So, Deleuze concedes
that his work on Nietzsche differs from others that try to be more faithful
to Nietzsche's intentions. On the more substantive point, however, Deleuze
thinks that the critical ethos must be turned against Nietzsche as surely as
Nietzsche turned it against Kant.

Can critique come to an end? That is, can philosophers ever get to the
bottom of the questions that Kant raises in the *Logic*? Deleuze's answer,
in *Nietzsche and Philosophy*, takes the form of a dogmatic skepticism: we
know that philosophy cannot find peace in the eternal or the historical. "If
philosophy's critical task is not actively taken up in every epoch philosophy
dies and with it dies the images of the philosopher and the free man."[139]
Philosophy wrestles with its time in thought. Two types of events spur the

philosopher into action. First, an event in the actual world jostles our mental faculties. The French Revolution of 1789, or the Bolshevik Revolution of 1917, or the events of September 11, 2001, destabilize common sense—or the harmonious accord of the mental faculties—and force the philosopher to remake mental order out of chaos. For Deleuze, there is no such thing as a philosophical method to lead us to eternally valid truths; there is only *paideia*, or cultural training, that teaches us to swim, so to speak, by throwing us in the ocean of the actual world.[140] As Foucault observes in his essay on Enlightenment, many philosophers and theologians have assumed that history has an overarching narrative or a *telos*. Deleuze agrees with Foucault's Kant that modern philosophy's task is to penetrate the singularity of its historical moment. Now that time has been unhinged from its ancient bearings—partly as a result of Kant's *Critique of Pure Reason*—philosophers must stand alert to today's difference from yesterday.[141] Yet philosophy is not only sparked by actual events; it is also moved by virtual events in the thinker's mind. For Deleuze, the human mind is not a *res cogitans* ontologically separated from one's material body, nor is it driven solely by instincts shared with other animals. The human mind is distinctly receptive to, and capable of transfiguring, cosmic forces that elude scientific observation. The human mind, in other words, straddles the historical and the untimely, its milieu and other (immanent) realms that provide new perspectives on one's time. Critique, then, is an ongoing task for human beings partially embedded in history.

In a conversation with Foucault published as "Intellectuals and Power," Deleuze specifies the critic's role in the political sphere. According to an earlier model—shared by both Plato and Kant—the critic has a right to judge the political realm because he is entirely removed from it. A philosopher's access to *a priori* truths—whether posited as existing in a transcendent realm of forms or immanently in the faculty of pure practical reason—legitimizes his perspective on the affairs of the cave or the sensible world. An alternate tradition—encompassing Machiavelli and Marx—asserts that philosophers as such have little power to steer history: they merely comment on it or serve as its midwife. For Deleuze and Foucault, on the contrary, critics have the power to act as a relay point between theory and practice. "The relationships between theory and practice are . . . partial and fragmentary."[142] Theories are largely composed of elements drawn from the historical sphere. Human practices, in turn, are partially shaped by the conceptual frameworks through which people view them and their purposes. Critics, then, treat theories as toolboxes that can contribute to the building of new institutions or as lenses that expose new vistas on the present and possible futures.[143] As makers of tools or cutters of lenses, critics need to be attuned to the problems and opportunities of their milieu.

One historical moment looms large in Deleuze and Guattari's work: May 1968.[144] Commenting on the upheavals in Paris among workers and students that, in effect, turned normal life upside down, Deleuze states: "There were a lot of agitations, gesticulations, slogans, idiocies, illusions in '68, but this is not what counts. What counts is what amounted to a visionary phenomenon, as if a society suddenly saw what was intolerable in it and also saw the possibility for something else."[145] Deleuze's task, in his technical language, was to counter-effectuate the events of '68.[146] On the one hand, in the actual experience of the events, there was a lot of foolishness, posturing, and thoughtlessness that is no more commendable because workers and students did it than it would be if perpetrated by police officers or judges. On the other, there was an event, an "ahistorical vapor," that emanated from that state of affairs and expressed a shared hope for a new world. In *Anti-Oedipus*, Deleuze and Guattari aimed to give voice to the prospects, in Foucault's words, for a "non-fascist life."[147] Yet this critical stance targeted leftists with fascist *moeurs*, or habitual ways of thinking and acting, as well as the more familiar targets of the political Right.[148] The Deleuzian critic has a Nietzschean "instinct for attack"[149]—against both conservative enemies of '68, as well as its participants who channel its surprising energies into rigid political categories, such as Maoists.

The critic, Deleuze states in *Nietzsche and Philosophy*, is both a creator of values and a criminal.[150] Critique emanates from an "active expression of an active mode of existence."[151] The critic creates values from a productive desire reaching out into the world, not from a lack or hunger for the attribution of established values or the recognition of others. Deleuze's notion of critique thus differs from the Kantian or Hegelian notions available in other variants of critical theory.[152] Why, though, does Deleuze describe the critic as a criminal? First, the critic must generate space for independent thought by renouncing established values, even those constitutive of his current identity. In *Thus Spoke Zarathustra*, Nietzsche describes this figure as the "man who wants to perish." Furthermore, once the critic succeeds in subverting established values and creating new ones, he fights for them against reactive forces. "There is no affirmation which is not *immediately followed by a negation* no less tremendous and unbounded by itself. . . . *Destruction as the active destruction of all known values* is the trail of the creator."[153] Even though the critic is motivated by an affirmative will to power, he must violate established codes and conventions and thus embrace the posture of the criminal.

Deleuze thus subverts Kant's image of the critic from the preface to the 1781 (A) edition of the *Critique of Pure Reason*. There, Kant institutes a court of justice to judge, among others, skeptical "nomads who abhor all permanent cultivation of the soil" and who have "shattered civil unity from time to time."[154] In an essay on "Nomad Thought," as well as the "Treatise on Nomadology" in *A Thousand Plateaus*, Deleuze sides with the philosophical nomads, such as Kierkegaard and Nietzsche, against the philosophical judges, such as Kant and Hegel. According to Deleuze's noology, or study of images of thought, State philosophers seek to codify laws, establish territories, and clamp down on joyful and experimental thinking. Deleuze sides with the "minor" authors in the history of philosophy who prefer to pursue "lines of flight" rather than give the established powers their blessing. Though Deleuze often qualifies his more incendiary statements in *A Thousand Plateaus*—he shares Kant's general assessment from his 1784 essay on Enlightenment that revolutions often perpetrate violence without changing mentalities—he agrees with Nietzsche that thought should be a battering-ram, or a nomad war machine, against common sense.

We are now in a position to compare Rawls's and Deleuze's inflections of Kantian courage. Both Rawls and Deleuze steer Kant's legacy in the direction of pragmatism. Pragmatism, generally speaking, naturalizes and historicizes Kant's conception of the transcendental.[155] Kant held that transcendental philosophy identifies the *a priori* conditions of possible experience common to all human beings. For Rawls and Deleuze, Kant's conception of the *a priori* is an unfortunate remnant of the Platonic legacy and should be dropped by critical thinkers, particularly after Darwin. Rawls's call for a Kantian political theory based upon an empiricist framework, in *A Theory of Justice*, and Deleuze's conception of transcendental empiricism, expounded most fully in *Difference and Repetition*, are both attempts to bring the Kantian ethos, or spirit, into contemporary philosophical circumstances. For both Rawls and Deleuze, Kantian courage manifests itself today as a willingness to question established ways of thinking and propose new theoretical frameworks. In their own ways, Rawls and Deleuze envision new trajectories for the Enlightenment. Throughout the book, we will consider different ways to describe Rawls's and Deleuze's contending visions. Here, I note that

Rawls and Deleuze express different sensibilities rather than necessarily divergent philosophical positions. There is no proof to convince a Kantian today to be more like a judge than a criminal, or vice versa. Nor can one argue conclusively that one should read Hegel over Nietzsche, or orient oneself by historical moments of founding (such as the New Deal in the United States) rather than unfounding (such as May '68). Paul Patton distinguishes Richard Rorty and Deleuze and Guattari by saying that the former advocates a "complacent pragmatism" and the latter promote a "critical pragmatism."[156] Though such binaries are problematic (as Patton acknowledges), they do indicate a different sensibility at work in authors such as Rorty and Rawls, on the one hand, and Deleuze and Guattari, on the other.[157] The Rawlsian temper, one might say, prefers Kant's cooler moments when he emphasizes the need for social order and regulation, whereas the Deleuzian temper is drawn to those moments in Kant when he subverts and perverts millennia old ways of thinking about the soul and God.[158] Neither Rawls nor Deleuze are more or less Kantian: they both express aspects of his legacy. Both thinkers, furthermore, complicate any simple dichotomy between them: Rawls modifies—scandalously, to some of his critics[159]—his principles of justice when he moves from the domestic to the international level in *The Law of Peoples*, and Deleuze's writings on creative jurisprudence, read in conjunction with his monographs on Bergson and Spinoza, may point the way to a new constitutional theory and analysis of institutions.[160] Still, Rawls and Deleuze differ in many ways, and the task for contemporary Kantians is how to preserve a productive tension between this tradition's apologetic, reformist, and revolutionary moments.

COMPLEMENTARY MOMENTS

In this section I will review how the different inflections of Kantian courage each contribute to the project of advancing the Enlightenment.

Kantian courage as apology inspires Kantians to present and defend Kant's doctrines in close to their original form. Kantians should feel pride and confidence in clarifying and advocating Kant's ideals, and those who do not personally adhere to Kant's principles can still profit from conversation with orthodox Kantians. Furthermore, from a Rawlsian or Deleuzian perspective, Kantians can play a vital role in an overlapping consensus or rhizomatic network of constituencies defending—from diverse perspectives—the shared values of liberal democracies. Further, Kantian militants can raise issues and spark debates in ways that John Stuart Mill commends in *On Liberty*, such as by forcefully questioning the grounds of any religious orthodoxy. The danger with an apologetic defense of Kantianism, however, is dogmatism. Kant often excoriates empiricist moral philosophers for corrupting healthy common sense. Intellectually, this approach can lead to dismissing or ignoring philosophers who do not think that moral distinctions arise from reason. Intellectual close-mindedness can translate into political imperialism. For many religious activists, the tendency of secularists to insist that enlightenment can only go in one direction—from religious superstition to philosophical atheism—infuriates.[161] If one sense of the German word *Vernunft* is to listen to the reasoning of others, then dogmatic Kantians can be unreasonable if they insist that any heteronomous morality is fraudulent.[162] Kantian apologists should have *a* voice in contemporary progressive political theory and politics, just not be *the* voice.

Kantian courage as jurisprudence empowers heirs of the Enlightenment to actualize its ideals. Kantians who comport themselves like Supreme Court judges express a reverence for the founding documents of the Enlightenment. In *Political Liberalism*, for instance, Rawls employs Kantian means to steer a path between Lockean liberty and Rousseauian equality. Though Rawls abjures Enlightenment liberalism as such, Rawls's political theory is unthinkable without the tools, blueprints, and raw materials of the Enlightenment tradition. Yet Rawls's willingness to diverge from the historical *Aufklärung* guarantees the continuing relevance of the Enlightenment. Though Wood acknowledges that Kant's theory of supernatural freedom is problematic, Rawls proposes a way to place Kant's practical philosophy in an empiricist framework. Rawls departs from the letter of Kant's philosophy in order to preserve its spirit for the twenty-first century. Furthermore, Rawls's emendation of his ideas to fit the language game of constitutional jurisprudence helps contemporary progressives implement those ideas. Rawls's reformist approach has influenced many progressive academics, politicians, Supreme Court judges, and journalists, and has thus furthered as well as transformed the ends of the historical Enlightenment.[163] Yet framing Kantian courage as a legalistic cast of mind is problematic for several reasons. First, it is elitist. Rawls insists that any citizen could reason as if she was a Supreme Court judge when making decisions about the constitutional rules of the basic structure of society. Yet Rawls's designation of the Supreme Court as the Exemplar of Public Reason, as well as his legalistic, abstract terminology, makes it appear that Rawls's audience is the philosophical guardians that Kant tries to circumvent in his 1784 essay on Enlightenment. There is also the fact that jurisprudence, even conceptualized pragmatically, still works within the confines of founding documents and legal traditions. Rawls notes that the United States Bill of Rights is vested by "the constitutional tradition of the oldest democratic regime in the world."[164] This may appeal to American progressives who honor the First Amendment protecting free speech, but institutional conservatism may protect less honorable ideals from scrutiny, such as gun control. Kantian courage as jurisprudence entrenches certain accomplishments of the historical and contemporary Enlightenment, but it does not necessarily cultivate an adventurous way of thinking about new and unforeseen problems.

Kantian courage as critique spurs political theorists to develop a restless cast of mind. For Kantians such as Deleuze, the critical theorist's task first and foremost is to breed discontent with the present and seek new avenues to move into the future. The intellectual advantage of this approach is that we are constantly receptive and motivated to interpret and evaluate our current mental habits and institutional practices. Kant, for instance, believed in a racial hierarchy and the critical ethos can help us abandon this hurtful, unscientific doctrine. Wood and Rawls agree up to this point, but Deleuze goes farther in problematizing themes or ideas closer to Kant's philosophical core. From a Deleuzian perspective, even cherished leftist ideals such as freedom and equality may need to be dropped or recast in surprising ways, say, by considering nonhuman assemblages as political actors.[165] In addition, the critical ethos can expand the range of voices in the political movement of the Enlightenment. Certain Enlightenment partisans try to align the Enlightenment tightly with, say, socialism or secular morality. Deleuze's thoughtful engagement with minoritarian-becomings—constituencies that fall between the cracks of traditional political imaginaries—helps us imagine a new Enlightenment. The problem with Deleuze's approach, however, is that its restlessness inhibits actualizing Enlightenment ideals. By placing philosophy on the side of the critic and criminal, Deleuze denigrates philosophers actually contributing to political movements. Deleuze qualifies this position somewhat in his later work, but he often argues that philosophers should view themselves as nomads rather than judges. A Deleuzian perspective is a valuable ingredient in progressive political thinking, but it clearly cannot be the sole or even dominant approach for a movement that wants to exercise power.[166]

To advance the Enlightenment today, we should exercise each moment of the courage that Kant calls for in his 1784 essay. First, we should apologize for the Enlightenment as an intellectual and political tradition that shapes how we, political progressives, think, feel, and act—without renouncing our right to rethink Enlightenment ideals even at a profound level. Second, we should sometimes play the part of responsible political agents—such as Supreme Court justices, or presidents, or legislators—and work to attain a fit between our ideals and our institutions—without imagining that we can take any topic off of the political agenda once and for all. Third, we should cultivate a "criminal" cast of mind that questions and laughs at established ways of thinking—without dwelling for so long in this space that we neglect the other roles that heirs of the Enlightenment must play. Kantian courage, then, is a comportment of mind that honors the achievements of the historical Enlightenment seeks to revise and actualize its ideals, and presses us to constantly rethink its fundamental commitments. In the following chapters, I elaborate what the exercise of Kantian courage looks like at the dawn of the twenty-first century.

2

Formulating Problems

Giovanna Borradori opens her book, *Philosophy in a Time of Terror*, by speculating on philosophy's relationship to history. According to the classical tradition of Plato and Aristotle, philosophy aims to grasp universal principles whereas history seeks knowledge of singular events. Most Western philosophers subsequently took for granted a gap between philosophy's quest for the universal and history's recording of the singular until the American and French Revolutions showed that the present and the future may radically depart from the ways of the past. Kant, living during this pivotal moment, largely held to the classical view that pure (practical) reason could influence historical events, and not the reverse, but in the generation following Kant Hegel argued that reason encapsulates as well as shapes the values of a particular community life (*Sittlichkeit*). The conflict between classical and modern conceptions of the relations between philosophy and history persists in contemporary debates about the role of political philosophy. For political activists such as Bertrand Russell, philosophy's role is to *apply* timeless truths to the controversies of the day. For social critics such as Hannah

Arendt, philosophy's role is to *engage* one's time in a dialogue that cannot be predetermined in advance. Borradori is not a mere spectator to this debate. The 9/11 attacks and the diplomatic and military responses they have precipitated demand a "reassessment of the validity of the Enlightenment project and ideals."[1] I agree with Borradori that the events of 9/11, as well as the broader collisions of certain understandings of Islam and the Enlightenment, call for philosophical sensitivity and creativity. The question remains, though, how should Enlightenment partisans identify the problems of the day that take account of 9/11 as well as other major historical events of the past two hundred years, including the publication of Darwin's *On the Origin of Species* and the Holocaust initiated in the historic heartland of the Enlightenment?

In this chapter, I consider how contemporary Kantians interpret the challenges and opportunities of the contemporary political and philosophical landscape. I begin by reflecting on three historical events that demand a reconsideration of the problems that Kant set for himself in the *Groundwork for the Metaphysics of Morals*. The problems are finding and establishing the supreme principle of morality in pure practical reason; engaging common sense to unearth the moral compass that it already possesses; and laying the foundation for a metaphysics of morals that encompasses both a doctrine of right and a doctrine of virtue. The historical events are Darwin's insight into human evolution that problematizes the notion of pure mental faculties; the Holocaust's display of the fragility of common sense; and the revelation of 9/11 that Euro-American political theorists need to forge alliances with religious activists around the globe to forestall further attacks from militant universalists. In this chapter, once again, I turn to Rawls and Deleuze for insight on how heirs of the Enlightenment may selectively appropriate elements from Kant's philosophy—more precisely, his metaethics—on how to proceed today. According to Rawls and Deleuze, the tasks facing contemporary Kantians are to offer a naturalized account of practical reason; address contemporary common sense in both a respectful and critical fashion; and envision pluralistic societies that include more diversity that Kant imagined—or could have imagined—in eighteenth-century Prussia. In the conclusion, I argue that Kant scholarship provides an elevated forum to discuss the future of the Left, and that Rawls favors the leftist ideal of freedom, or self-governing community life, and Deleuze the leftist ideal of liberty, or the individual's right to dissent or diverse from the group. The challenge for contemporary heirs of the Enlightenment is to forge just and stable societies as well as to appreciate lines of flight that confound established ways of living and thinking.

KANTIANISM AFTER DARWIN, THE HOLOCAUST, AND 9/11

A distinguishing feature of Kant's *Groundwork* is its lack of historical referents. Kant alludes to a handful of other philosophers but primarily to illustrate types of mistakes recurrently made by human reason. Kant's examples may presuppose an empirical content, but Kant frequently states that the *Groundwork's* aim—"the search for and establishment *of the supreme principle of morality*"[2]—can technically proceed without illustrations of its applicability. Like Plato in the *Republic*, Kant employs a minimal amount of sensory imagery to dramatize his argument without basing its conclusions on historical facts or empirical data. What is perhaps more surprising is a tendency of contemporary Kantians to maintain that Kant's problems remain, *mutatis mutandis*, our own—that is, that Kant's terminology may need to be updated, but the underlying problems are the same. Wood's attack on Kantian constructivists or "French literary theorists," for example, parallels Kant's attack on "popular moral philosophers" who extract moral concepts from intuitions or experience. For Wood, the names of empiricist adversaries may change over time, but the problem facing contemporary Kantians is the same essential one that Kant identified in 1785: to discover, justify, and actualize the supreme principle of morality.[3]

Kant's problems, I submit, are not our problems today. Just as Kant protested ecclesiastical authorities that sought to install permanent religious constitutions, we need to remain alert to the possibility that Kant's problems—and hence his solutions—do not fit our historical circumstances. This approach, though, is compatible with a willingness to learn from Kant how to formulate problems. In the subsequent sections, we consider how Kant frames his problems and how Rawls and Deleuze modify them. Before that, though, I wish to consider three historical events that contemporary Kantians need to address and that make a return to Kant impossible.

First, Darwin's *On the Origin of Species*, published in 1859, has rendered deeply problematic any appeal to *pure* practical reason. In an essay entitled "The Influence of Darwinism on Philosophy," John Dewey explains the philosophical sea change that occurs because of Darwin's insight into biological evolution. According to the ancients, the material world exhibits a certain regularity and a certain amount of variation; for example, animals are born and die but at widely different rates. For Plato and Aristotle, the formal activity that operates through a series of changes and holds them to a single course is an *eidos*, or a species. Given that our senses only illuminate the world of living and dying beings, the task of philosophy is to reach behind appearances and grasp the realities lying behind and beyond the processes of nature. Plato and Aristotle call the human faculty to perceive an *eidos* reason, and, on their accounts, this faculty is what distinguishes human beings from all other animals.[4] For two thousand years, scientists and philosophers assumed that the products of pure reason were more rigorous and truthful than anything that could be discovered in the empirical realm. Starting with the scientific revolution, however, men such as Galileo, Copernicus, and Kepler started to banish fixed and final causes from physics. For the early natural scientists, only patient and careful observation of the natural world could reveal its deeper patterns. Yet the scientific revolution of the sixteenth and seventeenth centuries did not penetrate the kingdom of plants and animals. In fact, scientific discoveries into the miraculousness of nature and its interconnected parts seemed to support the argument from design that preserves a role for God in a Newtonian universe. Yet Darwin's principle of natural selection removes the foundation of this philosophy. If all organic adaptations are due to constant biological variation and the death of those organisms unfit to survive and reproduce, then there is no "call for a prior intelligent causal force to plan and preordain them."[5] Darwin, in other words, provides a naturalistic explanation for the emergence of reason. Rather than a faculty implanted in human beings by a Divinity, reason is a faculty that emerges as do all other animal abilities, namely, through genetic variation and the continued survival of animals endowed with fortuitous genes.

What, then, does the future hold for philosophy if not the exercise of pure reason, either theoretical or practical? In his essay, Dewey identifies several ways that philosophy has to reorient itself after Darwin. First, philosophy has to foreswear inquiry into "absolute origins and absolute finalities" in order to focus on "specific values and the specific conditions that generate them."[6] Darwin shows that reason is a decidedly impure faculty that emerges gradually over time, in a complex relationship with the natural world, and thrives, or not, depending on how it helps human beings perpetuate the species. The task facing the Darwinian philosopher is to look at specifics: specific agents, specific interests, specific institutions, specific practices, and so forth. The Darwinian "genetic and experimental logic" still permits the practice of philosophy—now understood as the propounding of ideas for practice—yet humbles its claim to answer, once and for all, the question of what I, or we, ought to do.[7] Following from this point, the criteria for evaluating the success of philosophy changes. Once, philosophers determined success or failure by whether they penetrated the realm of *eidos*. In a post-Darwinian philosophical landscape, however, philosophers must evaluate ideas using only immanent criteria: such as, do they improve our education, ameliorate our manners, or advance our politics? For Dewey, we can only answer these questions by scrutinizing the empirical evidence.[8] Finally, "the new logic introduces responsibility into the intellectual life."[9] For classical or modern rationalists, *a priori* principles are valid regardless of what people think of them. Pragmatists, however, have a responsibility to diagnose the social conflicts of their times and propose ways to deal with them. Rather than analyze *a priori* concepts of pure reason, as Kant attempts in the *Groundwork*, Dewey recommends that philosophers employ their impure reason to help solve the distinct problems of one's time and place. Richard Rorty suggests that thinking through the implications of Darwin's *On the Origin of Species* means discarding Kant's two-world metaphysics, faculty psychology, moralistic terminology, and other vestiges of an earlier philosophical worldview.[10] A more interesting problem, suggested by the work of Rawls and Deleuze, is to recast Kant's ideas in a post-Darwinian framework, to save some of the normative and intellectual force of Kantian terminology while humbling its pretensions to purity or finality.[11]

The second major historical development that problematizes a return to Kant's practical philosophy in its original form is the Holocaust. In *Desolation and Enlightenment: Political Knowledge after War, Totalitarianism, and the Holocaust*, Ira Katznelson describes how the Holocaust threatened to expose the Enlightenment's rhetoric of liberty, fraternity, and equality as a web of lies: "Of all the developments from the outbreak of the First World War to the close of the Second, it was the Jewish nightmare that arguably made unrevised reaffirmations of Enlightenment impossible. The inclusion of Jews into western modernity on terms the American and French Revolutions first had propelled now had proved compatible with persecution and liquidation on a vast scale. Among the various offspring of Enlightenment, German liberalism and social democracy, Austrian modernism, and French Republicanism all had failed to stem horrors' tide."[12] The Holocaust overturned all civilizational norms. The Holocaust was also largely perpetrated and condoned by many "ordinary" Germans, including those who up to the

Holocaust interacted on friendly terms with Jews.[13] Clearly, Germans such as Adolf Eichmann who found a Kantian justification for their acts were poor readers of Kant.[14] The whole force of Kant's practical philosophy—particularly the formula of humanity in the *Groundwork*—demands that we recognize every human being's intrinsic dignity as a potential legislator of the moral law. Even conservative critics of the Enlightenment—such as Leo Strauss—argue that the Enlightenment contributed indirectly to the Holocaust by weakening religious traditions that may have provided a more effective bulwark against the barbarians who systematically slaughtered the Jews in the twentieth century.[15] Though some philosophers entertained the thesis that the Enlightenment contained the seeds of Nazism, the much more common and plausible thesis is that the Enlightenment failed to mobilize sufficient resistance to Nazi barbarism.

Yet the Holocaust did display a colossal failing of the common sense that Kant appealed to in his practical philosophy. In a chapter of *Kant and the Limits of Autonomy* entitled "Kant's Jewish Problem," Susan Meld Shell shows that Kant's ambiguous feelings towards Jews entered his moral philosophy, at various times, as ostensibly-rational conclusions rather than arbitrary prejudices. In the *Critique of Judgment*, for example, Kant argues that Judaism, in its ancient, iconoclastic form, is a superior moral religion than Christianity. In the *Religion within the Boundaries of Mere Reason*, Kant reverses course to assert, "Judaism represents all that Christianity must shed in order to become the true, moral religion of Jesus."[16] Kant's language takes several unfortunate turns, for example, when he calls for the "euthanasia of Judaism" in order for pure rational faith, embodied in Catholicism and Protestantism, to flourish.[17] Shell also shows that Kant helped propel the careers of several men, such as Johann Gottlieb Fichte, who would inspire Hitler and the Nazis.[18] The lesson here is not that Kant is a proto-fascist. The lesson is that there may not be a transhistorical moral compass embedded in common sense as Kant hoped in the *Groundwork*. Kant's common sense judgments about Judaism, we see in hindsight, made a (small) contribution to the rise of modern anti-Semitism in Germany and Europe. Philosophers may have no choice but to appeal to common sense judgments at several stages of their arguments. But after the Holocaust displayed the fragility and moral blind spots of common sense, Kantians need to rethink how to conceptualize and engage common sense today.

The third major historical development that calls for a rethinking of Kantianism is 9/11 and its aftermath. The significance of this event is that it dramatically displayed a larger historical development and the danger of a certain approach to solving it. The historical development is that modern societies are more religiously diverse than ever before. Königsberg in Kant's time, "was a frontier post of Lutheran German culture, adjacent to the religiously unreliable Baltic states and multireligious Poland, and confronted by the vast unknown of Russian orthodoxy." The immediate audience of Kant's philosophy—namely, his students at the University of Königsberg—was largely "destined to become Lutheran pastors, teachers, and academics."[19] Kant, of course, had a cosmopolitan sensibility and his philosophy may not be reduced to its historical context. Yet the backdrop of political thinking is very different today. One example is the rising presence of Muslims in Western Europe and North America. Muslims from the Balkans, Ottoman Empire, Syria, Lebanon, and Jordan emigrated to American cities such as Buffalo, Detroit, Dearborn, and Cedar Rapids in the late nineteenth and early twentieth centuries, and the American Muslim community increased with the arrival of emigrants from Europe, southwestern Asia, East Africa, India, and Pakistan after World War II.[20] Today, Islam is rapidly becoming Europe's "second religion" and attaining a larger presence in American society.[21] In Chapter 5, I consider in more detail how contemporary philosophers in the Enlightenment tradition are creating new vocabularies to describe and envision the future of these new religious communities. Here, though, we may note that the 9/11 attacks, as well as the worst responses by American forces at Abu Ghraib or Guantanamo Bay, demonstrate the danger of religious and secular fundamentalism. The challenge for contemporary Kantians is how to respond thoughtfully to the new religious pluralism without instantiating the darkest elements of Kant's practical philosophy, such as its insistence on the role of corporeal humiliation before the moral law.[22]

In an essay entitled "Of Power and Compassion," Shibley Telhami speaks of the need to build bridges of mutual understanding between different religious and political communities. Public opinion surveys indicate that many Muslims perceive American and European indifference to their lives and concerns. To prevent another atrocity along the lines of 9/11, it is essential that Americans and Europeans listen to Muslims and engage them in a respectful dialogue. According to Telhami, "public diplomacy must be present at the inception of any policy and must include dialogue and feedback. If the aim of policy is to send messages to others or to generate particular responses, it cannot succeed without understanding those others' aims, aspirations, priorities, and sensitivities."[23] The United States cannot defeat terrorism solely through military means. An effective foreign policy requires public diplomacy, and public diplomacy requires taking one's conversation partner's concerns seriously. Yet prudence is not the only reason to take this approach. Compassion, or morality, demands that powerful states or agents exercise restraint as well as care for our enemies who may become, one day, our friends. The lesson for Kantians is that we should constantly explore new ways to forge alliances against the forces that seek to impose their moral vision on the world. Thomas Pogge argues that Kant's doctrine of right can be endorsed by anyone who has an *a priori* interest in external freedom, and he offers as his example Kantians and Hobbesians. Does this analysis apply to all Muslims? Many Muslims? A few Muslims? These questions cannot be answered *a priori* and demand a careful intervention in contemporary political debates with Muslim interlocutors. The lessons of 9/11, in sum, seem to support the case for breaking apart and reassembling liberal political codes to fashion terms of political alliance across widespread religious, philosophical, and moral diversity.

RECASTING KANT'S PROBLEMS

History sets the background to philosophical reflection, but it does not determine what philosophers think. "History," Deleuze explains in *What is Philosophy?*, "designates only the set of conditions, however recent they may be, from which one turns away in order to become, that is to say, in order to create something new."[24] History throws problems at philosophers, provides preliminary resources to address them, and supplies an audience that can help make a philosopher's vision real. Yet philosophers may still decide how to frame their problems as well as how to articulate solutions. Contemporary philosophers influenced by Kant thus have a choice about how to frame the problems of post-Darwinian moral politics, post-Holocaust common sense, and post-9/11 political pluralism. We now turn to how Rawls and Deleuze interpret and recast Kant's problems in his practical philosophy.

Naturalizing Practical Reason

One of the great quandaries facing heirs of the Enlightenment is how to identify the source of normativity, that is, the origin of moral and political concepts and principles.[25] Many contemporary theorists frame this problem using the history of philosophy. Kant, as the paradigmatic thinker of the Prussian Enlightenment, redefines the classical definition of man as an *animal rationabilis*—a natural being capable of rationality.[26] For many strict Kantians, reason is the faculty that distinguishes human beings from other animals and is thus the locus of descriptive psychology and normative theory. Hume, as the paradigmatic thinker of the Scottish Enlightenment, holds, to the contrary, that human beings are creatures with heightened imaginative and sensitive capacities and that appeals to reason are misleading, if not positively harmful. Kant and Hume thus represent the leading figures in the cases for defining the Enlightenment as the Age of Reason or the Age of Sentiment. Yet an increasing number of political theorists recognize that both Kant and Hume provide at least one piece of the puzzle to thinking about the source of normativity. Kant provides a particularly rich vocabulary to describe the (apparently) uniquely human ability to transcend sense experience and think about ethical standards. Hume articulates a naturalistic explanation of moral development, evaluation, and deliberation that accords with a post-Darwinian scientific worldview. No prominent political theorist has yet claimed that the gap between Kant and Hume could be closed in an airtight synthesis—their visions are too divergent to resolve into one picture of the universe. Yet many political theorists today wonder how Kantian rationalism and Humean sentimentalism can be integrated into a compelling picture of how embodied human beings are capable of normative reflection that transcends one's time and place.[27] In this section, I review Hume's and Kant's official conceptions of reason before considering how Rawls and Deleuze frame the problem of naturalizing practical reason.

In *A Treatise of Human Nature*, Hume famously denigrates reason's powers. "We speak not strictly and philosophically when we talk of the combat of passion and of reason. Reason is, and ought only to be the slave of the passions, and can never pretend to any other office than to serve and obey them."[28] According to Hume, what actually moves people to act is pleasure or pain or the prospect of pleasure or pain. As embodied creatures with desires and aversions, we instinctively strive to maximize our pleasures and minimize our pains. Reason is the ability to determine the objects and means to achieve our ends. Reason influences our conduct "when it excites a passion by informing us of the existence of something which is a proper object of it; or when it discovers the connexion of causes and effects, so as to afford us means of exerting any passion."[29] Outside of the field of demonstrative reasoning, which determines the relations of ideas, as in mathematics or logic, probabilistic reasoning identifies "matters of fact" about whether particular objects exist that will satisfy our pleasure-seeking impulses and the most cost-efficient means to maximize our possession or use of such objects. Throughout the *Treatise*, Hume emphasizes that there is no categorical difference between fancy, imagination, understanding, and reason—the first two terms simply describe the less systematic and empirically verifiable operations of the mind, whereas the later two describe "the more general and more establish'd properties of the imagination," that is, the operations of the mind disciplined by the natural and social sciences.[30] One of the more astonishing implications of the *Treatise*, which Hume flouts before his rationalist adversaries, is that reason is not a distinctly human faculty—in fact, we appear to share it with a great many other animals. "To consider the matter aright, reason is nothing but a wonderful and unintelligible *instinct* in our souls, which carries us along a certain train of ideas, and endows them with particular qualities, according to their particular situations and relations."[31] Reason is an instinct humans may hone to augment their own power, but we boast without warrant when we identify ourselves as its sole possessor in the universe or that it motivates our actions. Despite humanity's propensity to self-flattery, we act because of passions and only retrospectively assign our volition to pure reason.[32]

Kant's practical philosophy can be read as a vindication of reason in response to Hume's skeptical assault on its sufficiency or adequacy as a moral source.[33] In the preface to the *Groundwork for the Metaphysics of Morals*, Kant states that it is "self-evident from the common idea of duty and of moral laws" that it is necessary to work out a "pure moral philosophy which is fully cleansed of everything that might be in any way empirical and belong to anthropology."[34] Kant's aim in the *Groundwork* is two-fold. First, he searches for the supreme principle of morality in *a priori* concepts of pure practical reason. That is, instead of looking to psychological propensities or habits as empiricists do, or looking to transcendent concepts of philosophical or theological perfection as rationalists do, Kant will investigate the pure sources of reason that lie within the thinking faculties of all rational beings. For Kant, it is essential that pure practical reason provide the guidance that—according to common sense notions of duty and moral laws—empiricist concepts cannot provide. Furthermore, Kant aims to establish the supreme principle of morality in a critique of pure practical reason that shows that these laws are, in fact, binding on imperfectly rational beings such as humans. In this argument, Kant will once again present an argument that applies to all rational beings and not just human beings as such. For Kant holds that "everyone must admit that a law, if it is to be valid morally, i.e., as the ground of an obligation, has to carry absolute necessity with it" and that, for example, "the command 'You ought not to lie' is valid not merely for human beings, as though other rational beings did not have to heed it."[35] In *The Invention of Autonomy*, J. B. Schneewind provides an explanation for why Kant insists that the metaphysics of morals applies to all rational beings—such as God, angels, and extraterrestrials—and not just humans. In these perplexing passages of the *Groundwork*, Kant participates in an early-modern debate between voluntarists and antivoluntarists. The voluntarists held that an omnipotent God was not required to obey the laws that applied to inferior beings. For voluntarists, God could choose to be benevolent in a way that humans appreciated, but God could also choose to act according to a humanly inscrutable wisdom. For the antivoluntarists, this picture of God as a tyrant makes it impossible for us to love him. Unbelievers such as Hume could simply sidestep this theological dispute. One of Kant's great achieve-ments, the one that makes it possible to describe him as the inventor of the modern conception of autonomy is the claim that human beings are God's equals, that is, the laws of reason apply to both equally. "The invention of autonomy gave Kant what he thought was the only morally satisfactory theory of the status of human beings in a universe shared with God."[36] For Kant, pure practical reason is the only normative source that can provide human beings with clear guidance on moral questions as well as secure our standing in the universe as beings deserving of respect and dignity.

The contrast between Kant and Hume may conceal important ways that their visions overlap and can possibly be combined.[37] Consider, for example, how Hume's complete account of practical reasoning in the *Treatise* com-plicates the assessment of reason as the slave of the passions. Hume's official position in the *Treatise* is that moral distinctions are derived from a moral sense and not reason. Hume's term for the moral sense is sympathy, con-noting the human ability to "feel with" another human's pleasure or uneasi-ness. Experience confirms that sympathy is a faculty shared by most sentient animals: "[T]ake a general survey of the universe, and observe the force of sympathy thro' the whole animal creation, and the easy communication of sentiments from one thinking being to another."[38] Human beings are like string-instruments that resonate together, in their joys and pains, and, as the metaphor suggests, this disposition may transmit itself between humans without the mediation of intellect.[39] It is thus noteworthy that Kant and Kantians reject a Humean appeal to sympathy, for sympathy combined with the human propensity to partiality may lead us to look favorably on family and friends even when they are acting immorally. And yet Hume's conception of reason in the *Treatise* may correct or reconfigure the passions in at least five ways.[40] Reason may *inform* us when a particular object upon which we attach our hope or fear, grief or joy, despair or security does or does not exist. Reason may *correct* our means-end reasoning so that we attain our ends in an efficient manner. In addition to these two vocations, reason may positively construct our passions in certain ways. Reason may *specify* the passions by rending an indeterminate desire more determinate, as when we transform a vague feeling of hunger into a specific desire for a particular food. Reason may *schedule* our passions so that we satisfy them in a timely manner. And reason may *weigh* our final ends so as to achieve a greater good over time rather than the immediate satisfaction of a desire here and now. According to Hume, passions are not unmediated pleasures or pains (impressions of sensation) but rather perceptions that have become ideas that then affect us, which is why they are called impressions of reflection.[41] The process of reflection assures us that human beings do not always or even very often act on pure impulse. Human beings have the ability to step back from their instincts and determine which course of action to pursue, and this faculty enables us to make more or less wise, more or less impartial, moral judgments, which, inevitably, are inspired by our sympathy for other human beings or, in cases of political justice, with the general interest of society. Hume's conception of reason is not a supernatural faculty, but it is one that empowers human beings to make choices with a degree of complexity and self-distancing apparently unavailable to other animals. That is why it is possible to hear "Kantian tunes on a Humean instrument," that is, to recognize Kantian insights about practical reasoning in, for example, Hume's account of intersubjective consensus achieved through the thought-device of the impartial spectator.[42]

There is also an important way in which Kant's conception of practical reason may be closer to Hume's than his polemical attacks on it might reveal. In the *Treatise*, Hume remarks, "moral philosophy is in the same condition as natural, with regard to astronomy before the time of *Copernicus*." Rationalists traditionally posit "without scruple" a new principle for every new phenomenon and conceal this move by arguing that it is simply the nature of the "intricate systems of the heavens."[43] Hume aims to eliminate this unscientific multiplying of hypotheses by turning his focus inward to discover the true principle of morality. "When you pronounce any action or character to be vicious, you mean nothing, but that from the constitution of your nature you have a feeling or sentiment of blame from the contemplation of it." Hume's Copernican revolution asserts that moral judgment "lies in yourself, not in the object."[44] Kant clearly disagrees that moral sentiment is the basis of moral judgment. But Kant does think that Hume was right "to establish a basis of moral knowledge independent of ecclesiastical authority and available to the ordinary reasonable and conscientious person."[45] For both Kant and Hume, human beings have internal resources, independent of natural or social context, to *know* the basis of right and wrong, to access the *source* of moral discernment, and to *self-motivate* to follow moral precepts without the coercive force of an external authority.[46] Like Hume, Kant does not think that practical reason's vocation is to access another world in which moral concepts and principles exist independently of rational agency. In the *Groundwork*, Kant remarks that practical philosophy is "in fact at a perilous standpoint, which is to be made firm, regardless of anything either in heaven or on earth from which it may depend or by which it may be supported."[47] In this sentence, Kant acknowledges that reason's status in the universe is more clearly defined by what it is not than what it is: it is not responsible for ascending to the heavens for moral laws, nor is it responsible for investigating the material world to formulate general precepts. In this concession, though, Kant acknowledges that Hume's Copernican revolution—in practical as well as theoretical philosophy—closes off certain philosophical options at the same time as it raises new problems. Philosophers must replace old conceptions of practical reason that try to read the heavens with new ones that appreciate (human) rational agency.

Kant and Hume, then, both embrace the ideal of reflective autonomy: the notion that human beings are capable of stepping back from the given to formulate principles that may then apply to the given.[48] The key difference between Hume and Kant is their answers to the question: where are we when we think?[49] According to Kant, reason is the faculty through which a human being distinguishes himself from all other things, even from himself insofar as he is affected by objects. For Kant, reason performs its vocation only if it removes us entirely from the world of senses: "reason, under the name of ideas, shows such a pure spontaneity that it thereby goes far beyond everything that sensibility can provide it, and provides its most excellent occupation by distinguishing the world of the senses [*Sinneswelt*] and the world of the understanding [*Verstandeswelt*] from one another."[50] The advantage of this approach is that it explains how human beings may transcend their historical milieu to articulate *a priori*—and hence universal—moral principles. The problem is that Kant perpetuates the medieval metaphysical tradition in which he was schooled at the University of Königsberg.[51] This tradition presents a portrait of the human being as a *homo duplex* divided between his higher, rational nature and his lower, earthy nature. This approach may recover Christian notions of free will, radical evil, and the "postulates" of God, the soul, and immortality in a Newtonian universe, but post-Darwinians demand functional explanations of how human capacities emerge as solutions to concrete problems. Post-Darwinians, in other words, demand a bottom-up explanation of how reason emerged in the human animal, whereas Kant perpetuates a top-down account of the relationship between reason and corporeality.[52] The challenge for contemporary Kantians is to explain how Kant's moral vision can be translated into a post-Darwinian framework. Hume, here, seems like a fitting antidote, insofar as he provides a naturalistic account of the moral sentiments and political notions such as justice, government, property, and political allegiance. Hume's method in the *Treatise*—"a cautious observation of human life"—comports with the modern empiricist sensibility.[53] The problem, however, is that Hume's thinking seems to transpire solely in this world and thus lacks a vantage point from which to criticize it. Hume's immanent account of thinking thus seems to accord with his conservative politics preoccupied, for instance, with protecting private property and established political authorities. The challenge for contemporary Humeans is to explain how Hume's theory of the moral sentiments can be transmogrified into a critical political theory, one capable of destroying traditions and prejudices and articulating new ideas and practices. How, in other words, is it possible to identify and sustain a normative source that is both immanent to the world and transcendent to it?

The task for contemporary progressive political theorists, in sum, is to offer a naturalistic account of practical reason. Rawls and Deleuze pursue this project in remarkably similar ways—though the differences are equally instructive. In *Lectures on the History of Moral Philosophy*, Rawls specifies the aspects of Hume's and Kant's philosophies that become stitched together in his own political theory. Rawls's conception of the reasonable is a Kantian-Humean hybrid that eludes traditional binaries in Anglo-American political philosophy, for example, between reading Kant through analytic or idealist lenses.[54] Similarly, Deleuze's early book on Hume, *Empiricism and Subjectivity: An Essay on Hume's Theory of Human Nature*, subtly introduces Kantian terms and concerns into the reconstruction of Hume's arguments.[55] Certain of the Humean-Kantian themes subsequently reappear in Deleuze's mature political theory.[56] Both Rawls and Deleuze, then, perform Kant and Hume scholarship for the larger end of describing mental faculties and normative frameworks in ways that are both normatively desirable and scientifically plausible. Next, I will consider how Rawls and Deleuze naturalize Kant's account of practical reason.

In *Political Liberalism*, Rawls emphasizes that liberal democracies may not demand that its citizens possess, acquire, or develop a strong conception of practical reason. A strong conception of practical reason asserts that rational agents who think about a certain question will arrive at a determinate answer, in the same way that mathematicians or logicians expect universal agreement for solutions to problems in their respective fields. In *A Theory of Justice*, Rawls identifies two problems with rational intuitionist theories: "first, they consist of a plurality of first principles which may conflict to give contrary directives in particular types of cases; and second, they include no explicit method, no priority rules, for weighing these principles against one another."[57] Rawls, here, presents in a brief and somewhat cryptic fashion Kant's critique of Plato in the *Critique of Pure Reason*. Plato aspired to abandon the world of senses and go beyond it on the wings of ideas: "He did not notice that he made no headway by his efforts, for he had no resistance, no support, as it were, by which he could stiffen himself, and to which he could apply his powers in order to get his understanding off the ground."[58] The problem with rational intuitionism, then, is that its explorations beyond the bound of sense have no necessary grounding in reality. Rational intuitionists may simply posit a supernatural reality and then identify different principles and methods that apply to the sensible world—but there is no way to falsify such judgments or to prove them scientifically. Rawls's attack on rational intuitionism in *A Theory of Justice* is a way to criticize fundamentalists who want their word (*logos*) to govern the polity. There is no way a just political order may select and enforce with the state's authority one rational intuitionist account of practical reason over its competitors. In *Political Liberalism*, however, Rawls changes his approach to rational intuitionism. In this text, he does not wish to disprove rational intuitionism or point out its key flaws, namely, indeterminacy and militancy. Rawls's hope is that the concepts and principles articulated through the constructivist procedure he outlines may gain the principled assent of rational intuitionists who arrive at similar conclusions following their own path. And yet Rawls's effort to appease rational intuitionists does not conceal the fact that in the case of conflict, a weak conception of the reasonable prevails over the strong. According to Rawls, advocates of a strong conception of practical reason—whether Platonic, Kantian, or religious—must recognize the burdens of judgment that seem to preclude universal agreement on the fundamental moral and philosophical questions. Stephen K. White thus argues that Rawls offers an account of *chastened reason* that disallows claims to adjudicate authoritatively between competing ontologies and the practical frameworks that they sustain.[59]

And yet it is important for Rawls that reason be the source of normative authority. In the terminology of Rawls's late work, rationality describes the capacity of single or unified agents to adopt, affirm, and prioritize ends and determine the most efficient way to attain them.[60] The rational, thus described, confirms to Hume's official view of reason as the slave of the passions. Rawls emphasizes that rational ends are not necessarily selfish, but this is a point that Hume concedes when he describes the calm, direct passion of the general appetite to good and aversion to evil.[61] Rawls willingly concedes that human beings are animals with refined instincts that, following Hume, we may call reason. But Rawls also thinks that reason—in German, *Vernunft*—has features overlooked by Hume's official account. In *Political Liberalism*, Rawls calls this set of features the reasonable. "What rational agents lack is the particular form of moral sensibility that underlies the desire to engage in fair cooperation as such, and to do so on terms that others as equals might reasonably be expected to endorse."[62] A reasonable agent willingly proposes and honors fair terms of cooperation and recognizes the burdens of judgment and accepts their consequences. Rawls attributes the origin of the idea of the reasonable to Kant. In the *Religion within the Boundaries of Mere Reason*, Kant distinguishes the "predisposition to moral personality" (which Rawls aligns with the reasonable) from the predispositions to humanity and animality (which Rawls aligns with the rational or the instinctual). And in the *Groundwork*, Kant distinguishes the categorical imperative (which originates from pure practical reason, or the reasonable) from the hypothetical imperative (which originates from empirical practical reason, that is, the rational).[63] Rawls's claim that in his political theory "the reasonable frames and subordinates the rational" seems to imply that the Kantian impulses in his political theory always and everywhere trump the Humean elements.[64] Yet in the *Lectures on the History of Moral Philosophy* Rawls contends that Hume's account of the "steady influence of the calm passions" may profitably be redescribed as "*calm* reason."[65] For Rawls, Hume's account of the calm passions, corrected by the distancing mechanism of the idea of the impartial spectator, may provide a functional equivalent of Kant's account of the reasonable. Hume himself does not have an account of practical reason—that is, a normative framework for thinking about what we ought to do—but his theory of the moral sentiments may be pressed to create one.[66] For Rawls, the reasonable may be described in the vernacular of both the Prussian and Scottish Enlightenments.[67]

Deleuze's first book, *Empiricism and Subjectivity*, raises the problem of naturalizing reason by establishing a contrast between Kantian transcendentalism and Humean empiricism. Philosophy in general "has always sought a plan of analysis in order to understand and conduct the examination of the structures of consciousness (critique), and to justify the totality of experience."[68] The difference between Kant and Hume is how they explain the vantage point from which to examine the structures of consciousness. Kantian critique aspires to a "methodologically reduced plane that provides an essential certainty"—the transcendental unity of apperception, or the transcendental subject—from which the subject may ask how it gives itself the given. The Kantian subject, in other words, stands outside of the material world and, from its transcendental plane, proposes concepts and principles that may then be applied to the world of sensibility. Deleuze, at various places, celebrates the fact that Kant's transcendental subject is divided by the line of time and that subjective transparency is impossible for embodied human agents. In other words, Kant's *Critique of Pure Reason* lays the foundation for philosophical investigations of the unconscious—which Deleuze himself will replicate in his own philosophy.[69] Yet the dominant strand in Kant's thinking—particularly the practical philosophy and its emphasis on freedom and responsibility—requires us to believe in a subject impervious to material or energetic flows. Humean critique, on the other hand, situates itself in a "*purely* immanent view" that holds that "the subject constitutes itself in the given."[70] In his effort to apply the experimental method to the moral sciences, Hume relies only upon careful observation to detail the means by which a mind becomes a subject, that is, how a collection of perceptions in the imagination becomes organized into a system. Yet Hume's philosophy may be interpreted as a form of mechanical naturalism that holds that the world and the brain are amenable in principle to precise mapping and explanation. In this case, Hume's "anatomy of human nature" would truly turn human conduct into a puppet show—just as Kant feared.[71] Deleuze's ethical vision differs from Kant's, but Deleuze does agree with Kant that a picture of a universe in which everything is mechanically determined fails to explain human thinking or ethics. Deleuze's very neologism of *empiricist critique* suggests that he wants clues from Kant on how to change empiricism so that it is better able to account for the layer of being that is real but beyond perception—what William E. Connolly calls the infrasensible.[72] *Empiricism and Subjectivity* thus initiates the philosophical endeavor that Deleuze calls transcendental empiricism—an approach that is less a static theory than a challenge to map and experiment with the naturally and socially inflected faculties of the mind.[73]

One of the remarkable features of *Empiricism and Subjectivity* is its account of practical reason. In this book, Deleuze arranges Hume's ideas to address the Kantian question: How does the mind become a subject?[74] That is, how does the mind—"a heap or collection of different perceptions"[75]— become a subject capable of deliberating and acting? To refute Kant's account of transcendental subjects, categories, and principles, Deleuze reconstructs Hume's position to show that Hume's theory of mental activity is as complex and nuanced as Kant's but embedded within a naturalistic worldview. Here are the key steps to Deleuze's account of the genesis of practical reason. The mind is originally filled with impressions of sensation—perceptual atoms, so to speak, that flood the imagination with an indistinct flux (what Kant called the manifold). Hume, though, is an associationist, not an atomist—that is, he recognizes that intuitions without a conceptual scheme are blind. This conceptual scheme is provided by the principles of human nature, namely, contiguity, resemblance, and causality. What "transforms the mind into a subject and constitutes the subject in the mind are the principles of human nature."[76] The mind becomes a subject as its principles habitually associate certain ideas and practices together: "We are habits," according to Deleuze's Hume, "nothing but habits—the habit of saying 'I.'"[77] Yet this assertion, provocative as it is, simply hands the phenomenological explanation of freedom to the Kantians. Surely many of us practically presuppose that we have choices about how to live our lives—can Deleuze's Hume offer no account of the experience of freedom other than as a surface effect of underlying mechanical processes? In fact, the most interesting passages of *Empiricism and Subjectivity* occur when Deleuze stretches Hume's theory to address the Kantian demand for an account of rational agency. Take Deleuze's account of how practical reason arises for embodied human beings struggling to create institutions (such as justice) to regulate their practical affairs. Human beings, motivated by passions, seek to institute procedures to codify the routines that make possible security and prosperity. Pure impulses do not suffice for creatures partial to kith and kin.

Fortunately, "nature provides a remedy in the judgment and understanding, for what is irregular and incommodious in the affections."[78] What, though, are judgment and understanding? They are not, for Deleuze's Hume, mental capacities unavailable to other animals—ants, bees, and beavers, in their own ways, coordinate their social activities. Yet judgment and understanding empower human beings to foresee the future, as well as to imagine the consequences of their actions on the pleasure or sadness of themselves and other people, in a way that differs from other animals. The reflection of human imagination "constitutes practical reason; reason is nothing other but a determined moment of the affections of the mind—a calm or rather calmed affection, 'grounded in a distinct view or in reflection.'"[79] Practical reason empowers human beings to invent social arrangements that do not already exist to serve our natural affections for other beings capable of feeling pain and pleasure.[80] "Practical reason is the establishment of a whole of culture and morality."[81]

Deleuze's conception of practical reason combines elements from both the Humean and Kantian traditions. The Humean component is that practical reason emerges from the imagination, or, more precisely, "a kind of twisting of the passion itself in the mind affected by it."[82] Nobody or nothing from above implants practical reason in human beings. Rather, the imagination responds to practical problems by twisting upon itself to determine new pathways and schemes to enrich human life. In *Difference and Repetition*, Deleuze applauds Darwin for raising the "question of knowing under what conditions small, unconnected or free-floating differences become appreciable, connected and fixed differences."[83] Darwin provides the scientific evidence to support Hume's claim that we attribute causality to objects and that, for example, we do not have to accept the cosmological argument that a more perfect being (God) is the necessary and sufficient cause of humanity. Rather, human beings and their distinctive capacities (such as reason) arose as a combination of individual differences—and that there is nothing determined *a priori* about the nature or conclusions of reason.[84] Hume, in other words, provides a functional or adaptive story about the emergence of practical reason. Yet Deleuze's conception of practical reason incorporates Kant's definition of practical reason as the faculty to "be by means of its representations the cause of the reality of the object of these representations."[85] In other words, Deleuze appreciates Kant's emphasis on the human capacity to transcend the given and change it. "Belief and invention are the two modes of transcendence," for Deleuze's Hume.[86] To invent, "each subject reflects upon itself, that is, transcends its immediate partiality" and takes a general survey of human affairs.[87] Deleuze's conception of practical reason is not identical to Kant's, particularly given Deleuze's concern that the discourse of representation imposes conceptual boxes on the given rather than receives it in its singularity.[88] Yet Deleuze does want to acknowledge the human capacity to question the given and imagine it otherwise. One way to describe this capacity is practical reason.[89]

For many contemporary philosophers, the project of naturalizing reason cannot get off the ground. Hilary Putnam states: "What is wrong with evolutionary epistemology is not that the scientific facts are wrong, but that they don't answer any of the philosophical questions."[90] For Putnam, what the mind does, in philosophy, is different than what the brain does, mapped by science. Kant's distinction between philosophy and natural science ensures that rational cogitation transpires in a qualitatively different realm than the lawful processes of nature. Yet Kant's defense of philosophy builds upon a two-world metaphysic that protects moral thinking from empirical vicissitudes, and the Darwinian account of human evolution has led us to doubt that the soul originates on a higher ontological plane.[91] The Kantian demand that moral thinking must take place in the realm of pure reason, combined with the scientific evidence discrediting the idea of a realm of pure reason, contributes to nihilism: the idea that since we lack what we must have, there is no point going on.[92] The demand that we choose between Kantian transcendentalism and Humean empiricism reflects a desire for a simple solution to a complex problem. Human beings are animals with the capacity to think of new ideas that may then affect how we live our lives. Kant and Hume provide complementary vocabularies to describe this mysterious faculty of embodied cognition. One of the best available options for contemporary philosophers thinking about normative sources after Darwin is to rub these paradigms together to spark new thinking. Someday, philosophers may envision other ways to identify the elusive part of human nature that produces practical concepts and principles. Today, however, philosophers must experiment with the traditions before us to approach the problem of naturalizing reason.

Confronting Common Sense

The second task facing contemporary Kantian political theorists is to confront common sense. Common sense provides the raw material—the fund of intuitive ideas, concepts, principles, judgments, and feelings—for subsequent philosophical reflection. Yet philosophy's task is to criticize common sense, that is, to evaluate which of its elements are worth unearthing and cleaning and which should remain buried or expunged. Two pressing questions face contemporary Kantians. How should philosophers balance their roles of clarifying and criticizing common sense? And how should philosophers describe contemporary common sense and envision alternatives to it? In this section, we consider how Kant bequeathed the problem of confronting common sense to his heirs, and then how Rawls and Deleuze recast this problem in contemporary circumstances, particularly after the horrors of the Holocaust have shattered faith in the inherent goodness of ordinary people.[93]

Kant describes common sense in two different ways in the *Groundwork*.[94] Common sense means *doxa*—commonly held positions about moral and political life. In Section I of the *Groundwork*, Kant explains that philosophers need to respect ordinarily held beliefs—such as the unconditional goodness of the good will—and consider it the foundation of their philosophical systems. In the *Critique of Practical Reason*, Kant explains that philosophy's role is not to invent a new morality at odds with common sense: "But who would even want to introduce a new principle of all morality and, as it were, first invent it? Just as if, before him, the world had been ignorant of what duty is or in thoroughgoing error about it."[95] What is philosophy's role, then, if common sense suffices for moral guidance? The need arises because human beings feel "a powerful counterweight against all commands of duty"—that is, a natural dialectic whereby imperfectly rational beings such as humans internally rationalize exceptions for ourselves to the moral law.[96] Common sense has an intrinsic propensity to confuse itself—to accede to its worst impulses and intellectual confusions—and popular moral philosophers exploit this confusion to justify principles arising from outside of common human reason. Philosophy's task is to help common sense see more clearly the moral compass that it already possesses at a fundamental level. Kant thus advises moral philosophers: "To stay with the judgment of common reason, and bring in philosophy at most only in order to exhibit the system of morals all the more completely and comprehensibly, and its rules in a way that is more convenient for their use (still more for disputation), but not in order to remove the common human understanding [*gemeine Menschenverstand*] in a practical respect out of its happy simplicity, and through philosophy to set it on a new route of investigation and instruction."[97] According to J. B. Schneewind, Kantians may view moral philosophy as an ambulance service to help common sense on those rare moments when it is confused by clarifying the principles that already reside within it.[98]

In Section II of the *Groundwork*, however, Kant complicates philosophy's relationship to common sense. "One cannot better serve the wishes of those who ridicule all morality . . . than to concede to them that the concepts of duty must be drawn solely from experience."[99] Philosophers should not equate healthy common sense with *doxa* because *doxa* clearly can be unhealthy. The problem with "popular moral philosophy" (*populären sittlichen Weltweisheit*) is that it misrepresents common sense—or, more precisely, it accurately represents common sense in its corrupt state. The true vocation of moral philosophy is to plumb common sense to discover the proper arrangement of mental faculties that produce and sustain good moral character or attunement (*Gesinnung*). Thus Kant enters the field of pure practical philosophy—that is, the terrain on which practical reason proceeds without any external influences—to discover the mental architecture that makes possible healthy common sense. Moral common sense, in the sense of a *sensus communis*, may be described as the harmonious accord of the faculties—whereby pure practical reason governs the soul and understanding, imagination, and sensibility play supporting and subservient roles.[100] Kant's complex relationship to common sense, we may note, replicates and diverges from Jean-Jacques Rousseau's. Rousseau famously taught Kant to honor the common man and to restore the "rights of humanity" in his philosophical endeavors. Rousseau provided the key to Kant's moral philosophy by arguing that human beings "make our own law and in doing so create the foundation for a free and just social order."[101] And yet, as Rousseau also recognized, nearly every human being we see in contemporary civilized societies has lost their natural innocence. Nobody's common sense today is pure. Rousseau hoped to recover our natural conscientious sentiments—either through politics (in the *Social Contract*) or education (in *Emile*). Kant, on the contrary, thought that we could never trust our natural sentiments—however purified—to provide adequate moral guidance.[102] For Kant, philosophy would always have to take a critical stance towards *doxa*.

Rawls frames the problem of confronting common sense through the idea of reflective equilibrium. "In a democratic society there is a tradition of democratic thought, the content of which is at least familiar and intelligible to the educated common sense of citizens generally."[103] The idea of reflective equilibrium posits that philosophers may construct political theories by dipping into the fund of implicitly shared ideas in a milieu and representing them in a propitious manner. Rawls's political theory begins by assembling elements from democratic common sense, namely, considered convictions at all levels of generality. "Such judgments we view as fixed points: one we never expect to withdraw, as when Lincoln says: 'If slavery is not wrong, nothing is wrong.'"[104] A considered conviction is a matter of the head and the heart, the mind and the passions: a sentiment. For Rawls, the philosopher begins the process of reflective equilibrium by collating such common sense positions and ends by testing his or her theories by how well they accord with common sense. In an early review of *A Theory of Justice*, Allan Bloom argued that Rawls was not a philosopher but "only the spokesman for a certain historical consciousness," namely, democratic liberalism.[105] Bloom worried that Rawls was a historicist and a relativist—a fear that would not have been allayed by late Rawls's more overtly political, rather than metaphysical, liberalism. And yet, a Rawlsian may reply, the common sense of advanced liberal democracies has been conflicted since the New Deal. Democratic citizens have not yet reached consensus over whether the state should play an active role in redistributing wealth or guaranteeing civil rights and liberties. Rawls, like Kant before him, may simply have been trying to provide liberal democratic common sense with a moral compass that it already possesses.

And yet, for Rawls, a political philosopher has a responsibility to weigh common sense from as many perspectives as possible and to contribute ideas to the fund of democratic common sense. Rawls clarifies this position with the idea of wide reflective equilibrium. A philosopher attains narrow reflective equilibrium when she provides a coherent system for the common sense convictions we already have. A philosopher pursues wide reflective equilibrium when she considers "the leading conceptions of political justice found in our philosophical tradition . . . and has weighed the force of the different philosophical and other reasons for them."[106] The idea of wide reflective equilibrium is a regulative ideal, for it presses human beings to achieve a comprehensiveness that can never be attained. For the *our* in this quote reaches to the past, to the future, and to other peoples and traditions. In this case, no philosopher can ever reach equilibrium or stasis because a new voice may always make itself heard. For Rawls, philosophy must have some connection to common sense to make itself intelligible or to motivate consent. Common sense provides philosophy with materials and traction. Yet philosophy's role is to provide a coherent framework for an ever-expanding pool of ideas, theories, and traditions, and to accomplish this role it may express familiar ideas and principles "in a somewhat different way than before."[107] Philosophy must select which elements of common sense to consolidate, which to discard, and what kind of framework to endorse—inventing one if need be. For Rawls, philosophy has a necessarily ambiguous relationship to common sense: forever seeking peace because it is forever at war.

A distinguishing feature of Deleuze's political theory is its overt antipathy towards the Kantian conceptions of common sense. Nietzsche presaged Deleuze's relationship to Kant in a passage from *The Gay Science*:

> And now don't cite the categorical imperative, my friend! This term tickles my ear and makes me laugh despite your serious presence. It makes me think of the old Kant who had obtained the "thing in itself" by stealth—another very ridiculous thing!—and was punished for this when the "categorical imperative" crept stealthily into his heart and led him astray—back to "God," "soul," "freedom," and "immortality," like a fox who loses his way and goes astray back into his cage. Yet it had been his strength and cleverness that had broken open the cage![108]

In the *Critique of Pure Reason*, Kant showed that human beings produce the categories and ideas by which we grasp the manifold, in the realm of knowledge, and orient ourselves, in the realm of practice. In Deleuze's words, "Kant sets up the critical image in opposition to wisdom: we are the legislators of Nature."[109] Insofar as he thinks that philosophers construct rather than discover concepts, Deleuze situates himself in the tradition of Kantian critique. Yet Kant's version of critique ultimately crawls back into the cage of the Platonic / medieval worldview that his theoretical work undermines. For Deleuze, as for Nietzsche, Kant respected the common sense of his time, namely, the Pietism of his family and eighteenth-century Königsberg in general. Kant tried to situate Christian ethics on a new foundation—pure practical reason—but he still insisted that his philosophy honored the spirit of Christianity. That is why Deleuze states in *Nietzsche and Philosophy* that "Kant merely pushed a very old conception of critique to the limit, a conception which saw critique as a force which should be brought to bear on all claims to knowledge and truth, but not on knowledge and truth themselves; a force which should be brought to bear on all claims to morality, but not on morality itself."[110] On this account, Kant embedded himself within Christian *doxa* and targeted the cannons of critique outwards rather than back on their source. A true critical philosopher never makes peace with *doxa*: the preeminent task of philosophy is to be *para*-doxical, that is, against one's time for the benefit of a time to come.[111]

Fortunately, for Deleuze, Kant provided a set of tools to dismantle common sense: the doctrine of the faculties. "One of the most original points of Kantianism is the idea of a difference in nature between our faculties."[112] Prior to Kant, faculty psychology—the study of the powers of the mind—often collapsed the faculties into one. Empiricist versions of faculty psychology argued that all of the mind's powers originated in sensibility, rationalist versions that the mind's powers are clear or obscure exercises of reason. Kant's epochal claim, in the *Critique of Pure Reason*, is that cognition requires the conjunction of active understanding and passive sensibility. Kant saw that knowledge (or morality, or aesthetic judgment) originates when human subjects, with their mental powers, confront a strange world that they can only grasp incompletely. Kant saw the mystery of human beings making their way in an ultimately unknowable universe, and his doctrine of the faculties diagrams the mental powers that make possible human knowledge, practice, and sensation.[113] In his presentation of the doctrine of the faculties, however, Kant introduced an acritical assumption that our mental powers somehow accord with one another in harmonious proportions. Kant trusted that in the realm of knowledge, understanding would legislate with its concepts and principles and the other faculties (reason, imagination, sensibility) would dutifully perform the roles assigned them, and that likewise in the realm of practice reason would dictate the moral law and the other faculties would schematize, typologize, and feel in the appropriate ways. Deleuze remarks that this approach merely transfers the responsibility for cosmic harmony from God to human beings: "Kant invokes a finalist and theological principle *in the same way* as his predecessors."[114] Yet Kant glimpsed, in the *Critique of Judgment*, a possibility that the faculties could be unhinged from common sense by powers that dwarfed the imagination or understanding. On occasions of the sublime, the imagination presents images of such power and magnitude that the understanding cannot grasp them and reason cannot explain them. At these moments, the faculties force each other to overstep their limits and become, in effect, new faculties. "The emancipation of dissonance, the discordant accord, is the great discovery of the *Critique of Judgment*, the final Kantian reversal."[115] Kant himself did not work through the implications of the *Critique of Judgment* for the rest of his critical philosophy. Yet Deleuze takes on the post-Kantian assignment of thinking through the possibilities of our mental faculties being involved in a constant struggle with the sensible world and each other. Deleuze lays out this project in *Difference and Repetition*, in which he defends philosophy's need for a doctrine of the faculties, but explains that Kant's transcendental idealism makes a mistake by freezing the faculties in an *a priori* system. Thus Deleuze proposes the idea of transcendental empiricism to envision the faculties as protean powers that arise through encounters between man and world. For philosophers need to be alert to the possibilities that new faculties may arise that break the cognitive, practical, and aesthetic shackles of common sense.[116] A transhuman philosophy will appropriate Kant's insights about mental powers and advance them beyond the borders that have traditionally defined mankind.[117]

Must a Deleuzian political theory simply oppose common sense? Despite the polemical tone of Deleuze's work in the 1960s, his later work—particularly *A Thousand Plateaus* and *What is Philosophy?*—expresses a more nuanced approach. All of the materials that philosophers use—conceptual personae, concepts, and planes of immanence—have some basis in a philosopher's historical milieu. Political philosophy is no exception. Political philosophers learn about historical figures (whose elements are recomposed in conceptual personae), inherited political concepts (which are rearranged in philosophical concepts), and political ideologies (which are restructured in philosophical planes of immanence). Take the concept of democracy. Political theorists at the beginning of the twenty-first century see that democracy is the default political ideal for numerous states and societies around the world. Deleuze's appeal to "becoming democratic" in *What is Philosophy?* suggests that he too recognizes the power and legitimacy of this idea. Yet, Philip Mengue argues, Deleuze's political theory—in its valorization of minorities, nomads, animal-becomings, and so forth—seems more aristocratic than democratic, more sympathetic to pursuing philosophical lines of flight than building a democratic consensus.[118] Paul Patton, though, explains Deleuze's two-pronged strategy of defending the ideal of becoming democratic and condemning the "meanness and vulgarity of existence that haunts democracies" today.[119] The key distinction is between democratic states of affairs that we see before our eyes in all their hypocrisies and oppressions and virtual democracies that contain potentialities that are both real but not yet actual. Philosophical concepts "fulfill their intrinsically political vocation by counter-effectuating existing states of affairs and referring them back to the virtual realm of becoming."[120] To counter-effectuate means to explore the latent possibilities in a concept that have not yet become actual, that is, to think about possible futures that have not yet become solidified in the present. Political philosophy thus requires collecting and scrutinizing common sense ideas and then experimenting with ways to recompose them in more promising ways. "Without history experimentation would remain indeterminate and unconditioned, but experimentation is not historical. It is philosophical."[121] In other words, political philosophy emerges out of political common sense, but its distinct vocation is to imagine how the ingredients could be recombined for a new earth and a new people.

In their confrontations with common sense, both Rawls and Deleuze are realistic utopians. To be realistic, philosophy must take an honest assessment of the materials at hand. Rawls plumbs the fund of democratic common sense to find the basic ideas, conceptions, judgments, and sentiments that form the basis of his political theory. Deleuze, too, practices a form of "geophilosophy" that has a symbiotic and tense relation with the philosophical opinions of one's nation.[122] Without some grounding in one's time and place, philosophy would lack content and importance. Yet philosophy's role is to combat historicity by imagining how our ideals could be better conceptualized and actualized. Both Rawls and Deleuze try to stretch the range of political possibilities in more promising directions. Realist utopians, Paul Patton explains, "draw on elements of present political normativity to suggest ways in which the injustice or intolerability of existing institutional forms might be removed."[123] For both Rawls and Deleuze, the future of the Enlightenment depends upon both surveying the empirical effects of ideals such as liberty and equality and imagining how the ideals may be recast.

Rawls's relationship to common sense seems to align with what J. B. Schneewind, in *The Invention of Autonomy*, calls the Pythagoras story in moral philosophy. The Socrates story tries to *find* the moral principles and concepts that human beings desire but lack. The assumption in such works as Plato's *Republic* is that no philosopher has yet discovered the idea of the good—but that failure is merely an incitement for philosophers to endeavor harder on the quest. The Pythagoras story, by contrast, holds that the basic truths of morality have always been known, on some level, but that they are often obscured, and the purpose of moral philosophy is to help common sense *rediscover* its moral bearings. On the Christian interpretation of the Pythagoras story, the source of obscurity is sin—or, on Kant's reformulation, the innate propensity to evil.[124] Rawls clearly does not subscribe to that version of the problem of evil—though, as his Princeton thesis on the meaning of sin and faith makes clear, it was not because he was unfamiliar with it.[125] Rather, Rawls's political theory addressed the massive failure of democratic common sense during the Weimar period.[126] "A cause of the fall of Weimar's constitutional regime was that none of the traditional elites were willing to cooperate to make it work. They no longer believed a decent liberal parliamentary regime was possible. Its time had passed."[127] One lesson of the fall of the Weimar constitutional regime in 1933 was that philosophers—such as Nietzsche[128]—had corroded faith in the viability or desirability of liberal democracy. Rawls finds inspiration in the Kantian idea that "human beings must have a moral nature . . . that can understand, act on, and be sufficiently moved by a reasonable political conception of right and justice to support a society guided by its ideals and principles."[129] Rawls believes that people, deep down, are capable of articulating and honoring just political standards. Rawls's faculty psychology—in its thicker version (in Section III of *A Theory of Justice*) or thinner (in *Political Liberalism*)—holds that most people are capable of acting reasonably. Rawls also has faith that given favorable historical circumstances—including the nourishment by responsible liberal democratic philosophers—democratic common sense may flourish. One reason that Rawls writes in such an abstract style is precisely to unearth democratic citizens' "shared political understandings" rather than to inflame passions.[130] For Rawls, the task of political philosophy today is to buttress democratic common sense against its many enemies.

Deleuze subscribes to the Nietzschean view that philosophy should be untimely, that is, outside of and contrary to *doxa*. Common sense, Deleuze explains in *Difference and Repetition*, is stupid—only recognizing things that can be cut up into its conceptual carts—and mean—denigrating singularities that resist its conceptual impositions. "In so far as the practical finality of recognition lies in the 'established values,' then on this model the whole image of thought as *Cogitatio natura* bears witness to a disturbing complacency."[131] Why, though, doesn't Deleuze hope to convert common sense to a better vision? That is, could we at least think of the possibility of a good, joyful philosophy changing enough people's opinion to bring about an affirmative *doxa* based upon a relatively harmonious accord of the faculties (even if not the ones that Kant espoused)? David Reggio argues that Deleuze's political vision can only be understood if one places it in the post–World War II French intellectual milieu consumed by the question of rebirth. "In this postwar environment he joined with colleagues in heralding a post-apocalyptical mock-biblical age, re-creating the world through this double movement of catastrophe and revelation, birth and rebirth."[132] After witnessing the horrors of World War II—in which his brother died on a train to Auschwitz—Deleuze may have doubted that the masses could be courageous thinkers and actors. Here, we may see a genuine tension over the course of Deleuze's intellectual career—between a recurrent interest in the occult and the hermetic tradition and a commitment to philosophy's project of demystification; between a sympathy for isolated and misunderstood geniuses such as Spinoza, Proust, Nietzsche and a desire to forge democratic assemblages; between a political program committed to "vacuoles of non-communication" and a tempered appreciation for the role of established institutions; in short, between a hatred for common sense as such and a recognition that a liberal democratic common sense is a valuable thing.

How, then, should contemporary Kantians confront common sense?[133] I do not think that Rawls's and Deleuze's projects can be collapsed into a single vision. The Enlightenment benefits from a tension between its moderate pole—committed to solidifying a healthy common sense committed to democracy, liberalism, and pluralism—and a radical pole—always pointing out blind spots (about say, the treatment of unfamiliar minorities) and raising new possibilities to enrich collective life. According to William E. Connolly, the contemporary Left benefits from a torsion between a politics of being and a politics of becoming, a politics committed to establishing and preserving just social arrangements, and a politics attentive to considering new ideas and experiments in living.[134] Furthermore, as John Stuart Mill notes, very few minds are sufficiently "capacious and impartial" to achieve a perfect balance between conservative and revolutionary impulses: in practical politics, it is better to allow combatants to present their perspectives under competing banners.[135] The challenge for the contemporary Left, then, is to recognize the importance of both respecting liberal democratic common sense and solidifying its considered convictions and challenging liberal democratic common sense and perforating its categories and proposing new ones.

Envisioning Pluralism

The third problem facing contemporary political theorists is to envision the contours and limits of pluralistic societies. In *Political Liberalism*, Rawls makes a distinction that has now become commonplace in Anglophone political theory. Enlightenment liberalism envisions a society in which all citizens ideally agree on the basis of political morality and the principles of the constitutional order. Citizens may disagree on the details of a meaningful life and how to interpret constitutional principles, but these disagreements transpire on a shared moral foundation, such as Kant's metaphysics of morality. Political liberalism, on the contrary, envisions a political order in which most citizens agree to the terms of political cooperation for whatever reasons they wish. Political liberals do not care why citizens propose and honor just political principles: the important thing is that the citizens act and speak in a civically responsible manner. Political liberals, then, do not think that political morality demands that citizens become Kantians all the way down. What, then, do political liberals such as Rawls and Deleuze take from Kant?[136] In this section, I show how Rawls and Deleuze think that Kantian courage demands that Kantians should address the fact of reasonable pluralism in liberal democratic societies.

Kant's vision of pluralism is famously opaque and controversial. Take, for example, Kant's conception of a metaphysics of morals. In the *Groundwork*, Kant proposes to search for and establish the supreme principle of morality that will, in turn, serve as the foundation of a metaphysics of morals.[137] One might suppose that Kant sees a tight fit between morality and politics, and that the categorical imperative in the realm of moral philosophy might simply be restated as the universal principle of right in the political realm. Yet in the *Metaphysics of Morals*, Kant distinguishes ethical lawgiving—that concerns the will's incentives, or why one performs an action—and juridical lawgiving—that only addresses what one does, regardless of the moral or pathological incentives at work.[138] The question that still perplexes scholars is whether Kant's conception of juridical lawgiving is loosely or tightly connected to his more robust moral philosophy.

In an essay entitled, "Is Kant's *Rechtslehre* a 'Comprehensive Liberalism?'" Thomas Pogge presents a case that Kant's political theory may apply to all citizens in a pluralistic society and does not presuppose agreement with his accounts of the categorical imperative or transcendental idealism. According to Pogge, Kant's argument at the beginning of the *Rechtslehre* is both simple and persuasive. Kant begins by thinking about the concept of right, that is, the concept of a law that maintains borders between each person's domain of external freedom. Upon analyzing this concept, Kant arrives at the universal principle of right: "Any action is *right* if it can coexist with everyone's freedom in accordance with a universal law."[139] This principle permits any action that can coexist with an appropriate sphere of freedom for every other person and prohibits—through the coercion of the state, if necessary—any action that infringes upon another's domain of personal freedom. Pogge likens Kant's principle to a rule that governs any possible game among citizens competing and cooperating with each other in social life. As such, this rule may appeal to anyone who sees the benefits of rule-governed social cooperation, including Hobbesians who may scoff at the details of Kant's moral philosophy. Pogge thinks that Kantians may disagree with whether Kant's *Rechtslehre*, in its entirety, proposes fair terms of social cooperation. Yet Pogge thinks that Kant—and contemporary Kantians—may "be rather pleased that so substantial a result can be derived from so slender a basis," that is, that a basic constitutional principle can be formulated merely by thinking of the idea of *Recht*.[140] For Pogge, Kant's liberalism is freestanding of any complex or controversial metaphysical or moral doctrine.

For other interpreters, however, Kant's political philosophy is permeated by his moral and theological presuppositions. In his study of early modern German philosophy, *Rival Enlightenments*, Ian Hunter contends that Kant was a participant in the tradition of the metaphysical Enlightenment. After the religious warfare of the seventeenth century, philosophers branched off in two main directions. Members of the civil Enlightenment, such as Christian Thomasius and Samuel Pufendorf, argued that the state's role was to guarantee security by deconfessionalising society, that is, by placing strict boundaries around the political authority or intellectual prestige of the religious metaphysicians who had contributed to Europe's recent carnage. Members of the metaphysical Enlightenment, such as Leibniz and Kant, on the contrary, argued that the state had a crucial role in inculcating religious morality and raising the prestige of university metaphysicians. Yes, Kant's *Rechtslehre* merely touches upon the state's coercion of physical bodies. But Kant's *Religion within the Boundaries of Mere Reason* polemicizes for a new philosophical elite to publicly proclaim rationalized religious truths. Kant tries to take power from the civil jurists and the religious orthodox and hand it to the new priestcraft: philosophical biblical interpreters. "Kant's program thus preserves the longstanding role of university metaphysics as the intellectual architect of confessional society; that is, society conceived of as a single 'true visible church,' or, as the morally perfecting 'kingdom of God on earth.'"[141] According to Hunter, Kant provides a way to preserve the crux of Christian morality and confessional politics in a post-Newtonian, post-Westphalian universe—namely, by grounding the authority of Kantian morality and politics on pure practical reason rather than empirical observations or biblical revelation. Yet Kant's *Rechtslehre* is controversial to anyone who does not think that constitutional principles may be derived in an *a priori* manner. From Hunter's perspective, arguments such as Pogge's try to induce belief in a metaphysical moment in which principles of right appear as self-evident rather than as the product of hard-won political and jurisprudential battles. For Hunter, too many contemporary Kantians militate for a quasi-confessional politics behind the veneer of abstract philosophy. Rawls and Deleuze disagree with Hunter on many things, including the latter's inattention to elements within Kant's philosophy that rebel against medieval metaphysics as well as Hunter's secularist assumptions about philosophy and politics. But they would agree with him that Kant's vision of religious pluralism is unduly narrow. In what follows I consider how Rawls and Deleuze revise Kant's problem of formulating a theory of justice for pluralistic communities.

Rawls frames his problem in *Political Liberalism* as that of constructing a political conception of justice, not a comprehensive moral doctrine such as Kant's. Rawls's first set of reasons for abandoning Kant's original aspirations is more academic than political. Kant argued that pure moral philosophy could have the same rigor and precision as logic: the categorical imperative, after all, may be interpreted as a restatement of the principle of noncontradiction. For Rawls, however, many philosophers today recognize that reasonable people—confronted by the burdens of judgment—disagree about the ultimate ends of life and thus should exercise forbearance in using the state's authority to impose upon all citizens one moral, philosophical, or religious system. When people make hard decisions about, say, political legislation, they are likely to disagree on what evidence counts, how to weigh the evidence, what the criteria mean, and what the relevant precedents are. This is not to say that legislators do not have to make choices—it just means that reasonable legislators must acknowledge that they have likely not solved the problem once and for all. Furthermore, normative frameworks themselves—say, between those of different religions—are likely to conflict about important matters and no society has room for all ways of life. Reasonable citizens and philosophers, in sum, hold that "individual and associative points of view, intellectual affinities, and affective attachments, are too diverse, especially in a free society, to enable those doctrines to serve as the basis of lasting and reasoned political agreement."[142] Rawls's religious and conservative critics often point out that Rawls seems to court dogmatism in precluding militant interpretations of natural right or natural law.[143] Rawls tries to address this point by acknowledging that reasonable citizens have a wide latitude in what they believe and say in the nonpublic spheres of life. Yet Rawls also thinks that political philosophers who study the history of political philosophy have a right to be deeply skeptical that any one thinker or school has arrived at the incontrovertibly right answers to the most important questions about the soul, its origin, its fate after death, and so forth.

Rawls's second set of reasons for relinquishing talk of a metaphysics of morals is the historical experience of the past two centuries. Rawls identifies two facts that reasonable people have become aware of since Kant's time. The fact of oppression is that a "continuing shared understanding on one comprehensive religious, philosophical, or moral doctrine can be maintained only by the oppressive use of state power."[144] Rawls acknowledges that Enlightenment philosophers recognized this fact when looking at the Catholic Church's violent suppression of heresy during the Middle Ages, most notably in the Inquisition. Yet Enlightenment philosophers thought that oppression could be eliminated if the right, secular, doctrine became the supreme law of the land. What we realize today, according to Rawls, is that Enlightenment philosophers made their own contributions to the horrors of the past two centuries. This is not to say that liberal democrats share the same moral culpability as Stalin, Hitler, or Pol Pot. But it is to say that dogmatic liberal democracy has its own moral blind spots that come from treating alternate viewpoints as heretical. According to Rawls, Kantians need to drop the language of *a priori* moral or juridical codes and present themselves as pragmatists who may make their own valuable contribution to political discourse. They may take this step confidently if they recognize the fact of reasonable pluralism, that is, that in modern democratic societies the majority of citizens have shown a willingness to cooperate even in the face of persistent moral disagreement. There is no reason to criticize Kant on this score: he could not have anticipated the shape of twenty-first century pluralism in countries such as the United States of America, England, or France. Nor can contemporary Kantians say once and for all what the contours of pluralism will take in such countries in the future. Yet contemporary heirs of the Enlightenment must be amenable to changing the terms of political cooperation if new constituencies present a reasonable case for change.

What is at stake in the idea of a political conception of justice? From Kant, Rawls takes the idea that a theory of justice articulates the basic principles and standards to govern the relations between citizens in a well-ordered society. In *A Theory of Justice*, Rawls described the principles of justice as fairness as akin to categorical imperatives, but perhaps in the face of critics who charged him with betraying Kant's notion of the *a priori*, Rawls dropped such language in *Political Liberalism*. Yet the modified Kantian position remains the same: the principles of justice are effectively (if not ontologically) the supreme laws of the land. From Hume, however, Rawls takes the idea that the rules of justice are a human invention necessary to confront the circumstances of justice (natural scarcity, human acquisitiveness), and from Hegel, the idea that rules of justice apply to the basic structure of society (the background political and economic order). For Rawls, a political conception of justice, unlike Kant's metaphysics of morals, concerns human beings in a particular milieu, namely, modern, industrialized societies. Finally, Rawls folds a pluralistic sensibility into his notion of a political conception of justice that he attributes to the influence of Isaiah Berlin. According to Berlin, pluralists are committed to ethical political standards while also shouldering the burden of listening to other perspectives.[145] A political conception of justice, then, is political in the sense of being open to public debate and negotiation. In sum, Rawls's problem in *Political Liberalism*— "how is it possible for there to exist over time a just and stable society of free and equal citizens, who remain profoundly divided by reasonable religious, philosophical, and moral doctrines?"[146]—is not Kant's in the *Rechtslehre*. A political conception of justice is historically inflected, designed for deeply pluralistic societies, and subject to contestation—it is not *a priori*, applicable to every rational being as such, or universal.

In *A Thousand Plateaus*, Deleuze crafts the problem of political pluralism by constructing the concept of the rhizome. On its face, the rhizome is an anti-Kantian concept. Kant appears briefly in *A Thousand Plateaus* as a state philosopher who sanctifies the powers that be and demands agreement on a narrow conception of morality. "Ever since philosophy assigned itself the role of ground it has been giving the established powers its blessing, and tracing its doctrine of faculties onto the organs of State power. Common sense, the unity of all the faculties at the center constituted by the Cogito, is the State consensus raised to the absolute."[147] Here, Deleuze restates in cryptic form the charge he leveled against Kantian philosophy in *Nietzsche and Philosophy* and *Difference and Repetition*. Kant saw that the human mind is much more complex and embedded in earthy materiality than earlier philosophers, but he contained the revolutionary implications of this vision by demanding that all rational beings recognize the apodictic demands of pure practical reason. In the terminology of *A Thousand Plateaus*, Kant is an arboreal philosopher who permits disagreement among rational beings only on the condition that they agree on certain moral presuppositions. In other words, people may branch out into different moral, religious, or philosophical doctrines only on the condition that they emerge from the same rational trunk. For Deleuze, Kantian liberalism perceives only a very narrow range of disagreement: unreasonable constituencies are those who threaten the true harmony of the faculties or the reigning opinions about good and evil. Deleuze's entire goal in *A Thousand Plateaus* appears to be the construction of a philosophical war machine to attack the Kantian foundations of liberal democracies in the name of allowing joyful assemblages, or rhizomes, to flourish. Yet this interpretation misses Deleuze's subtle debts to Kant's critical philosophy—evidenced by his March 1978 lectures on Kant just two years before the publication of *A Thousand Plateaus*—or the ways in which Deleuze may be read as an immanent critic of liberal democracy. How, then, can the concept of the rhizome be seen as extending rather than destroying the insights of political liberalism?

In *A Thousand Plateaus*, Deleuze offers a definition of the rhizome and several principles embedded in the concept that may be fleshed out for contemporary political theorists.[148] Rhizomes are "acentered systems, finite networks of automata in which communication runs from any neighbor to any other, the stems or channels do not preexist, and all individuals are interchangeable, defined only by their *state* at a given moment—such that the local operations are coordinated and the final, global result synchronized without a central agency."[149] Political action requires coordination to be effective. For Western political theorists, trees offer the common sense model of political action: everyone in a political body agrees on certain core planks even if they disagree on secondary matters—this is what makes movement, or growth, or solidity, possible. Rhizomes, however, lack a center or a predetermined plan. Like an English garden, rhizomatic pluralism empowers a certain wildness or indeterminacy to flourish. "Any point of a rhizome can be connected to anything other, and must be."[150] There is no top or bottom in rhizomatic politics in the same way that the classical Marxist party places the communists atop the proletariat or the proletariat above the bourgeoisie. Rather, rhizomatic politics demands that individuals and constituencies connect with other political orders to construct provisional coalitions and agencies. There is no solid boundary for rhizomatic politics; fluctuating political bodies, or what Deleuze also calls multiplicities or assemblages, are "defined by the outside, the line of flight or deterritorialization according to which they change in nature and connect with other multiplicities."[151] Political bodies are essentially protean, attaining a certain density or cohesion at the same time that they necessarily fall apart. In political terms, individuals and constituencies are always in an unstable relation of force that precludes entire agreement or identification. Political bodies, furthermore, are not defined by their ideologies alone—rather, political bodies have multiple layers that enable and undermine the rest. "A rhizome ceaselessly establishes connections between semiotic chains, organizations of power, and circumstances relative to the arts, sciences, and social struggles."[152] To map the political universe, one needs to attend to the ways in which plural constituencies interact on the levels of ideas, institutions, on the street, in the academy, in conversations, through public pronouncements, and so forth. Finally, "a rhizome is not amenable to any structural or generative model."[153] According to Deleuze's ontology, there are no transcendent or intrinsic structures that make things such as bodies or languages possible. There are processes of structuration and generation, but these are always distinct combinations of singularities that can never be perfectly replicated. This means, in turn, that political scientists cannot trace the political order without contributing their own artistic vision to the map they produce. Rhizomatic pluralism is both a description of how politics always transpires as well as a call for appreciating multilayered, acentered politics.

What are the implications of the concept of the rhizome for thinking about political pluralism? One possibility is that Deleuze envisions a tight fit between his ethics and his politics. A Deleuzian, in this case, would be somebody who entirely embraces the vision of *A Thousand Plateaus*: namely, a mechanosphere composed of abstract machines and concrete assemblages, or a universe composed of bodies and things in perpetual states of re- and decomposition. Only the most enthusiastic Deleuzian thinks that Deleuze discovered the truth supposed to govern all moral, philosophical, or religious visions—and it is hard to see how this interpretation fits with Deleuze's call for acentered systems. Another possibility is that the concept of the rhizome simply fails to present a vision of a coherent politics. Many Marxists—including Alain Badiou, Peter Hallward, Michael Hart, Antonio Negri, and Slavoj Žižek—accuse Deleuze of celebrating the deterritorializing flows of capitalism and weakening the strength and cohesion of the proletarian party.[154] Yet these arguments simply assume that political bodies must have a firm ideology and a militant structure and ignores how political bodies are always adding and losing members, shifting their intellectual positions, and imbricated in complex relations with other political bodies. Far better, for Deleuze, to grasp the rhizomatic nature of already existing politics in order to determine how better to intervene in tipping political bodies in a more joyful direction. To translate Deleuze's philosophy into contemporary terms, one might say that rhizomatic politics today means mapping liberal democrat politics—the reigning political order today—to determine how best to create beautiful gardens, or social orders, in which the best available type of pluralism might flourish. A rhizomatic politics may militate for economic justice, environmental sustainability, racial or sexual justice, and other traditional concerns of the Left: it just remains critically responsive to new forces that might compel leftists to rethink their vision of pluralistic societies.

How, more precisely, may Deleuze's idea of the rhizome change Rawls's idea of a political conception of justice? First, political liberals may give up the idea that a political order needs constitutional principles, as it were, set in stone. Both Rawls and Deleuze, as shown above, give up the idea that political theorists may access a transcendent or ideal realm of concepts and principles that govern moral and political practice. Yet whereas Rawls thinks that political theorists may, for political purposes, use the idea of "once and for all" to designate principles or judgments that one cannot imagine amending, Deleuze's rhetoric incites perpetual experimentation.[155] Rawls, when pressed, acknowledges that wide reflective equilibrium compels political theorists to consider new theories of justice, whereas Deleuze explicitly proposes a "model that is perpetually in construction."[156] Deleuze urges political liberals to relinquish the "State model of thought" in which Kantians take center stage in political debates on the left. Instead, the idea of the rhizome presses political liberals to embrace a decentered vision of pluralism in which multiple constituencies craft provisional terms of political alliance.[157] Furthermore, the idea of the rhizome—exemplified by biological entities such as crabgrass, dandelions, and potatoes—is much earthier than Rawls's idea of a political conception of justice. Rawls, one might say, is still beholden to an intellectualist model of pluralism, where constituencies agree primarily on the level of ideas (doctrines, conceptions), whereas Deleuze draws attention to the multiple layers of being in which individuals and groups—themselves porous entities—interact.[158] Deleuze's idea of the rhizome explains how political liberals need to engage friends and enemies through concepts, percepts, affects, and so on. From a Deleuzian perspective, this type of interaction is already taking place: it is not a question of glamorizing the emotive or physical layers of politics. Rather, political theorists need to widen their apertures to perceive the many ways that plural forces interact.[159] Finally, the idea of the rhizome helps political theorists be on the lookout for new constituencies striving to cross the threshold of public recognition. Rawls proposes to forge a political conception of justice by assembling ideas from the common sense of democratic political culture. What happens, though, when new beings want to break through common sense to make their voices heard? The idea of the rhizome helps pluralists look for buds, as it were, that may be nurtured to find expression in a diverse polity—though, as Deleuze emphasizes in *A Thousand Plateaus*, rhizomes may also include the worst forms of personal or collective identity that need to be eradicated before they attempt to destroy the garden. A rhizomatic political conception of justice needs to distinguish valuable contributors to societal diversity from potentially dangerous invaders. There is no way to fashion *a priori* principles for this type of pragmatic politics: one needs to survey carefully the political terrain—its constituencies and forces and their interaction—and determine collectively how to proceed. Lest this discussion seems too abstract or utopian, one might note that rhizomatic politics are already happening in Europe and North America as political orders adjust to growing Muslim communities who want a say in democratic mores and laws. The idea of the rhizome contributes to the idea of a political conception of justice by pointing out that liberals do not and cannot—without extreme violence—hold the center of global debates about political and religious pluralism, that the fate of pluralism will not be settled by intellectual arguments alone, and that heirs of the Enlightenment must be amenable to changing their ideas and principles to forge alliances with other peoples.

Kant contributes little directly to the pluralist imaginary of paradigm thinkers in contemporary Anglophone or Continental political theory. Neither Rawls nor Deleuze think that contemporary political theorists should strive to formulate a metaphysics of morals, much less polemicize for Kant's. The first set of reasons is philosophical: Kant still holds out hope for an *a priori* code that may govern the ethical and juridical spheres, whereas post-Darwinians recognize that concepts and principles are "only working hypotheses" that human beings develop through a constant interaction with the natural and social environment.[160] Philosophically, it seems impossible to transcend the material world entirely to determine theories of justice, though human beings do have the capacity to transcend in some capacity their immediate *habitus*. Contemporary Kantians can thereby imagine pluralistic societies that both mirror currently existing societies and stretch elements in new directions. By naturalizing and politicizing Kant's conception of the transcendental, Rawls and Deleuze hold that human beings may construct new categories to facilitate productive forms of political cooperation. The second set of reasons to abandon Kant's aspiration to formulate a metaphysics of morals is political: an *a priori* theory of justice announces on its face, as it were, that is refuses to consider empirical data when laying out doctrines of personal or collective morality. Deleuze counters: "We're tired of trees. . . . They've made us suffer too much."[161] A metaphysics of morals makes people suffer by saying that they are unreasonable when they refuse to honor pure practical reason as the highest source of moral principles. One of the most remarkable features of contemporary Kant scholarship is the paucity of serious engagements with non-Christian religions. Or, stated more positively: some of the most interesting work in contemporary Kantian political theory is among those who consider how the Enlightenment needs to shift to dialogue respectfully with voices that Kant could afford to ignore in the eighteenth century.[162] For Rawls and Deleuze, the best way to honor Kant's legacy is to exercise the courage to address our own problems. Today, that means creating ideas—such as a political conception of justice or the rhizome—to consider how plural communities can interact respectfully on matters of shared concern and fend off common threats.

THE FUTURE OF THE LEFT

Is it possible to envision a new Left, or a new Enlightenment, that somehow combines all of the different post-Kantian traditions into, say, a poststructuralist political liberalism? This book is clearly motivated by the guiding idea that Rawls and Deleuze—or the Anglophone and Continental philosophical traditions more broadly—may enrich each other, particularly as they determine how Euro-American liberals may engage diverse constituencies around the globe. Yet I contend that the Enlightenment benefits from pitching a broad enough tent for different styles of philosophy with different aims. To give this idea more content, I propose to take up a contrast from David Hackett Fischer's study, *Liberty and Freedom: A Visual History of America's Founding Ideas*. Despite the common practice of using liberty and freedom as synonyms, particularly to define one of the major ideals of the Left, Fischer shows that these terms have dramatically different origins and subsequent uses. In what follows, I argue that Rawls is more concerned with freedom, Deleuze with liberty, and that the Left benefits from the charge between these ideals.

The etymology of freedom and liberty, Fischer explains, reveals that the terms originally meant, and still do to some extent, dramatically different things. The term freedom originates from the Proto-Indo-European word *priya*, meaning dear or beloved, which forms the root of such terms as the Norse *fri*, the German *frei*, the Dutch *vrij*, the Celtic *rheidd*, and the English *friend*. To be free means to be part of a tribe united by kinship and bound by certain rules that gives its members rights (from the Proto-Indo-European root **reg-*, "to put straight"). For the Norse families who fled kingship to colonize Iceland in the ninth century, for example, "freedom meant the rule of law, the power to choose one's own chief, and the right to be governed and judged by a local assembly called the *Thing*."[163] The word freedom comes from northern Europe and means joining a self-governing group. To be free means the power to do something with others in a united community.

The term liberty originates from southern Europe and means the power to be left alone from the community. Liberty comes from the Latin *libertas*, which in turn stems from the Greek *eleutheros*, which means a condition of being independent or distinct. In ancient Greece and Rome, "most people were born in a condition of prior restraint, to which liberty came as a specific exemption or release."[164] The liberty to speak in an assembly, or the liberty to vote and govern, implied a stratified society in which some people were mobile and capable of distinguishing themselves, and other people (the vast majority) were not. The term *freedom*, in sum, privileges the group and its self-governance, and the term *liberty* privileges the individual and his or her excellence. One of the remarkable features of the history of the United States, Fischer argues, is that it has blended these two concepts—and their background assumptions—into an inherently tense political vocabulary. On the whole, this has been a good thing: "What made America free, and keeps it growing more so, was not any single vision of liberty and freedom but the interplay of many visions."[165] Though Fischer writes as a historian concerned with the fate of one country, I wish to consider how the liberty-freedom contrast illuminates different strains of post-Kantian political theory.

How is Rawls committed to the ideal of freedom? Consider the conclusion of *Justice as Fairness: A Restatement* in which Rawls explains how *A Theory of Justice*'s idea of a well-ordered society survives Rawls's turn toward political liberalism. While it is true that citizens in such a society do not share final moral ends, "they do affirm the same political conception;

and this means that they share one basic political end, and one with high priority: namely, the end of supporting just institutions and giving one another justice accordingly, not to mention the other ends they must also share and realize through their political cooperation. Moreover, in a well-ordered society the end of political justice is among citizens' most basic aims by reference to which they express the kind of person they want to be."[166] At the end of his career, Rawls gave up hope or expectation that all citizens could affirm the ideal of moral autonomy all the way down. Or rather, he thought that it would be unreasonable to demand that all citizens interpret justice as fairness through Kantian lenses and that political liberals would have to exercise more modesty in their interactions with citizens of other faiths. Yet Rawls believed that it was of the utmost importance that all citizens—or at least an educated majority—embrace constitutional essentials. Furthermore, he thought that constitutional essentials included a principle guaranteeing all citizens a minimal level of primary goods to exercise their liberties. That is why Rawls presents his late theory of justice as a political liberalism rather than a libertarianism: liberalism, on his account, still requires viewing the less fortunate as members in a collective endeavor of self-governance. Thus in his restatement of justice as fairness Rawls presents a case for property-owning democracy: a revolutionary idea in early twenty-first–century United States, but one that expresses a collectivist impulse.[167] For Rawls, political liberals have to protect civil rights and liberties, but in a political order that brings people together in their ideas regarding political justice and in their material possessions through progressive economic redistribution. For Rawls, freedom is the condition of and a consequence of a just political order.

How does it make sense to describe Deleuze as a liberal? One reason is that Deleuze, like John Stuart Mill in *On Liberty*, extols the "absolute and essential importance of human development in its richest diversity."[168] Deleuze's protest against arboreal political thought resonates with Mill's warning against the tyranny of the majority that enslaves the soul as well as the body. The key difference between Deleuze and Mill is that the latter is concerned with human flourishing, whereas the former thinks that this category places arbitrary and unfortunate limits on the ways in which human beings can change their nature. Consider, for example, the contrast between majorities, minorities, and minority-becomings in *A Thousand Plateaus*: "The majority in a government presupposes the right to vote, and not only is established among those who possess that right but is exercised over those who do not, however great their numbers; similarly, the majority in the universe assumes as pregiven the right and power of man. In this sense women, children, but also animals, plants, and molecules, are minoritarian. . . . It is important not to confuse 'minoritarian,' as a becoming or process, with a 'minority,' as an aggregate or a state."[169] According to Deleuze, politics contain three types of bodies. A majority is the standard against which all other bodies are measured: it is defined less by a numerical advantage than a state of domination. A minority is a definable aggregate in relation to the majority: it is the inferior force in a relation of domination. A minority-becoming, or a minoritarian-process, eludes predetermined criteria: it is a flow that goes between entities in the process of forming something new. One could imagine, for instance, a political body that contains a majority religion (Protestantism), minority religions (Catholicism, Judaism, and Islam), and minoritarian religions (Wickens, heretical sects). At several key points in *A Thousand Plateaus*, Deleuze acknowledges that the politics of majorities and minorities are vitally important: Without protection for established identities all political action would disintegrate into chaos.[170] Yet the whole force of *A Thousand Plateaus* is to help us perceive minority-becomings and appreciate their power and ethical importance. A Deleuzian political calculus may "have its own compositions, organizations, even centralizations; nevertheless, it proceeds not via the States or the axiomatic process [of the global economy] but via a pure becoming of minorities."[171] It is only partially true that Deleuze extols "vacuoles of noncommunication" that simply break away from established norms, common sense, and the striated space of the global political-economic order.[172] Deleuze views minority-becomings as supplements to, not replacements for, ordinary politics. What is clear, though, is that a Deleuzian politics favors the liberty of singularities to the freedom of collectivities.[173]

For over two hundred years, Kantians have been divided over whether to interpret his philosophy as libertarian or socialistic, concerned ultimately with the rights of the individual or with building the right type of community, appreciative of each person's dignity or insistent that all rational being's will in the right way. In this book, I am concerned with a recent chapter in this debate, namely between Rawlsians who favor freedom and Deleuzians who favor liberty. Of course, there are elements in each paradigmatic thinker that can be assembled to present a contrary case: Rawls values each person's liberty to say, believe in, and practice their own conception of the good (within limits) and Deleuze sees the need for democratic-becomings that bring communities closer to the egalitarian ideal. Yet Rawls's arguments for stable and just communities and Deleuze's invocations of minority-becomings pick up two important strands in the Enlightenment legacy: its moderate and radical elements.

I now turn to how Rawls and Deleuze construct political theories to address the problems detailed in this chapter.

Constructing Theories

In a recent book titled *Is Critique Secular?*, Talal Asad and Judith Butler debate whether Kant, or the Enlightenment more broadly, may still serve as a resource to critical political theory. Asad argues that Michel Foucault is wrong to valorize Kant, the Enlightenment, secular reason, or the modern West. Foucault's late defense of the Enlightenment is "surprising coming from a genealogist, because it sets aside the need to think through the various historical determinants whose effect . . . has been a diversity of 'critiques.'"[1] In his essay, Asad documents how the Greek concept of critique has been transformed by successive Western authors, including the Cynics, the church fathers, Bayle, Kant, Hegel, Marx, neo-Kantians, Pope Benedict XVI, and ultimately contemporary academics for whom "*professional* critique . . . has less to do with the right of free speech than with the reproduction of intellectual disciplines."[2] For Asad, the concept of critique has been and continues to be used to marginalize other discourses—including political Islam—that may be reflective but do not share Kant's aspiration to establish a court of pure reason. Of course, Butler concedes, philosophers and political actors have used the rhetoric of critique to bludgeon alternate points of view and forestall rather than promote intercivilizational dialogue. Yet is this all that critique entails? Butler notes, first, Foucault never equates the critical ethos with Kant's doctrines or the modern, secular West, and second, he does not think that modern Westerners have to defend uncritically the ideals of the eighteenth-century Enlightenment. Regardless of Kant's intentions, Foucault holds that "if critique is incessant and does not stop happening, then critique can turn on the concept of reason itself."[3] Kant himself may have sought the universal conditions of possibility of theoretical, practical, and aesthetic judgment, but Foucault tries to "transpose a Kantian procedure onto a historical scheme."[4] In sum, Butler argues that Foucault discards (many of) Kant's doctrines at the same time as he embraces the critical ethos and selectively reappropriates Kant's metaethics. But how does that play out for contemporary political theorists who wish to advance the Enlightenment tradition? That is, even if we acknowledge that Kantian political theory has to adapt to historical developments, how do we proceed today?

In this chapter, I consider how Rawls and Deleuze take up Kant's metaethics to construct timely political theories. First, I consider how Rawls and Deleuze conceptualize the idea of constructivism and defend it against critics who accuse them of corrupting Kant's pure moral philosophy. In the heart of the chapter, I consider how Rawls and Deleuze use constructivism to fabricate their political theories, namely, by performing four activities: inventing a conception of the person, laying out a plane, constructing theories, and evaluating theories. Finally, I consider how the project of constructivism may be renewed for the twenty-first century by combining Rawlsian and Deleuzian insights. Rawls, I contend, participates in the moderate branch of the Enlightenment that seeks common cause with citizens of faith, and Deleuze extends the tradition of the radical Enlightenment that advances the Spinozist project of demystifying religion. Without wishing to collapse the differences between their visions, I suggest that liberal democrats may broaden the range of materials that they use to construct new political theories, including shifting intuitions about the Muslim presence in Western societies. This project, I suggest, can get us started on making new political theories for our increasingly interconnected world in which diverse faiths must envision new ways to coexist agonistically, peacefully, and fruitfully.

THE IDEA OF CONSTRUCTIVISM

Immanuel Kant opened up a new prospect for political philosophy in the *Critique of Pure Reason*. In the preface to the B (1787) edition, Kant proposed to shift philosophy's focus from the object to the subject in the same way that Copernicus forced astronomers to factor in their own motion in the calculations of heavenly bodies.

> Up to now it has been assumed that all our cognition must conform to the objects; but all attempts to find out something about the *a priori* through concepts that would extend our cognition have, on this presupposition, come to nothing. Hence let us once try whether we do not get farther with the problem of metaphysics by assuming that the objects must conform to our cognition, which would agree better with the requested possibility of an *a priori* cognition of them, which is to establish something about objects before they are given to us.[5]

Kant agreed with Plato that philosophers should pursue metaphysics—the study of *a priori* concepts and principles. Unlike Plato, however, Kant thought that philosophers must look inward rather than outward to discover the basic conceptual apparatus through which we apprehend knowledge. In other words, Kant's defense of metaphysics involves a new appreciation of subjectivity and its powers to organize the manifold into coherent objects that human beings can experience. The basic insight of constructivism, according to Tom Rockmore, is that "the knower construct, constitute, make, or produce its cognitive object as a necessary condition of knowledge."[6] Kant himself thought that the *Critique of Pure Reason* enumerates "all of the ancestral concepts (*Stammbegriffe*) that comprise the pure cognition in question."[7] Yet post-Kantian German idealists criticized this very claim itself and highlighted the contextual, historic, linguistic, and material features of the human cognitive apparatus. For many philosophers writing "in Kant's wake," the specifics of Kant's system are much less important than the active terminology he bequeathed to describe the philosophic enterprise: to create concepts, to legislate principles, to construct frameworks, and so forth.[8]

Rawls describes the basic insight of constructivism in his essay, "Themes in Kant's Moral Philosophy." Rawls proceeds by setting up a contrast between rational intuitionism and Kant's moral constructivism. Rational intuitionism holds that human beings may use their faculty of reason to acquire knowledge of a moral order of values that is "prior to and independent of our conceptions of person and society."[9] On the one hand, Kant agrees with rational intuitionists—such as Samuel Clarke, Richard Price, Henry Sidgwick, and G. E. Moore—that moral concepts and principles are gleaned by the human faculty of reason and do not simply reside in the natural world. On the other hand, Kant opposes the cosmology of rational intuitionism. Rational intuitionists believe that moral concepts and principles originate outside of our self-understanding. Even though rational intuitionists prize the faculty of reason to transcend the material world and enter a higher order of things—such as Plato's realm of forms or Leibniz's hierarchy of perfections—they still think that human beings need to get their moral guidance from elsewhere, that is, they endorse moral heteronomy. Though Rawls overtly mentions Kant's philosophical opponents, Rawls tacitly lays out the theological stakes of Kant's project: Kant's ideal of moral autonomy challenges all religious doctrines that hold that moral laws originate in the divine will. Kant's *Critique of Practical Reason*, Rawls elaborates, sets forth a radically new agenda for practical philosophy. Paraphrasing the passage on the "paradox of method" in Chapter II ("On the Concept of an Object of Pure Practical Reason") of the second *Critique*, Rawls explains: "Rather than starting from a conception of the good given independently of the right, we start from a conception of the right—of the moral law—given by pure (as opposed to empirical) practical reason. We then specify in the light of this conception what ends are permissible and what social arrangements are right and just."[10] Kant's Copernican revolution in moral philosophy occurs when philosophers start with a conception of the right rather than a conception of the good. What is at stake in this distinction? A conception of the good originates outside of us. Moral concepts and principles, in this case, are given to us. That is why rational intuitionists have a sparse conception of the person: the key aspect of human nature is that we be able to recognize the moral law once it is revealed to us or we learn about it. A conception of the right, on the other hand, originates in the human faculty of pure practical reason. The moral law is something that *we* write: a point that Kant emphasizes in the third formulation of the categorical imperative (the formula of autonomy). It is only once we write the moral law, according to Kant, that we are then able to determine the objects that result. On Rawls's reading, then, Kant develops a more robust faculty psychology than rational intuitionism because the cosmological status of the person has suddenly become elevated. Our faculty of reason does not simply read moral and political truths in the nature of the universe; rather, reason constructs our ideas of right and justice that we may then use to shape the human world. Rawls elaborates on Kant's moral constructivism by laying out a procedure that displays the main steps in Kant's thinking in the *Groundwork*.[11] For Rawls, however, one may detach Kant's notion of constructivism from his moral doctrine. Kant's great insight is that human beings may construct their own practical concepts and principles by reflecting upon their own self-identity (as persons) and their shared life (in society).

In *What is Philosophy?*, Deleuze presents a case for philosophical constructivism largely through a direct and indirect engagement with the Kantian legacy. Deleuze takes for granted two of Kant's great theses in the *Critique of Pure Reason*. First, concepts are not transcendent entities that we discover through theoretical reason. "Concepts are not waiting for us ready-made, like heavenly bodies. There is no heaven for concepts."[12] If modern philosophy's task is to overturn Platonism, then Kant's Transcendental Dialectic is exemplary in its assault on Platonic (or Christian) conceptions of the soul, freedom, and God. Deleuze thus agrees with Kant that philosophy cannot be defined as the contemplation or recollection of eternal verities.[13] In addition, Deleuze embraces the basic premise of Kant's metaphysics of experience in the Transcendental Analytic, namely, that concepts arise from the spontaneity of thinking. Deleuze thus offers a Kantian definition of philosophy as "the art of forming, inventing, and fabricating concepts."[14] Kant sometimes vacillates on whether concepts represent a mind-independent reality—in which case philosophers should strive for verisimilitude—or construct reality as best we can understand and move within it—in which case philosophers may exercise creativity.[15] Deleuze, with Nietzsche, pushes the constructivist thesis as far as possible, arguing that post-Kantians should make and create concepts rather than polish and purify them. Deleuze presents this view in his gloss on Kant's Copernican revolution in *What is Philosophy?*: "Thinking is neither a line drawn between subject and object nor a revolving of one around the other. Rather, thinking takes place in the relationship of territory [*territoire*] and earth [*terre*]. Kant is less a prisoner of the categories of subject and object than he is believed to be, since his idea of Copernican revolution puts thought into direct relationship with the earth."[16] Deleuze distinguishes Kant's official position from a subterranean theme in his thinking. Kant's official position is that philosophy traces the relationship between subjects, objects, and representations.[17] Kant's Copernican revolution, on this account, maintains that subjectivity is the most important part of this equation (rather than objectivity). For Deleuze, however, Kant's subject/object distinction perpetuates a Platonic distinction between ontological realms. In other words, Kant wants to ensure that there is a part of human nature—the transcendental subject—that is not affected by the material conditions of existence. For Deleuze, however, completing Kant's Copernican revolution entails putting "thought into direct relationship with the earth." What does this mean? For Deleuze, one needs to radicalize Kant's assault on transcendence and consider what it means to think and act in immanence. Human beings are embodied creatures permeated by "unformed, unstable matters."[18] We live and think on the ever-changing and flowing earth. Yet we also have the ability to construct theoretical frameworks—or territories—that enable us to orient ourselves in thinking and acting. For Deleuze, the best way to take up Kant's legacy is to practice a "transcendental empiricism" that enables us to create concepts in an experimental relationship with the world. Deleuze hesitates to use Kantian terminology to describe his position because of the way that Kant and many post-Kantians imprison thought in an idealistic framework that prohibits tactical intervention into, or conceptual transformation of, our thinking.[19] Yet Deleuze still calls himself a constructivist because he endorses the Kantian insight that *we* are the legislators of nature and our practical concepts and principles.

In a fascinating parallel, both Rawls and Deleuze articulate versions of political constructivism meant to apply to a specific milieu, namely, contemporary liberal, pluralistic, and capitalistic democracies. Consider, for example, Rawls's famous claim that his political theory, justice as fairness, is political, not metaphysical: "This is because, given the fact of reasonable pluralism, citizens cannot agree on any moral authority, whether a sacred text, or institution. Nor do they agree about the order of moral values, or the dictates of what some regard as natural law. We adopt, then, a constructivist view to specify the fair terms of social cooperation as given by the principles of justice agreed to by the representatives of free and equal citizens when fairly situated. The bases of this view lie in fundamental ideas of the public political culture."[20] On the one hand, citizens are autonomous, politically speaking, insofar as they are responsible for legislating the laws of the land—including constitutional principles that have often been presented as originating from a higher, nonhuman source. Rawls's idea of political constructivism announces on its face the Kantian insight that political reason is "self-originating and self-authenticating."[21] Thus Rawls opposes moral realists who claim to know the *a priori* rules to govern the political order:

human beings in their role as citizens, and only such beings, legislate the laws of the land. On the other hand, Rawls disagrees with Kant that rational beings may construct the fundamental principles of the moral and political order once and for all. Political constructivism, unlike moral constructivism, plumbs an admittedly impure source: the public political culture. Kant's transcendental idealism may have postulated a conception of the person as an imperfectly rational being that sustains an account of universal and necessary moral and political principles; in his late work, though, Rawls announces that a politically viable methodology must appeal to a source that all reasonable citizens can judge: experience. Political constructivism, may rearrange experience in surprising ways—a naturalized account of practical reason still permits philosophers to transcend immediate perceptions to think about just social arrangements. Yet political constructivism will disappoint Kantians who perpetuate Kant's dichotomy between pure and impure moral philosophy.

In *What is Philosophy?* Deleuze similarly employs the notion of constructivism to negotiate the divide between history and becoming. History, Deleuze explains, provides the concrete setting for our actual lives and thoughts. For Deleuze, there are several major variables that determine the nature of our historical era. The first and most important is capitalism. Capitalism functions as "an immanent axiomatic of decoded flows (of money, labor, products)" that encircles the globe.[22] Capitalism seeks to constitute and capture everything in the world as either "naked labor" or "pure wealth."[23] Capitalism becomes instantiated and regulated in several different types of nation-states, including the one privileged at the center of the world economy: democracy. Just as the classical Greek city-state was a hospitable home for the rise of philosophy, modern democracies foster the type of creative thinking necessary for both philosophy and capitalist management. Finally, history seems to favor the rise of human rights protocols that seek to combat the ideology of fascism. It is notable, however, that in *What is Philosophy?* Deleuze criticizes the historical features of capitalism, democracy, and human rights (or liberalism). We experience shame "before the meanness and vulgarity of existence that haunts democracies, before the propagation of these moments of existence and of thought-for-the-market, and before the values, ideals, and opinions of our time."[24] By stating that he feels shame before the gap between ideals and practices, Deleuze expresses dismay at how these potentially revolutionary concepts have been poorly thought and actualized.[25] For Deleuze, the way to escape historical determinism and philosophical cynicism is to think becoming. Becoming designates the ahistorical vapor within history that gives rise to new concepts and practices. "What History grasps of the event is its effectuation in states of affairs or in lived experience, but the event in its becoming, in its specific consistency, in its self-positing as concept, escapes History."[26] History sets the limits and conditions for what we can think, feel, and do, but becoming describes the inherent potential within human beings (and other entities) to transform those limits and conditions. For Deleuze, political theorists must attend to both history and becoming, what is and what may be, the peoples and the territories that currently inhabit the globe as well as the new peoples and earths on the horizon. Constructivism is an exercise in utopian thinking that is alert to both the now-here (history) and the no-where (becoming). Like Rawls, Deleuze thinks that political theorists should create lenses to make sense of the real world as understood by liberal, democratic common sense. Deleuze just presses harder than Rawls does on the role that experimentation plays in philosophy—the need, in other words, to challenge common sense to think or see things it may otherwise ignore.

I will now consider how Rawls and Deleuze respond to their critics who think that their conceptions of constructivism are impure and thus incapable of offering clear, consistent, and ethical political guidance.[27] In *Political Liberalism*, Rawls explains how political constructivism both retains and transforms the idea of objectivity. Rational intuitionists defend metaethical realism, in part, because it seems to provide humanity with certain essential elements for human flourishing, including objective moral and political standards. In *Political Liberalism*, Rawls explains how political constructivism provides the functional equivalent of realist standards. In practice, political constructivism establishes a public framework for thought that ensures public agreement about constitutional essentials; provides a concept of correct judgment; specifies an order of reasons; ensures that society's objective standards trump subjective points of view; fosters agreement about constitutional essentials among democratic citizens; and explains the possibility of reasonable disagreement. In our daily lives, political constructivism provides the same guideposts as metaethical realism. "Given a background of successful practice over time, this considered agreement in judgment, or narrowing of differences, normally suffices for objectivity."[28] Yet metaethical realists may surely point out that objectivity seems to demand an anchoring in reality, or objective standards may be revised as soon as somebody does not like what they force him to do. A pragmatic account of objectivity, for realists, is an absurdity, akin to truthiness. For Rawls, this objection simply overlooks how Kant has transformed the purpose of philosophy. Kant originates the idea that reason is self-originating and self-authenticating.[29] What this means is that reason may not ground its principles and canons outside of itself. Clearly, though, this position will seem solipsistic to those participating in philosophical or theological traditions that demand a cosmic guarantee for the veracity of our concepts. Kant's position, though, is that no such cosmic guarantee is possible, and that "one of philosophy's tasks is to quiet our distress at this thought."[30] Rawlsian objectivity is going to be closer to positive law than natural law, but the fault is not Rawls's incorrect reading of Kant, but the implications of Kant's Copernican revolution in philosophy. After Kant, we simply cannot know that our theories will provide an accurate representation of reality; but that assigns us the awesome responsibility of making our own concepts to facilitate human flourishing. Political constructivism is one way that human beings may write a political constitution, so to speak, given that we have not found one in the heavens (politically speaking).

In *What is Philosophy?* Deleuze describes the status of philosophical concepts in an account of geophilosophy. Deleuze describes at least two options modern philosophers have once they relinquish the Platonic aspiration for objective idealism. The German style of philosophy is to reconquer the Greek plane of immanence. That is, German philosophers seek to impose order on the unruly chaos of the earth. But rather than impose a pattern found in the stars, German philosophers shape the manifold according to their own transcendental subjectivity. Subjective idealism and objective idealism differ on the origins of theoretical frameworks, but they concur that theoretical frameworks must be permanent, or objective. "A mania for founding, for conquering, inspires this philosophy; what the Greeks possessed Autochtonously, German philosophy would have through conquest and foundation, so that it would make immanence immanent *to* something, to its own Act of philosophizing, to its own philosophizing subjectivity."[31] Kant's *Groundwork*, for Deleuze, would be a paradigmatic attempt to establish a ground (*Grund*) beneath the shifting earth of popular moral philosophy. The other way to proceed philosophically is in the English style. For empiricists such as David Hume, we acquire concepts through the contraction of habits. The English embed thinking in the material existence of life, unlike the French and Germans who obsess about a nonempirical *cogito*. The English collect and organize concepts that arise naturally from our contracted habits and customs. For the English, philosophical contingency is just a fact of life: the English are "nomads who treat the plane of immanence as a movable and moving ground, a field of radical experience, an archipelagian world where they are happy to pitch their tents from island to island and over the sea."[32] Kant himself would have liked to tame the philosophical nomads and barbarians, as he famously explains in the preface to the first edition of the *Critique of Pure Reason*. Yet Kant's Copernican revolution places thought in direct contact with the earth, which means that all of our attempts to ground philosophy are liable to shift as self-reflective human beings rethink their individual and collective identities. In other words, Kant is closer to Hume than he would like: the concept of the transcendental both humbles the Platonic claim to access the transcendent and empowers human beings to produce the concepts that make possible experience. For Deleuze, removing the Platonic residue from Kant's Copernican revolution leads to the notion of transcendental empiricism, which forthrightly acknowledges that concepts are human constructs liable to permanent reworking. Concepts, for Deleuze, are tents: that is, human inventions that transform elements from the natural world to provide a (fragile and mobile) habitat for human beings. There is no such thing as a pure concept or a pure tent: there are only conceptual alloys that mix the given and the philosophical.

In a notebook entry from the 1870s, Nietzsche describes the post-Kantian philosophical condition as well as the joys and dangers of notions such as constructivism. Unpacking this paragraph gives us a clue to Rawls's and Deleuze's ambitions, as well as the issue dividing them from their Kantian counterparts. Nietzsche writes: "Man's longing to be completely truthful in the midst of a mendacious natural order is something noble and heroic. But this is *possible* only in a *very relative sense*. That is tragic. That is *Kant's tragic problem*! Art now acquires an entirely *new* dignity. The sciences in contrast are *degraded* to a degree."[33] Kant's tragic problem, for Nietzsche, is at the heart of the *Critique of Pure Reason*. In the Transcendental Analytic, Kant develops a logic of truth that expounds the concepts and principles that make possible experience, and in the Transcendental Dialectic, Kant exposes and corrects the illusions that mislead reason. Stated in general terms, Kant agrees with the classical definition of truth as the agreement of cognition with its object.[34] What, though, are the objects that we are capable of knowing? In the Transcendental Aesthetic, Kant explains that space and time are merely forms of intuition that do not correspond to things-in-themselves.

Time, as well as space, is "merely a subjective condition of our (human) intuition (which is always sensible, i.e., insofar as we are affected by objects), and in itself, outside the subject, is nothing."[35] Kant's transcendental idealism presupposes that objects are not spatiotemporal even though human beings necessarily experience them that way. To rectify this deeply counterintuitive notion, Kant explains that transcendental idealism is compatible with empirical realism. Empirical realism "grants to matter, as appearance, a reality which need not be inferred, but is immediately perceived."[36] Kant does not want to deny the truth of natural science or common sense belief in the reality of external objects. Still, intellectual honesty compels Kant to acknowledge that the transcendental object that grounds outer appearances and inner intuition is "neither matter nor a thinking being in itself, but rather an unknown ground."[37] Kant's tragic problem, then, is that human concepts do not match up to reality. Human concepts grasp the manifold as transmitted by sensation and filtered through the forms of intuition and the schema of the imagination, but what things are in themselves eludes the power of human comprehension. The sciences are thereby degraded: we cannot extend our knowledge beyond the bounds of sense to things in themselves. Even the primary qualities that early moderns attributed to objects become, for Kant, merely human ways of organizing the flux of sense perception. Yet art acquires a new dignity. Human concepts are artifices, or molds, that we use to arrange perceptions into coherent wholes. Nietzsche, here, plays on two senses of the term tragic. From a Platonic, Christian, or Kantian perspective, tragedy signals defeat and despair. Kantian critiques of constructivism reflect a fear that we are losing what makes us human, that constructivism leads to nihilism. Yet Nietzsche endows tragedy with a positive connotation that he recovers from the Greeks. A tragic conception of art acknowledges that human concepts are lies, strictly speaking, but that they have the potential to affirm and enhance life. The Nietzschean tragic is "pure and multiple positivity, dynamic gaiety."[38] Though Kant sought to contain his tragic problem (particularly in his pure moral philosophy), Kant's Copernican revolution empowers each generation of philosophers to construct theories to organize the political manifold in ways that serve their needs. There are multiple ways to do this—and there are no guarantees that we will get it right. For constructivists such as Rawls and Deleuze, however, Kantian courage demands that we confront this challenge in both its frightening and enchanting dimensions and go about creating concepts to help us understand and move within the late-modern political world.

THE ACTIVITIES OF CONSTRUCTIVISM

Kant's Copernican revolution assigns human beings the responsibility to create their own concepts and principles to make sense of the political realm. The Kantian ethos, we may say, empowers political theorists such as Rawls and Deleuze to dare to be wise (*sapere aude*), where wisdom connotes facing the great problems of the day and creating concepts and principles accordingly. Rawls and Deleuze turn to Kant, however, not merely for inspiration, but for guidance on how to create political theories. The idea of constructivism is not, properly speaking, a method, a step-by-step mental sequence that necessarily leads to the same result, in the way that a highway always terminates in the same destination.[39] Kant may have envisioned his practical philosophy as having the same precision and logical rigor as geometry—but that side of Kant's thinking does not interest Rawls and Deleuze. Rather, the idea of constructivism is an open concept that may and must be filled in with the theorist's own intellectual interests, ethical passions, political concerns, and, most broadly, tacit knowledge accumulated over time in a particular milieu.[40] The idea of constructivism historicizes, naturalizes, and politicizes Kant's metaethics. The primary reason that Rawls and Deleuze take up the idea of constructivism, however, is because it works. That is, Kant gives sage advice about how to create new political theories. To paraphrase Rawls: Kant's importance for contemporary political thinkers is that he teaches us how to philosophize rather than a static philosophy.[41]

In this section, I describe the mechanics of constructivism.[42] Though constructing political theories always requires inspiration, so to speak, one can still identify certain activities necessary to build a post-Kantian political theory. Here is how Rawls and Deleuze isolate the four activities of constructivism.

Inventing Personae

The first and most important activity in political constructivism is to invent a conception of the person. A conception of the person provides an answer to the question that Kant designates as the central one of philosophy: What is man?[43] A conception of the person fulfills many of the same roles that Hume ascribes to a theory of human nature ("the capitol of the human sciences"). A conception of the person describes our mental faculties that then enables us to determine what we may know, what we ought to do, and what we may hope. A conception of the person helps us set the parameters for human cognition about logic, mathematics, and natural science and enables us to think more profoundly about the moral, political, and artistic arrangements that accord with our self-conception. Once we possess a conception of the person, we may then determine the categories that condition our political vision and the principles that determine how we ought to proceed in the world. As I will show, refining a Kantian conception of the person is the surest way to introduce a new Kantian political theory into the world.

Why, though, does Kantian political theory emphasize personality rather than human nature? What is at stake in this apparently minor terminological distinction? The issue, from a Kantian perspective, is what fills in the two concepts. The human being, according to Kant, is a child of nature. We are born with certain biological and mental features that define us as human beings. We can develop aspects of our humanity—including our faculty of instrumental or theoretical reason—but we cannot change human nature.[44] A conception of the person is different. Derived from the Greek root *persona* ("character in a drama," "mask"), a conception of the person is amenable to transformation as we decide what kind of role we wish to play in society. Before Kant, philosophers and theologians tended to think that human beings were made in the image of God. Kant's Copernican revolution, however, empowers us to view ourselves as self-constituting in a fundamental way.[45] In the *Groundwork*, Kant starts with a conception of the person defined as a "universal concept of a rational being in general" (*allgemeinen Begriffe eines vernünftige Wesen überhaupt*).[46] There are theological reasons why Kant wants to identify principles that apply to God and extraterrestrials as well as human beings.[47] Kant also seeks to fix the definition of personality to encapsulate the side of humanity considered wholly intellectually (and thus immune from revision or corruption).[48] Constructivists, however, detach Kant's insight into the self-defining nature of personality from the theological and moral strictures that Kant places around it. For Kantians such as Rawls and Deleuze, our reflective self-identities have changed over the course of the past two centuries and our political theories should reflect that.

Political constructivism, according to Rawls, begins by assembling materials from the public political culture, including, crucially, a conception of the person. Rawls elicits this conception of the person from democratic common sense. "We must have some material, as it were, from which to begin," and Rawls collects this material from democratic common sense, that is, such a society's "fund of implicitly shared ideas."[49] Rawls's political philosophy thus starts from an empirical anthropology that displaces it from the orthodox Kantian tradition. For Rawls, however, political philosophy does not need to grapple with the theological debates that troubled Kant and that exacerbate conflicts between democratic citizens; furthermore, Kant's image of man as *homo duplex*—divided between a noumenal and phenomenal nature—seems philosophically anachronistic after Darwin. Rawls's conception of the person exemplifies one instance of Rawls's larger project of recasting Kant's dualisms "within the scope of an empirical theory."[50] For political and philosophical reasons, then, Rawls paints a portrait of the person that freely uses the pigments available in popular political discourse. On the other hand, Rawls exercises discretion in which aspects to highlight or ignore in his conception of the person. Rawls extracts his material "from our everyday conception of persons as the basic units of thought, deliberation, and responsibility," but then adapts it for a political conception of justice.[51] Rawls's critics have charged him with either falling prey to historicism— simply giving a philosophical veneer to the common sense of our time[52]—or ignoring the empirical evidence that most democratic citizens (particularly religious conservatives) do not share his conception of the person.[53] Both criticisms miss how Rawls seeks to present a conception of the person that both represents us *and* shifts our self-assessment. Rawls asks us to endorse his political psychology upon "due reflection."[54] Rawls's theory of the person, then, is not Kant's, but in its emphasis upon political self-assessment and self-constitution, it is Kantian.

Rawls invents, or rather reworks, a conception of the person as the citizen. Rawls takes this idea, and many of its attendant notions, from everyday speech, and Rawls explicitly situates his political theory within a tradition of democratic discourse about how citizens should balance their individual desires and political responsibilities. Yet Rawls's political psychology reframes democratic intuitions about citizenship within the terminology (and conceptual framework) of Kant's moral psychology. Rawls describes the citizen, for example, as plied by his rational and reasonable natures. Rationality describes human means-end reasoning necessary to achieve our nonpublic ends and satisfy our personal interests. Rationality, here, corresponds to Hume's official account of reason in the *Treatise*. The democratic citizen is also, according to Rawls, reasonable. The reasonable designates the willingness to "propose and honor fair terms of cooperation" as well as to "recognize the burdens of judgment."[55] Rawls aligns the reasonable with Kant's notion of pure practical reason that, in its essence, holds reciprocity as the key to fair (moral or just) dealings with other rational agents. Rawls restricts the meaning of the term reasonable, however, to merely the political virtues, including the virtue of tolerance for other moral faiths that willingly abide by the constitutional order. Rawls's conception of the person, then, is neither purely immanent nor capable of pure transcendence: the citizen is both in his time and capable of finding a higher vantage point within it (in part, by abstracting from it using the help of Kantian terminology).

In *What is Philosophy?* Deleuze exhibits little of Rawls's restraint in stating that constructivism must invent—rather than elicit or extract from common sense—conceptual personae. Deleuze acknowledges that philosophers need to ground conceptual personae on psychosocial types.[56] Psychosocial types are not necessarily specific people, but they do play a role in a given society's structures and functions. A psychosocial type can be, for example, a judge, a police officer, a migrant, an exile, or a citizen.[57] By reflecting upon flesh and blood psychosocial types, a constructivist ensures that her political theory will connect with empirical reality (or at least not exist as pure fancy). Conceptual personae, however, are what spur thinkers to create concepts or theories that do not simply mirror common sense. For Deleuze, it can be misleading to say that philosophers invent conceptual personae given that they sometimes seem to have a life of their own; like Socrates's *daemon*, conceptual personae often appear unbidden to philosophers. Yet philosophers are willing to dialogue with these voices; in fact, they need them to think. Conceptual personae are "intercessors, crystals, or seeds of thought."[58] "A particular conceptual persona, who perhaps did not think before us, thinks in us."[59] Conceptual personae mediate between the philosopher and his or her concepts and theories; conceptual personae pose questions, propose solutions, forge new concepts, express irreverence, and push the philosopher's thinking in new and surprising ways. Conceptual personae show thought's terrain: where thinking flees, or deterritorializes, traditional habits and opinions, and where thinking creates, or reterritorializes, new ideas. For Deleuze, constructivism expresses philosophical autonomy, but the *autos* is fractured between a relatively congealed side (the philosopher's subjectivity) and the conceptual personae who jostle for space in the thinker's mind.

In *A Thousand Plateaus*, Deleuze invents the conceptual persona of the Body without Organs (BwO). Deleuze defines the BwO as "already under way the moment the body has had enough of organs and wants to slough them off" and offers as examples "drug users, masochists, schizophrenics, [and] lovers."[60] The BwO is, strictly speaking, not an autonomous subject but a "set of practices"[61]; on the other hand, the BwO performs the functions assigned to a conceptual persona in *What is Philosophy?*: to dramatize a voice in one's head to spark thinking. Deleuze takes the idea of the BwO from Antonin Artaud's 1945 radio program, "To Have Done with the Judgment of God." On this program, Artaud declares war on the organs and the organism that unifies and orders them according to a preexisting plan ("the judgment of God"). Artaud's polemic targets transcendent theologies, clearly, as well as philosophies that install one organ—such as reason (*logos*, *Vernunft*)—above the passions and desires. Artaud criticizes what Derrida calls logocentrism, and employing the BwO as one's main conceptual persona seems to ensure that *A Thousand Plateaus* fits within the Romantic tradition. Despite using a term designated to shock us into thinking, Deleuze immediately qualifies the role that the BwO plays in his philosophy. The BwO "swings between two poles, the surfaces of stratification into which it is recoiled, on which it submits to the judgment, and the plane of consistency in which it unfurls and opens to experimentation."[62] The BwO is stratified. The BwO has certain faculties (reason, understanding, imagination) that play assigned roles in different domains of human existence (knowing, desiring, feeling pleasure and pain); that is, the BwO has common sense. The BwO has a fairly stable identity as a person (subjectivity), an unconscious that overlaps with psychoanalytic structures (signifiance), and a physical body in which the organs perform necessary functions such as breathing and digesting (organism). The BwO corresponds, most generally, to the psychosocial type of the normal human being in any given society. The purpose of the BwO, though, is to spur us to dismantle the strata—intellectual habits, political predispositions, familial loyalties, and so on—that lock us into stagnant ways of being in the world. Deleuze does not say that the BwO can attain an unmediated intellectual access to reality: Deleuze still works within the Kantian framework of the transcendental.[63] But he does think that human beings can experiment with the categories or ideas that organize the unruly manifold (the plane of consistency), and that new ideas can enhance our thinking, ethics, and capacity for joy. The BwO inspires philosophers to press against the limits of convention without denying the need for limits to preserve mental, emotional, physical, and political bodies.

How do the conceptual personae of the citizen and the BwO compare? First, both of them are, in their own ways, politically autonomous. They refuse, in Rawls's words, to "view the social order as a fixed natural order, or as an institutional hierarchy justified by religious or aristocratic values."[64] The citizen and the BwO personify the Kantian insight that we can shape the social order according to our own faculty of practical reason. The modern nature of these conceptual personae comes into clearer focus when we consider how many classical and theological conceptual personae—such as Socrates in the *Republic*, or Moses in the Torah—try to discover the ideas or laws to govern human life. Rawls and Deleuze assign their conceptual personae the responsibility of making categories and principles for the political realm. Second, both the citizen and the BwO are plied between their social and individual natures, their roles as members of larger political bodies (citizens) as well as eccentric bodies that do not conform to social conventions. The third similarity between the citizen and the BwO is that they are both capable of freedom: negative freedom to tear themselves away mentally and sometimes physically from their milieu; positive freedom to embody or pursue self-chosen paths; and critical freedom to transgress the limits of their current identity.[65] Rawls and Deleuze invent the conceptual personae of the citizen and the BwO, as I will demonstrate below, to address the same basic question: how should individuals and political collectivities balance political responsibility to self-governance with a desire to depart, on occasion, from the majority consensus? How, in other words, to balance the democratic concern with enforcing the majority's norms and the liberal concern with sheltering individuality and singularity?

Yet the citizen and the BwO clearly express different philosophical sensibilities. For Rawls, the reasonable frames the rational absolutely. Rawls acknowledges that our nonpublic interests give meaning to our lives. "Rational agents may have all kinds of affections for persons and attachments to communities and places, including love of country and nature"—and to dismiss these rational commitments would drain life of much of its meaning.[66] Yet the great values of the political demand that nonpublic loves must submit to the authority of political reasonableness. Rawls employs the ideal of the citizen to ensure that at each stage of his theory construction "the reasonable frames and subordinates the rational."[67] The Rawlsian citizen always follows democratic common sense. The BwO, instead, maintains tension between her commitments to the general will and her desire to explore new avenues of self- and collective-fashioning. Most of the time, the BwO goes along with the demands of society. She may even choose to follow unconditionally (as best she can) certain social codes; she is not necessarily evil.

But she views all laws as positive laws that may be revised or transgressed to enhance joy and diminish sadness. The BwO expresses a flexible ethical sensibility rather than follows a rigid moral code.

The citizen and the BwO, in sum, reflect the different assignments that Rawls and Deleuze give to political theory. For Rawls, political theory needs to buttress democratic common sense against the assaults perpetuated by unreasonable people, including fascists and certain libertarians, religious fundamentalists, and moral skeptics. The lesson of Weimar Germany, for Rawls, is that philosophers need to exercise political responsibility and defend the liberal democratic constitutional order. The conceptual persona of the citizen helps political liberalism determine how best to achieve that goal. For Deleuze, on the contrary, philosophy's role *qua* philosophy is to challenge *doxa*, even if it is democratic. Democratic rule, for Deleuze, can degenerate into what Tocqueville and Mill called tyranny of the majority. The BwO challenges democratic complacency and thoughtlessness and proposes new ways of thinking, feeling, and acting. The citizen and the BwO, in sum, both conceptualize the need to balance collective order and individual freedom: it is just that the citizen favors the former and the BwO the latter.

Laying Out a Plane

The first activity of constructivism is to specify *who* we are when we think about politics. The second activity is to describe *where* we are when we think politically. How, though, to describe this mental terrain? The dilemma is this: if we describe this space in the terms of, say, neuroscience, then we have lost the ability to advance a philosophical rather than a psychobiological argument. A purely scientific explanation of thought's location would relinquish the perspective necessary for philosophic critique. On the other hand, Kant's critical philosophy insists that we cannot know where we are when we think only that there is such a place. Kant grappled with this question throughout his life, describing the space of thought, variously, as the noumenal realm, the world of understanding (*Verstandeswelt*), and the intelligible world (*intelligible Welt*). How to portray thought's location puzzles virtually all post-Kantians and ensures that their work will always be vulnerable to critique as being either too immanent or too transcendent, too historicist or too otherworldly. Still, for political theorists such as Rawls or Deleuze it is necessary to lay out a plane of thought that is both scientifically plausible and capable of providing a critical vantage point. In this section,

I focus on how Rawls describes the original position and Deleuze unfurls a plane of immanence.

Rawls's problem, in *Political Liberalism*, is to construct a political theory that helps us envision the possibility of a just, stable, and tolerant society of free and equal citizens. Rawls famously situates himself in the social contract tradition of Locke, Rousseau, and Kant. As part of this tradition, Rawls must describe where citizens go when they legislate the fundamental charter of political society. "We must find some point of view, removed from and not distorted by the particular features and circumstances of the all-encompassing background framework, from which a fair agreement between persons regarded as free and equal can be reached."[68] This sentence encapsulates the difficulty that Rawls faces in trying to describe the point of view of political constructivism. Rawls is drawn to the Kantian idea that the original contract is a mere idea of reason that any reasonable and rational being can enter by thinking as if she were a legislator acting on behalf of the united will of an entire people.[69] In *A Theory of Justice*, Rawls thus describes the point of view of the self-reflecting citizen as analogous to that of the Kantian noumenal, or intelligible, realm.[70] For Rawls's early critics such as Michael Sandel, *A Theory of Justice* replicates the Kantian metaphysics that Rawls seeks to avoid. Addressing this point in his later work, Rawls acknowledges that the all-encompassing background framework unavoidably colors one's point of view. Just as Rawls extracts his idea of the rational and the reasonable from everyday speech, the description of where we go when we think also bears similarities to empirical models such as the United States' 1787 Constitutional Convention. Yet even late Rawls opposes Hume's thesis in his 1784 essay, "Of the Original Contract," that conventions and interests—not abstract notions of right or justice—are the real ground of political obligation.[71] The Humean perspective—based entirely, in principle, on the historical record—minimizes humanity's capacity to transcend its time and place in thought. In *Political Liberalism* Rawls tries to find a middle ground between Kant and Hume by, for instance, describing the original position as a device of representation. The original position presents, or mirrors, how we currently think about our political order; the original position also *re*-presents, or transforms, our thinking to reflect new considerations introduced by the philosopher. Rawls is agnostic on how we are able to transcend the all-encompassing background: we may be able to do it through pure practical reason, but it might also be possible to use the type of disciplined imagination we exercise when we play a game of Monopoly or follow the plotline of a Shakespeare play.[72] The point is, for Rawls, human beings are able to enter a space of thinking that both reflects and transcends the political order of the day.

Rawls places the citizen on the mental terrain of the original position.[73] For the purposes of my argument, I wish merely to focus on how Rawls envisions this notion as a "means of public reflection and self-clarification."[74] For metaethical realists, the terrain of thought corresponds to reality: the Platonic philosopher can no more rearrange things in the realm of forms than he can change the truths of mathematics. For constructivists, however, we design our mental topography to reflect our own deepest interests and aspirations. And that is what Rawls does when he places the citizen in the original position. The original position mirrors our rational nature, insofar as we desire to maximize the all-purpose means, the primary goods, that enable us to achieve our life plans. By placing the rational parties of the original position behind a veil of ignorance, we also model our reasonableness, a willingness to offer fair terms of cooperation to our fellow citizens and to acknowledge the inevitable plurality of moral, philosophical, and religious doctrines that arise in free societies. The original position models the citizen's freedom to choose principles that govern the basic structure of society and to take responsibility for honoring those principles. By placing each and every citizen in the original position, furthermore, the original position models the equality of democratic citizens. Rawls's frequent description of the original position as a mirroring or modeling device should not conceal how strange this place is supposed to be. Yes, Rawls states that we may enter the original position at any time simply by reasoning according to the conditions it places on arguments. Yet the religious image of the veil suggests that we should proceed with "holy awe" when we think about our responsibilities in this powerful, mysterious place.[75] The original position is a mental platform built by reflective human beings to exercise political autonomy.

In *What is Philosophy?* Deleuze specifies the role that a plane of immanence plays in philosophical constructivism. The plane of immanence "constitutes the absolute ground of philosophy, its earth or deterritorialization, the foundation on which it creates its concepts."[76] The plane of immanence, firstly, is an *image of thought*, an image of what it means to think and the possibilities open to conceptual personae. The major tradition of philosophy, on Deleuze's account, describes the plane of immanence as a "program, design, end, or means."[77] Metaethical realists, we may say, want to ensure that thought can only move along predetermined paths. Deleuze's aim is to portray a mental landscape that is both open to new and surprising events in the world as well as to the autopoetic features of philosophy. The plane of immanence selects elements from the material conditions of its existence, the history of philosophy, and common sense—the plane of immanence is always a patchwork of inherited and original materials. The plane of immanence provides a structural framework that organizes concepts and houses the conceptual personae—the plane of immanence acts as a sieve to prevent thinking from degenerating into chaos.[78] Furthermore, the plane of immanence is an open system that constantly regenerates itself as conceptual personae change, ideas or concepts emerge, or historical or philosophical variables shift in and for the philosopher. The plane of immanence is a mobile earth rather than a stable ground, a mental layer of existence imbricated in the moving flows of the chemical-biological-physical-political world. Secondly, a plane of immanence is an account of the *substance of being*. For Deleuze, a philosopher cannot describe thought's location without also describing its place among the other layers of reality. Deleuze thinks that philosophers must grapple with ontology even if they accept the critical thesis that reality is ultimately inaccessible to human intuition. Human finitude ensures that there will be many ways to diagram planes of immanence: "we can and must presuppose a multiplicity of planes, since no one plane could encompass all of chaos without collapsing back into it."[79] A Deleuzian plane of immanence presents a mental and physical world of order emerging temporarily and precariously out of chaos.

In *A Thousand Plateaus*, Deleuze situates the BwO on a plane of consistency[80] that differs in the mind of each reader: "The field of immanence or plane of consistency must be constructed. This can take place in very different social formations through very different assemblages (perverse, artistic, scientific, mystical, political) with different types of bodies without organs. It is constructed piece by piece, and the places, conditions, and techniques are irreducible to one another. The question, rather, is whether the pieces can fit together, and at what price."[81] We may extrapolate from this passage several features of a political plane of consistency. First, a plane of consistency is connected, though irreducible, to a social formation. To envision the landscape on which a conceptual persona walks, leaps, builds, thinks, and so forth, political theorists need to appropriate elements from their historical and material milieu. Though Deleuze disagrees with key planks of the Marxist tradition—including the notion that history proceeds through class conflict and arrives, necessarily, at communism—Deleuze does think that philosophers need to study the concrete conditions of society. Second, we have a choice about how to lay out philosophical planes of immanence. We can choose which features of our historical milieu to accentuate or diminish in our mental landscapes. Each of us constructs a plane of immanence "piece by piece" by assembling elements from art, science, mysticism, politics, and other sources. That is why Deleuze rejects the Marxist notion of ideology: It determines in advance the theoretical options available to political agents. If there are only two conceptual personae—the bourgeoisie and the proletariat—on a plane of consistency embedded in capitalism, then there is only one correct way to think. For Deleuze, however, political agents operate on a more complex physical and mental geography. Third, the plane of immanence imposes a certain order upon the world that enables us to see coherent bodies interacting with each other (rather than chaos); but, fourth, the plane of immanence opens our eyes to the ways that borders between entities are porous and that assemblages interlock. The plane of consistency is not the plane of organization: a crude and rigid way to organize thought and reality. Finally, there are no preexisting criteria to determine whether a plane of consistency is good or bad: We can only lay planes out and think through their opportunities and dangers they present to philosophy.

One hundred years from now, Deleuzian political theorists may describe planes of immanence in ways that we cannot foresee. In *What is Philosophy?*, however, Deleuze helps us fill in the picture of where the BwO resides: in a world that espouses the ideals of democracy, liberalism, and human rights but practices stupidity and cruelty in the service of universal capitalism.[82] Fortunately, the BwO can (partially) escape the cave of historicity through the help of philosophy, art, and science—each of which provides resources (concepts, percepts, or functions, respectively) to see aspects of reality occluded by common sense. The BwO, in other words, can range far and wide to find materials to build theories to analyze and confront late-modern capitalism.[83]

Both Rawls and Deleuze grapple with the problem of where we are when we think. Rawls's original position and Deleuze's plane of immanence are both accessible to anyone willing to think—where thinking involves both imaginative and rational components. Furthermore, both Rawls and Deleuze hold that we need to posit a mental plateau to give us a vantage point from which to criticize a global capitalism that distributes resources unfairly, punishes individuals or groups that do not conform to the logic of the market, and ravages the natural world.

There is, however, a major difference between Rawls's and Deleuze's theoretical planes. Rawls places parties in the original position behind a thick veil of ignorance: "the parties are to be understood so far as possible solely as moral person and in abstraction from contingencies."[84] Rawls defends the thick veil of ignorance on Kantian grounds: we restrict information about the parties in the original position to ensure that the principles selected to govern the basic structure of society are fair. In principle, Rawls describes the parties in the original position with just enough information to give content to the principles of justice, analogously to how Kant in the *Groundwork* employs the formula of the universal law of nature (FLN)—rather than the more rigorous and abstract formula of universal law (FUL)—to help embodied creatures conceptualize what it means to test maxims by categorical imperatives. Even though Rawls contextualizes his theory of justice in the historical milieu of contemporary (liberal, democratic, pluralist, capitalist) societies, Rawls still aspires to pure procedural justice. He aspires to cleanse the original position of empirical contingencies that favor one type of citizen over another. Deleuze's mental landscape, on the contrary, is richer in concepts and images. For Deleuze, ethical thinking requires a wide rather than a narrow lens, with as much comprehension of complexity and interconnectedness as we can manage. Each BwO, in principle, lives and thinks on a singular plane of immanence that must be mapped out with the precision of a cartographer or painter. There are tradeoffs for each approach: Rawls's narrow and abstract political philosophical vocabulary has a greater chance of wide-spread appeal, but Deleuze's political thinking stretches the range of the politically imaginable. Rawls's mental landscape, to conclude this section, retains many features of Kant's noumenal realm, whereas Deleuze's mental landscape is Nietzschean in its wildness.

Constructing Theories

The third activity of constructivism is to construct concepts and principles, that is, to make theoretical lenses. The first two activities have set the stage for the third. The first presents a mental portrait that reflects one's deepest interests and aspirations as well as the situation one finds oneself in the world. This self-portrait does not simply describe who one actually is, but rather how one considers oneself at one's best. Constructivists view identities as works-in-progress, which is why it makes sense to say that constructivists invent a conception of the person. The second activity places the conception of the person on a mental landscape. Once again, constructivists describe this landscape in ways that both resonate with, and alter, common sense conceptions of our current condition. The third activity of constructivism actually sets the construction of concepts and principles in motion by thinking about the actions of the conceptual persona on the terrain of thought. Once one determines what the conceptual persona does, then one has clearer insight into what one ought to do. Rather than gain theoretical knowledge of what the moral laws are independent of human nature, one constructs concepts and principles to express philosophical personalities. Using the help of conceptual personae and planes of thought, one constructs categories and rules to arrange the political universe and help one proceed within it.

The philosophical example *par excellence* of constructivism at work—at least for Rawls and several of his students—is Kant's procedure in Section II of the *Groundwork*. Initially, Kant presents a portrait of humanity as "reasonable and rational persons endowed with conscience and moral sensibility, and affected by, but not determined by, our natural desires and inclinations."[85] This conceptual persona has a higher nature (encompassing reasonableness, conscience, and moral sensibility), a lower nature (including affective desires and inclinations), and a power to choose—what Kant called the *Willkür*—between higher or lower desires whenever they conflict. With this portrait in place, Kant situates the reasonable and rational being on a plane with two levels. The immanent level represents the "normal conditions of human life and our situation as finite beings with needs in the order of nature."[86] On the purely immanent level, human beings are not much different from other animals besides having a more refined intelligence, or empirical practical reason. For Kant, however, humans differ from other natural creatures by a capacity to transcend our animality in thought. This transcendent plane enables us to consider whether to will the "perturbed social world" that would arise if we acted according strictly to our empirical practical reason.[87] Kant proceeds to construct a moral theory in the *Groundwork* by thinking through how a reasonable and rational natural being, living with other humans yet capable of transcending his individual perspective, would formulate his own moral laws and objectives. Kant thereby constructs, in Rawls's words, a four-step categorical imperative procedure as well as a sequence of six conceptions of the good that encapsulate the thinking of such a being (who is really us as represented in thought). The Rawlsian description of Kant's moral philosophy takes liberties with Kant's text. Kant states explicitly that "all morality, which needs anthropology for its *application* to human beings, must first be expounded completely, independently of anthropology, as pure philosophy, i.e., as metaphysics."[88] For Kant, we need to determine the concepts and principles of a rational being in general before we then apply them to human beings. From a Rawlsian perspective, however, a literal reading of Kant's text wins the scholarly battle at the cost of rendering his philosophy less plausible and relevant today. For Rawls, it does not make sense, after Darwin, to try to discover the moral laws in a common reason shared by God, angels, and humans. For Rawls, naturalizing Kant's procedure in the *Groundwork*—including by starting with a conception of the person as a self-reflective human being rather than as a pure rational essence—enables us to renew Kant's thinking for contemporary circumstances.[89] The constructivist reading shows how Kantians, by modifying Kant's moral psychology or the context of the conceptual persona, can build new political theories.

In *A Theory of Justice*, Rawls presents one account of the principles constructed by the citizen in the original position. The thought-process here can be told as a story. Rational parties, behind the veil of ignorance, do not know where they will be placed once they have finished legislating in the original position. Therefore, they will seek to guarantee that all citizens have certain protections from the potentially despotic will of the majority or minority. Therefore, the first principle of justice as fairness is: "Each person has the same indefeasible claim to a fully adequate scheme of equal basic liberties, which scheme is compatible with the same scheme of liberties for all."[90] Once the citizen has sufficiently protected her higher-order interests, she will want to make sure that she is not punished or rewarded for arbitrary reasons from realizing her full potential. The second principle of justice as fairness, then, is that offices and positions within the basic structure of society will be "open to all under conditions of fair equality of opportunity."[91] Finally, the citizen will want to ensure that she has all-purpose means necessary for her to exercise her religious or philosophical liberty as well as vocational potential. The third principle therefore states that social and economic inequalities "are to be to the greatest benefit of the least-advantaged members of society (the difference principle)."[92] In his account of justice as fairness, Rawls's thinking parallels Kant's in the *Groundwork*. The equal basic liberty principle is a perfect duty that brokers no exceptions. The principle of fair equality of opportunity and the difference principle are imperfect duties that should be enacted with all deliberate speed. Rawls's justice as fairness and Kant's metaphysics of morals, furthermore, are based on the notion of reciprocity: that rational beings, or citizens, should construct principles that are acceptable to others viewed as equal to oneself in a fundamental way, whether as political beings or moral beings as such. Rawls's justice as fairness, however, frames its principles in ways that reflect the conditions of its creation. The principle of equal basic liberty incorporates the accumulated historical understanding of the meaning of rights—as codified in US Supreme Court cases and Euro-American moral philosophy; the fair equality of opportunity principle acknowledges patterns of racial, sexual, and religious discrimination; and the difference principle recognizes the power of a property-owning democracy to produce and redistribute wealth.

In *Political Liberalism*, Rawls modifies his political theory to account for the problem of reasonable pluralism. Now, citizens in the original position perceive that other citizens, in other original positions, are constructing their own theories of justice. Late Rawls's conception of the person attends to value pluralism and the need to cooperate with citizens of other faiths and political convictions. Thus late-Rawls presents justice as fairness as but one member of "a family of reasonable political conceptions of justice."[93] The Rawlsian citizen still constructs the principles of justice as fairness, but she is still willing to collaborate with other political liberals who specify certain rights and liberties, prioritize freedoms, and assure citizens the minimum all-purpose means to exercise their liberties.[94] The Rawlsian citizen in the original position, furthermore, becomes aware that other peoples on the global horizon adhere to political visions that may not be liberal but that may still be described as decent. To construct principles meant to apply to the globe, the citizen conjectures what principles will be acceptable to other liberal peoples as well as decent peoples who are nonaggressive, honor human rights, have an independent judiciary, and stipulate a common good idea of justice. In *The Law of Peoples*, Rawls thus constructs a theory of global justice to complement justice as fairness and political liberalism. Rawls may disappoint liberals who hope to transfer the principles of justice as fairness to the globe.[95] For Rawls, however, theorists must be free to reconstruct their political visions to help us grasp new developments in the domestic and international political arenas. Rawlsian theory prizes, in principle, the right to construct new theories to grasp new philosophical and political developments.

Deleuze exercises this right in a spectacular way in *A Thousand Plateaus*. In this text, Deleuze constructs a political theory by thinking through the concepts and principles appropriate to a BwO on a plane of immanence—or, we might say, the theory appropriate for liberal democratic citizens who are torn between experimenting with new ideas and practices but who also appreciate the need for social stability. Here is one formulation of a Deleuzian political theory, presented as an answer to the question, "how do you make yourself a body without organs?": "This is how it should be done: Lodge yourself on a stratum, experiment with the opportunities it offers, find an advantageous place on it, find potential movements of deterritorialization, possible lines of flight, experience them, produce flow conjunctions here and there, try out continuums of intensities segment by segment, have a small plot of new land at all times."[96] Deleuze's political theory is normative: it articulates ought claims, or principles, that specify how we should emulate the conceptual persona of the BwO. We may extract several principles from this passage. First, we need to survey our personal and social situation. Human beings are segmentary animals: we divide our lives into different spatial and temporal strata that provide some order and cohesion to our lives. Deleuze's first piece of advice is to exercise a cartographer's skill and map out the social stratum as well as our place on it. In a contemporary context, this could mean studying the globalized economy, the *de jure* and *de facto* operations of the political system, and popular culture. To "lodge yourself on a stratum" signifies that political theory always takes place in a particular (social, historical, economic, political, cultural, familial, individual) context and that we need to scrutinize that context if we are to shift it in productive ways. The second principle is to experiment with the opportunities offered by our stratum. From the Latin word *experiri* (to test, to try), to experiment means to push against the limits of our individual and collective bodies. To experiment, to deterritorialize, to pursue a line of flight, to produce flow conjunctions—each of these formulations gets at the need to expand or open up our borders if we are to grow and experience the fullness of life.[97] To experience the benefits of global capitalism, we need to reduce tariffs and open national borders to immigrants; to gain the wisdom of different parts of the world, we need to reduce political or cultural exclusivities that prevent people from visiting or settling in our country; to enrich our culture with different languages, religions, and ways of life, we need to perforate established practices and worldviews. For Deleuze, self-creation and enhancement require selective self-destruction—reterritorialization and deterritorialization are mutually entwined. The third principle, however, is that we must exercise care to become a joyful, rather than a sad, BwO. If we obliterate our strata or segments, then we run the risk of dying and destroying the possibility of future experiments. We can also think that we are experimenting when we are, instead, opening our bodies up to microfascisms that destroy social bodies from the inside. Unlike in his earlier books, such as *Anti-Oedipus*, in *A Thousand Plateaus* Deleuze emphasizes the need to exercise the "art of caution" when fashioning ourselves as BwOs. To "have a small plot of new land at all times" implies that we must appreciate the benefits of contemporary liberal democracies that provide, all things considered, advantageous strata on which to live and experiment, individually and collectively. For Deleuze, like Rawls, constructivism reworks political traditions from the inside rather than somehow exercising a Nietzschean radical choice that pretends to create new concepts and principles out of thin air.[98] Deleuzian political theory can be read as both liberal and democratic and deeply dissatisfied with contemporary societies.

In *What is Philosophy?* Deleuze explains why constructivism expresses an internal dynamic that all but guarantees that theory construction will never end. Each of the three activities considered so far—inventing personae, laying out planes, and creating concepts and principles—can be affected by internal eruptions or external disruptions. That is, constructivism works "blow by blow" in which the blows emerge either from within or outside of the philosopher.[99] Deleuze explains how each variable in constructivism affects the equation that produces new concepts and principles: "There are innumerable planes . . . and they group together or separate themselves according to the points of view constituted by personae. Each persona has several features that may give rise to other personae, on the same or a different plane: conceptual personae proliferate. There is an infinity of possible concepts on a plane. . . . They are created in bursts and constantly proliferate."[100] Conceptual persona are the voices in one's mind that suggest new ideas of how to live, think, act politically, visualize the world, and so forth.[101] Philosophers can invent new conceptual personae in the same way that authors create new characters, as the expression of psychic forces that can never be fully measured. What often happens, though, is that philosophers situate conceptual personae on new planes—for example, democratic societies in a state of emergency—which then produces new conceptual personae—such as statesmen or demagogues—and new concepts and principles—such as societies of control or nomadic war machines. Or, the philosopher expresses a new idea that the conceptual persona then explores. There are innumerable points of entry for an idea, fact, historical opinion, nutrient, or personal idiosyncrasy to start us thinking. Constructivism can be renewed whenever a philosopher, for whatever reason, modifies a variable that demands the production of new theoretical frameworks.

Rawls's and Deleuze's political theories converge and diverge in instructive ways. Metaethically, both Rawls and Deleuze are constructivists; they hold that human beings self-reflectively create the lenses through which we know the political realm. Rawls and Deleuze elaborate *how* they have constructed their own political theories and, thereby, how their readers may tinker with the machinery that produced them. Unlike metaethical realists, Rawls and Deleuze expect future disciples to invent new conceptual personae, imagine new planes of thought, and create new political theories. Rawls's and Deleuze's political metaphysics are like open-code software that can be transformed by anyone with the skill and initiative to participate in the common endeavor. Politically, both Rawls and Deleuze construct theories that navigate between preserving the status quo and bringing about a new state of affairs. The first set of principles is often stated tacitly: Rawls and Deleuze trust that normal politics will advance rational ends or protect the integrity of the social body. The second set of principles expresses the utopian vision at work: Rawls seeks to make society more reasonable by protecting civil rights and liberties, bringing about racial, gender, and religious equality of opportunity, and hitching society's progress to the fate of the least fortunate, and Deleuze promotes chiseling at political norms to create the possibility of more joyful political bodies. Rawls and Deleuze are both left egalitarians: They think our destinies interconnect and that one cannot become a fully autonomous citizen or a joyful BwO on one's own. Rawls and Deleuze are also both liberals: They think that individual citizens and BwOs must be granted extensive latitude to chart their own life's course as best they can—on the condition that they do not violate the same right for others.

Rawls's and Deleuze's theories, however, manifest different political sensibilities. In the original edition of *A Theory of Justice*, Rawls states that the principles of justice as fairness are "categorical imperatives in Kant's sense" for they apply "to a person in virtue of his nature as a free and equal rational being."[102] Late Rawls distances himself from such language to emphasize the many different ways that citizens can understand the foundations of the common principles of justice. Yet late Rawls's conception of the person must still be governed by reasonableness—a willingness to adhere to a political conception of justice—and not rationality—means-end thinking to actualize a doctrine of the good. For Rawls, principles of justice must be treated *as if* they are natural laws even if, under philosophic pressure, he concedes that constructed laws are always open, in principle, to revision. Deleuze, however, sees politics as fraught with hard, ambiguous choices. For Deleuze, there is no way to determine *a priori* how to become a BwO. There are no metaphysical principles that can say when, for instance, to permit a foreign religion to thrive within one's borders and when to repress it. The "test of desire" is always ongoing: One must carefully examine whether one's social experimentations are producing positive or negative consequences.[103] Advice such as the following—"keep an eye out for all that is fascist, even inside us, and also for the suicidal and the demented"[104]—would strike Rawlsians and many Kantians as hopelessly vague and impressionistic. Deleuze radicalizes the Aristotelian point, however, that the terms of political science must match the precision of the subject matter, and that politics is inherently complex and ambiguous. For Deleuze, even the term *reasonable* retains a medieval political outlook that, ironically, Kant helps bury even as he tries to perpetuate it. Or, perhaps better, Deleuze embraces the Nietzschean point that we must live and think dangerously—testing out new ideas and practices courageously though not recklessly. However one describes the pedigree informing Rawls's and Deleuze's political theories, they illustrate the wide range of political visions made possible by constructivism.

Evaluating Theories

The final activity of constructivism is to evaluate the theories that have been constructed. For metaethical realists, the only germane evaluation of a theory is whether it is true or not—if it is true, it should be adopted, if not, it should be rejected. For constructivists, however, this dichotomy does not work; all theories are, strictly speaking, false—given that our forms of intuition, space and time, are merely human ways of experiencing things that do not hold true of things-in-themselves. How, though, do constructivists determine whether one theory is better than another? And how do constructivists determine that the process of constructivism must be reactivated? The answers to these questions must combine affective and reflective components. We are embodied creatures motivated by passions. Yet passions, according to Hume, are impressions of reflection, that is, feelings that are shaped, or reflected, by our thoughts. The salient question for Rawls and

Deleuze, then, is how do our theories affect our passions. Yet Rawls and Deleuze differ on how to evaluate answers to this question—the former's criteria are more Kantian and the latter's more Spinozistic.

Kant's methods of grounding theories, for Rawls and Deleuze, are deeply problematic—more reflective of his realist aspirations in moral philosophy than his constructivist insights first developed in the *Critique of Pure Reason*. Dieter Henrich has shown that Kant pursued, over time, two general strategies to justify the moral law.[105] Initially, Kant sought to prove, or deduce, the moral law from incontrovertible theoretical propositions. In his notebooks (*Nachlass*) from the 1770s, on through to Section III of the *Groundwork* (1785), Kant sought to find a starting point, a principle, that nobody could plausibly deny and that would lead, through similarly incontestable premises, to the conclusion that the moral law necessarily applies to imperfectly rational beings such as humans. In the *Groundwork*, Kant identified this principle as the common sense assumption that our cognition only reaches appearances and not things in themselves. "The legal claim (*Rechtsanspruch*), even of common human reason, on freedom of the will is grounded on the consciousness and the admitted presupposition of the independence of reason from all merely subjectively determined causes."[106] Kant's argument in the *Groundwork*, though notoriously obscure, can be summarized as follows. Everyone recognizes a distinction between appearances and reality. We can only make this distinction because we have negative freedom, an ability to think and act independently of alien causes, including our sensible natures. Negative freedom would be lawless, however, and not freedom as such, unless we are also capable of acting on the moral law identified in Section II of the *Groundwork*. Therefore, the fact that we can distinguish appearances and reality makes us aware of our faculties of negative and positive freedom that thereby deduces the moral law, or proves that the law is binding upon us. At the end of the *Groundwork*, however, Kant expresses doubts about whether his deduction has succeeded in making comprehensible the absolute necessity of the unconditioned moral law.[107] In the *Critique of Practical Reason* (1788), Kant thereby reverses course and argues that we know the moral law first, which subsequently gives us insight into its ground of freedom. The moral law is the *ratio cognoscendi* of freedom, and freedom is the *ratio essendi* of the moral law.[108] The moral law is a fact upon which we can deduce subsequent judgments about freedom, virtue, right, religion, and other practical matters. "The moral law is given, as it were, as a fact of pure reason of which we are *a priori* conscious and which is apodictically certain."[109] As numerous commentators since Hegel have observed, the doctrine of the fact of reason seems to contravene Kant's demand, in the *Critique of Pure Reason*, that all ideas must subject themselves to public and rational scrutiny. Kant's claim that the moral law is apodictically certain thus seems to bring him closer to the religious tradition he excoriates for trying to exempt itself from the fiery test of critique. In his efforts to deduce or vindicate the moral law, Kant seems to retreat from the implications of his Copernican revolution to the orthodoxies of rational intuitionism or theological dogmatism.

Rawls has an ambiguous relationship to Kant's method of authenticating the moral law in the *Critique of Practical Reason*. On the one hand, Rawls explicates and defends Kant's coherentist account of authentication. According to this notion, each form of reason, and its attendant concepts and principles, is authenticated if it can be shown how it fits within a coherent account of the constitution of reason as a whole.[110] In his essay "Themes in Kant's Moral Philosophy" Rawls specifies how Kant assigns certain functions to various aspects of reason that interlock to provide a comprehensive account of our faculty psychology. The understanding provides categories and principles that make possible experience of objects in space and time. Pure speculative reason generates the ideas that make possible systematic scientific knowledge. Empirical practical reason organizes our desires and inclinations into a conception of happiness. And pure practical reason is authenticated by the fact of reason. Together, this account displays the unity of reason, guaranteed by pure practical reason's primacy as the determining ground of all the other faculties. Why does Rawls praise Kant's coherentist doctrine?[111] Kant's coherentist account of authentication demands coherence only among our pure mental faculties, not our impure sentiments—and this distinction is precisely one of the dualisms that Rawls, like Hegel and Dewey, seeks to overcome in Kant's moral philosophy. Furthermore, Kant's doctrine of the fact of reason illustrates why Kant's comprehensive moral doctrine does not work as a political conception of justice—many reasonable people will prefer to ground their ethics or morality on a different source. On the other hand, then, Rawls proposes to modify Kant's coherentist doctrine profoundly—by contending that a theory is authenticated only if it helps us, particular people in a historical context, achieve coherence among our thoughts and passions. Rawls's term for his naturalized account of Kant's coherentist doctrine is the idea of reflective equilibrium.

The idea of reflective equilibrium proposes to evaluate theories by how well they help us enrich the vision of politics that we already have. That is, the idea of reflective equilibrium helps us achieve coherence among our concepts and principles on several affective-intellectual levels, from specific thoughts about people and events, to common sense habits of thinking about issues or topics, to our considered convictions about general matters, up to our most abstract concepts and principles. Rawls describes the procedure of reflective equilibrium as follows.[112] First, we collect "considered political judgments at all levels of generality."[113] For Rawls, we have no choice but to start from where we are: embodied creatures who, to a large degree, think in the linguistic terms and judgments of our historical culture. On this point, Rawls is closer to Hume or Wittgenstein than Kant; Rawls does not think that we discover any purely rational truths through philosophical introspection. In the second step, however, Rawls argues that philosophers can isolate, from among our political judgments, "considered judgments or convictions."[114] Here, philosophers already exercise a power of choice in determining which judgments express our deepest convictions and which represent our superficial commitments or intemperate thought-imbued feelings (what Hume called violent passions). In the third step, the philosopher constructs a political theory that advances concepts and principles that systematically organize our considered convictions. In the previous section, I demonstrated how Rawls assembled certain ideas—such as the ideas of the citizen and society—as materials, which he then transformed, through the idea of the original position and the thought process of political constructivism, to fashion certain principles of justice. In the final step of reflective equilibrium, we need to test how well the theory sustains coherence among our concepts, principles, judgments, common sense convictions, and feelings. By explicitly drawing upon contingencies throughout the procedure, Rawls renounces the Kantian project of trying to ground his theory in apodictic facts. The idea of reflective equilibrium justifies a theory in a nonfoundational way: "The most reasonable political conception *for us* is the one that best fits all our considered convictions on reflection and organizes them into a coherent view. *At any given time*, we cannot do better than that."[115] To evaluate a political theory, according to Rawls, we have to determine how well it helps us understand and navigate our particular historical circumstances.

Is the idea of reflective equilibrium conservative? That is, does Rawls protect common sense from critical enquiry by installing it as both the genesis and terminus of evaluation?[116] In this case, the regulative ideal of coherence would serve the same function for Rawls as it did for Kant: placing arbitrary limits on critique's power to assess everything, including commons sense views of morality or political justice. Rawls insists, however, that the ideal he advocates is *wide* reflective equilibrium. Political philosophy, for Rawls, must begin by collecting ideas from the public political culture if it is to have traction among the majority of citizens to support a political conception of justice. The idea of public justification requires that we proceed from some consensus to ensure social and political cooperation. In the second and third steps of the reflective equilibrium procedure, however, philosophers should extend themselves to consider a myriad of ways to frame political things. "Taking this process to the limit, one seeks the conception, or plurality of conceptions, that would survive the rational consideration of all feasible conceptions and all reasonable arguments for them."[117] We cannot actually do this, according to Rawls, but we can aspire to the next best thing: to evaluate our theory of justice in light of the major traditions of political thought. In principle, we should aspire to reevaluate our theory as new traditions of political thought emerge, including from around the world (and not just a necessarily vague *us*). For Rawls, the idea of public justification rests uneasily alongside a philosophic imperative to open ourselves to rethinking our political ideals and categories.

Deleuze expresses a consistent antipathy to Kant's method of deducing or proving his doctrines. For Deleuze, the drive to justify expresses the worst impulse in Kant's moral philosophy, namely to defend established values through repressing alternate ways of viewing and acting within the world. In *Kant's Critical Philosophy*, Deleuze repeatedly notes that Kant appeals to "facts" to justify his theoretical and moral doctrines.[118] In *Difference and Repetition*, Deleuze explains why Kant's recurrent appeals to facts is problematic: Kant relinquishes his ability to criticize the given, in this case, traditional values. "Kant traces the so-called transcendental structures"—such as the fact of reason—"from the empirical acts of a psychological consciousness."[119] Kant tries to hide "this all too obvious procedure"—by denying, for instance, that the fact of reason makes itself known through sensual feelings or moral sentiments—but critical thinkers should be suspicious that Kant consistently extols core notions of Christian ethics—including freedom, God, and immortality—on rational grounds.[120] "Kantian Critique is ultimately respectful: knowledge, morality, reflection and faith are supposed to correspond to natural interests of reason, and are never themselves called into question."[121] From a Deleuzian perspective, Kant offers a coherentist account of justification that evaluates mental faculties and subjective judgments by how well they cohere with common sense. Deleuze, however, thinks that philosophy betrays its fundamental mission of breaking with *doxa* when it simply or primarily clarifies judgments according to the mandates of common sense. Deleuze expresses this sentiment in a late essay entitled, "To Have Done with Judgment": "Judgment prevents the emergence of any new mode of existence. For the latter creates itself through its own forces, that is, through the forces it is able to harness, and is valid in and of itself inasmuch as it brings the new combination into existence."[122] Deleuzian philosophers should be critically responsive to new forces seeking to create a space for themselves in the political order.[123] New constituencies are, by definition, going to appear strange to established constituencies, and Kant's—and, to a lesser degree, Rawls's—demand that alien ways of life conform to facts and common sense threatens to establish a punitive political order. That is why Deleuze, at his most polemical, seems to renounce the project of justification: it seems unlikely if not impossible for a new political vision to satisfy sufficiently the criteria of established political doctrines.

For Deleuze, however, it is essential that philosophers evaluate their creations, even if they cannot justify them apodictically.[124] In *A Thousand Plateaus*, Deleuze explains why one should be willing to wear the glasses that he has constructed: "Find your body without organs. Find out how to make it. It's a question of life and death, youth and old age, sadness and joy. It's where everything is played out."[125] Deleuze, here, is stating that we should evaluate his, or any other, theory by immanent criteria. Transcendent criteria—such as good and evil, or true and false—presuppose that human beings can access eternal or metaphysically real laws or categories. Immanent criteria, on the contrary, assume that human beings can only evaluate different ways of living in this world. In *Spinoza: Practical Philosophy*, Deleuze defines the meaning of joy and sadness: "we experience *joy* when a body encounters ours and enters into composition with it, and *sadness* when, on the contrary, a body or an idea threaten our own coherence."[126] When we form positive encounters with other bodies—say, when we learn another language, delight in another cuisine, or collaborate on a common political project—then we experience joy, or youthfulness, or heightened vitality. Conversely, when we form negative encounters with others, our life force drains and we experience sad passions. We still need normative criteria to help us chart our life's course, but we should consider using the ethical duality of good and bad rather than the moralistic one of good and evil. Deleuze promotes his political theory in *A Thousand Plateaus* as helping us best realize the means and the stakes of becoming a joyful BwO.

Is Deleuze's political theory purely aesthetic? That is, does Deleuze appeal solely to images, or poetry, and renounce the whole philosophical project of using reason to justify its concepts or principles? For Deleuze, this question presupposes a Kantian (or Platonic) understanding of reason that he seeks to elude. Deleuze situates himself in a minor tradition of philosophy that considers reason subservient, so to speak, to the *conatus* (Spinoza), passions (Hume), or will to power (Nietzsche). According to this tradition, every animal, including the philosopher, "instinctively strives for an optimum of favorable conditions in which to fully release his power and achieve his maximum of power-sensation."[127] For Deleuze and his philosophic predecessors, human instincts and desires propel our movement in the world and reason simply helps us determine suitable objects for our desires or the most propitious way to attain those objects. This is not to say that reason—or the human capacity for reflection and foresight—is unimportant. In *A Thousand Plateaus*, for instance, Deleuze recommends the exercise of practical reason in becoming a BwO: "Dismantling the organism has never meant killing yourself, but rather opening the body to connections that presuppose an entire assemblage, circuits, conjunctions, levels and thresholds, passages and distributions of intensity, and territories and deterritorializations *measured with the craft of a surveyor*."[128] According to Deleuze, human beings need to exercise prudence in distinguishing experiments that amplify human perception, cognition, desire, happiness, power, or joy from those that separate human beings from their power and spread sadness. To measure individual and political bodies with the craft of a surveyor demands a trained intellect. To study the interrelationship between different bodies also implies that the individual and the collectivity, ethics and politics, are mutually imbricated: one cannot become a joyful BwO on one's own. From a Kantian perspective, Deleuze's principles seem to be hypothetical imperatives: either rules of skill that help us achieve determinate ends or counsels of prudence that over the long-run tend to facilitate human happiness. Deleuze would not deny these charges, but he contests the assumptions that undergird them. For Deleuze, ethical thinking requires many of the same skills that Kant assigns to the *sensus communis* in the *Critique of Judgment*: an ability to think for oneself (rather than be governed by fears or superstitions), a facility to think in the position of others (through philosophic exercises that help one become broad-minded, such as by entering a plane of immanence), and the ability to think consistently (by forging a coherent plane of immanence). We need to think, to evaluate, in ways that attend to the complexity of the world.[129] This position does not need to lead to fascism or nihilism; on the contrary, liberal democracies, among all possible political regimes, tend to "substitute the love of freedom . . . for the affections-passions of fear, hope, and even security."[130] For Deleuze, immanent criteria such as joy and sadness, combined with the human faculty of reason, tend to support political liberty and freedom, and that may be their best (or only) justification.

Constructivism ultimately recommends that we evaluate political theories pragmatically. Kant himself drew a sharp distinction between pure moral philosophy (based upon the conception of the rational being as such) and pragmatic anthropology (based upon the study of human beings—earthly creatures endowed with reason).[131] For Kant, the former discipline finds and establishes moral concepts and principles in pure practical reason, and the latter discipline considers how best to inculcate them in corporeal beings. Rawls and Deleuze, however, try to overcome the dualisms in Kant's philosophy, including by attending to the mutual relationship between our thoughts and our passions, our mental frameworks and their historical-material milieu. Kant tries to ground his practical philosophy on a fact of reason that humiliates our corporeal nature.[132] Rawls and Deleuze, on the contrary, try to find more nuanced criteria that respect both our affective and reflective natures. Rawls, we saw, proposes the idea of reflective equilibrium to evaluate how well a political theory achieves coherence among our thoughts, opinions, judgments, and feelings. Deleuze, in turn, proposes the criteria of joy and sadness to determine how well our theoretical and political arrangements increase or decrease our individual and collective power. Both Rawls and Deleuze think that political theories must promote the individual's desires (or rationality) as well as collective responsibilities (or reasonableness). For better or worse, constructivists cannot deduce or prove the validity of their political theories with the certainty that Kant demanded in the *Critique of Practical Reason*. From the constructivist perspective, however, this is not because of a failure of will; it is, rather, because Kant's Copernican revolution assigns human beings the responsibility to construct their own political theories, and there is no way to assure that our concepts or rules will match up with the universe's articulations. We evaluate our theories through trial and error.

Constructivists, however, have different tastes. In *What is Philosophy?* Deleuze describes taste as the philosophical faculty of coadaptation. Constructivists invent personae, lay out planes, and construct theories—but taste is the mysterious power in the background that determines the success or failure of each activity. "Philosophical taste neither replaces creation nor restrains it. On the contrary, the creation of concepts calls for a taste that modulates it."[133] Kant, in the *Critique of the Power of Judgment*, and Hume, in "Of the Standard of Taste," acknowledge the role of taste in aesthetic and moral judgments but aspire to formulate criteria of universal validity regarding, say, statements of beauty or moral approval. Deleuze, on the contrary, defines the faculty of taste as "an instinctive, almost animal *sapere*" that ensures a plurality of political visions.[134] Political philosophers evaluate theories using categories such as "Interesting, Remarkable, or Important"—but these are essentially contestable concepts.[135] Rawls does not flag the contestability of his political theory in the same way that Deleuze does. Rawls explicitly employs an abstract political vocabulary that makes possible political consensus.[136] Using inflammatory or poetic rhetoric would defeat Rawls's purpose of forging political alliances among reasonable comprehensive moral doctrines. Yet Rawls's ideal of wide reflective equilibrium promotes philosophical dissatisfaction with currently existing theories of justice. For Rawls, there is no way to end the debate over political theories once and for all—and the decision of when to temporarily suspend the process of reflective equilibrium to act or judge politically will depend upon the character—or taste—of the political actor or theorist. Both Rawls and Deleuze, then, acknowledge an idiosyncratic component of political theory that cannot be purified through reason. Yet, as should be clear by now, Rawls and Deleuze have disparate philosophical tastes. Rawls seeks to rise above the political fray, like a Supreme Court judge, and Deleuze identifies with the nomads who chart new courses for thought and life. Rawls has a taste for power, and Deleuze has a taste for adventure. In the next section, I dig deeper into the reasons for Rawls's and Deleuze's differing philosophic tastes and consider how to renew the process of constructivism incorporating elements from both Rawlsian and Deleuzian political theory.

VARIETIES OF CONSTRUCTIVISM

One can see why Rawls and Deleuze are drawn to the notion of constructivism. The Enlightenment as a movement prizes humanity's ability to chart its own destiny in the universe. Rawls and Deleuze take to heart Kant's enjoinder that we should exercise the courage of our own understanding and make our own political theoretical lenses. Autonomy, though, is hard. We grow up in a certain historical environment—with determinate economic, political, social, cultural, and linguistic structures—that shapes our thoughts profoundly. The *autos* seems to be pervaded by the *heteros*—we in the Euro-American political tradition, for instance, employ a vocabulary largely drawn from Greek, Latin, and Judeo-Christian roots. How is it possible to be self-legislating when historical and material ingredients permeate the self? Kant's metaphysics of morals prizes the human ability to escape the world of sense entirely by entering the noumenal realm or a functional equivalent. For Rawls and Deleuze, however, this is the side of Kant's philosophy that faces the medieval world and preserves the spirit of Christianity. Rawls and Deleuze prefer to pursue Kant's intimations of a new way of being in the modern world—including the notion of constructivism that outlines a loose method of building new conceptual frameworks that inevitably retain traces of their historical conditions of possibility. In the final section of this chapter, I consider how the project of constructivism can be renewed again for the twenty-first century.

To understand the prospects of future constructivisms, we would do well to consider the relationship between Rawls's and Deleuze's political theories. Here, I propose to employ a certain set of conceptual distinctions proffered by Jonathan Israel in *Radical Enlightenment: Philosophy and the Making of Modernity 1650–1750*. According to Israel, the Enlightenment—despite linguistic, geographical, philosophical, political, and personal differences— converged on a common set of presuppositions: "The Enlightenment . . . not only attacked and severed the roots of traditional European culture in the sacred, magic, kingship, and hierarchy, secularizing all institutions and ideas, but (intellectually and to a degree in practice) effectively demolished all legitimation of monarchy, aristocracy, woman's subordination to man, ecclesiastical authority, and slavery, replacing these with the principles of universality, equality, and democracy."[137] The Enlightenment project gained consistency by what it fought against: traditional doctrines that sought to impose a single worldview on all human beings. The critical spirit weighed and rejected doctrines pervasive in the medieval era, including the natural rights of kings to govern subjects, men to govern women, priests to govern laymen, lords to govern serfs, and so forth. In the face of philosophical and theological efforts to ground these doctrines on how things really are, the

Enlightenment philosophers argued that human beings have a say in how we view and do things. For Enlightenment philosophers such as Locke, Hume, and Kant, skepticism was a valuable disposition to challenge metaethical realism and its attendant practical dogmatisms. Yet the Enlightenment's critique of heteronomy was conjoined with a defense of autonomy. Enlightenment philosophers, in general, defended the right of peoples to constitute their own political order, as well as of individuals to choose their own moral, religious, or philosophical faith. The Enlightenment came together, broadly speaking, in defense of democracy and liberalism. There was, of course, a spectrum of views between cautious republicans and radical democrats, social conservatives and libertines. Yet Enlightenment philosophers believed that the old theoretical lenses had been broken and that human beings had the power to create new ones. Rawls and Deleuze endorse each of these characteristics of the Enlightenment: a critique of moral, political, philosophical, and religious authoritarianism; a defense of self-governance individually and collectively; and the confidence that human beings may construct political theories to help them grasp and confront their historical moment.

The historical Enlightenment, according to Israel, was divided along moderate and radical lines. The moderate Enlightenment included prominent figures such as Newton, Locke, Leibniz, Thomasius, and Wolff. This Enlightenment "aspired to conquer ignorance and superstition, establish toleration, and revolutionize ideas, education, and attitudes by means of philosophy but in such a way as to preserve and safeguard what were judged essential elements of the older structures, effecting a viable synthesis of old and new, and of reason and faith."[138] The moderate Enlightenment walked a fine line: It promoted the scientific cast of mind, but it also argued that this mental disposition was compatible with the spirit, if not the letter, of moral, political, and religious traditions. The moderate Enlightenment waged a war on two fronts: against ecclesiastical and political authorities, who sought to reestablish the *ancien régime*, but also against radicals who thought that the scientific worldview was incompatible with revealed religion. In a word, the moderate Enlightenment respected Christianity even as it criticized elements of its doctrines and historical practice. According to this criterion, Rawls falls squarely within the tradition of the moderate Enlightenment. Rawls's complex relationship with Christianity becomes apparent in his posthumously published essay, "On My Religion." In this essay, Rawls explains why he abandoned the Episcopalianism in which he was raised and for which he considered, during college, joining a seminary. In June of 1945, several events converged to shake Rawls out of his orthodox convictions: a Lutheran pastor's absurd claim that God aimed American bullets at the Japanese and not the reverse; a friend's death that could just as easily have been Rawls's; and the evil of the Holocaust. After the war, Rawls retained a certain fideism, but he began to doubt many Christian ideas of right and justice. The notions of sin, heaven and hell, and salvation by true belief "depict God as a monster moved solely by God's own power and glory."[139] The Inquisition displays the tendency of salvational religions to perpetuate cruelty: "I came to feel that the great curse of Christianity was to persecute dissenters as heretics."[140] The focus on individual salvation permits Christians to acquiesce in evil, as in the case of the German resistance movement worrying (wrongly) over the permissibility of assassinating Hitler. Together, these factors led Rawls to lose his faith.[141] Yet Rawls concludes his reflections by insisting on mutual respect among religious faiths. Rawls cites Jean Bodin's *Colloquium of the Seven* as his model. In this text, Bodin, a believing Catholic, stages a dialogue among a natural philosopher, a Calvinist, a Muslim, a Catholic, a Lutheran, a Jew, and a skeptic. At the end of the dialogue, the speakers agree to stop trying to refute or convert each other and to encourage one another to present and listen to the other's views respectfully. Rawls draws several lessons from Bodin's text, including the need to incorporate tolerance into any reasonable moral conception, the importance of exercising public reason—or the virtue of refraining from displaying one's full religious convictions when discussing common political matters—and the need to judge people by their deeds rather than their words.[142] Despite his own personal views, then, Rawls constructs principles that he imagines would be acceptable to reasonable Christians—a point that he emphasizes in a late interview with *Commonweal*: "I make a point . . . of really not discussing anything, as far as I can help it, that will put me at odds with any theologian."[143] Rawls's political theory is not Christian per se, but it does construct lenses compatible with how reasonable Christians already view the world.[144]

In the seventeenth and eighteenth centuries, however, the radical Enlightenment sought a more profound break with Christianity. This Enlightenment "rejected all compromise with the past and sought to sweep away existing structures entirely, rejecting the Creation as traditionally understood in Judeo-Christian civilization, and the intervention of a providential God in human affairs, denying the possibility of miracles, and reward and punishment in an afterlife, scorning all forms of ecclesiastical authority, and refusing to accept that there is any God-ordained social hierarchy."[145] The founder of the radical Enlightenment, according to Israel, was Baruch Spinoza—the hero, as it turns out, of Deleuze's *What is Philosophy?* Why does Deleuze, in this text, call Spinoza the prince of philosophers?[146] Deleuze situates Spinoza's accomplishment in the history of Western philosophy presented as a struggle over how to interpret the relationship between immanence and transcendence. Plato poisoned the history of Western philosophy at the same time as he initiated it. Plato began the philosophical project of constructing concepts—including ones central to Deleuze's philosophy, such as ideas. Yet Plato insisted, at least exoterically, that above the immanent field of experience there is an ontological plane that grounds our ideas. For Plato and Neo-Platonists, there must always be a One beyond the One, a pure realm of ideas above the impure world of experience.[147] Christian philosophy takes up and modifies this idea, acknowledging a limited sphere in which the human intellect can be creative, but insisting that philosophy "be strictly controlled and enframed by the demands of an emanative and, above all, creative transcendence."[148] From a Spinozist perspective, however, Christianity stifles the philosophic spirit—when it does not actively condemn and persecute it. Descartes and Kant initiate modern philosophy by insisting that the human mind produces its own ideas rather than receives them from a higher source. Yet Descartes and Kant still insist that immanence must be judged from a higher plateau—although this time, this plateau is identified as the *cogito*, or the transcendental subject, rather than a transcendent order as such. "Kant discovers the modern way of saving transcendence"—by placing the ideational framework in the Subject (the transcendental unity of apperception) rather than the Object (now placed behind the cognitive veil of the noumenal realm).[149] For classical philosophers such as Plato, and modern philosophers such as Kant, there is an ideational dimension of the universe that transcends the material one. Spinoza's philosophy was and is radical for two reasons. Ontologically, Spinoza denies that a transcendent order must be superimposed upon immanence. Spinozist metaphysics posits one substance that presents two sides to us, extension and thought, in which beings can be mapped by their modes and types, affects and speeds. Spinoza "knew full well that immanence was only immanent to itself"—and that humanity could therefore discard many of the two-world doctrines that now appear indistinguishable from theological superstitions.[150] Politically, this suggests that the notion of natural right must be radically reconfigured. For the ancients, natural right meant that the few human beings who could transcend the immanent world possessed the right to govern the ignorant—a hierarchical doctrine easily appropriated by the Christian and feudal order. For Spinoza, on the contrary, "everyone's primal desire to be happy in their own way must be treated as strictly equal in any realistic discussion of society and politics."[151] Spinoza's conception of natural right suggests that democracy is the political regime most congruent with human nature.[152] Despite his debts to Spinoza, Deleuze does not think that the radical Enlightenment culminates with the *Ethics* or the *Theological-Political Treatise*. Spinoza's great accomplishment was to posit *the* plane of immanence: a one-world metaphysics, albeit a world of multiple layers and means of expression. Contemporary Spinozists can extend Spinoza's project by mapping the One-All with new concepts and principles. Spinozists "can and must presuppose a multiplicity of planes, since no one plane could encompass all of chaos without collapsing back into it."[153] To construct these new planes, Spinozists can draw upon the metaethics of Spinoza's great critic: Kant. Deleuze's political theory thus oscillates between two projects: to construct lenses that can be shared by many constituencies in the democratic political garden, and to make lenses for Spinozists who seek to understand a world of pure immanence.

The historical Enlightenment, in hindsight, benefited from the tension between its moderate and radical wings.[154] The radical Enlightenment pressed the action: arguing that the Bible be read as a historical-material document; presenting the first public defense, since Greek antiquity, of democracy as the most natural form of government; demanding freedom of speech and expression as well as liberty of conscience (for Christians and nonbelievers); and, in principle, exposing all inherited ideas and practices to critique. Yet the radical Enlightenment by itself was vulnerable to persecution: Israel's book details how conservative religious and political authorities persecuted Spinozists and tried to wipe their names from the history books. The moderate Enlightenment hesitated to endorse Spinoza's purely immanent framework—wondering, for instance, how it was compatible with free will—but the moderate Enlightenment did shelter its more radical sibling from the harshest forces of the clerical right. The moderate Enlightenment translated the ideas of the radical Enlightenment into a more comprehensible and acceptable language for the authorities and the general populace. The moderate Enlightenment also actualized aspects of the vision of the radical Enlightenment—making democracy a legitimate and viable form of government in the modern world, although not to the same extent and on the same timetable as the radical Enlightenment. There were of course tensions and recriminations between members of the rival Enlightenments, but *the* Enlightenment benefited from cultivating both responsible and experimental members.

The contemporary Enlightenment, then, can learn a lesson from the historical Enlightenment. We ought to appreciate the contributions of both moderates and radicals, Rawlsians and Deleuzians. Rawls constructs a political theory that both collaborates with reasonable Christians and defends the right of nonbelievers to participate in the political system. Rawlsian political liberalism expresses a somewhat conservative sensibility—in which members of the judiciary bear a heavy responsibility in articulating political values—but political liberalism does, in principle, recognize a philosophical responsibility to listen to radical voices. Political liberalism also seeks to actualize in the basic structure of society many of the ideals originating in the radical Enlightenment, including the right to free speech and a concern with the material preconditions of a functioning democracy. Deleuze's political theory, following the lead of its radical predecessors, constantly looks on the horizon for new issues. Whereas political liberalism employs a narrow range of abstract conceptions to maximize its chances of forming an overlapping consensus on a just political order, Deleuzian political theory embraces the responsibility to construct new concepts to best understand new and surprising events in the world. Deleuzian political theory both accepts and expresses dissatisfaction with the Left's political vocabulary of democracy, liberalism, socialism, and tolerance. Whereas Rawls brackets certain issues from political liberalism (the family, the environment), Deleuze constructs a philosophic framework to help us think about how to shift our political perceptions and actions. Deleuze's advice to "gently tip the assemblage," for instance, presses political liberals to both secure the conditions of a just, stable, and tolerant society as well as to open that society to new ideas, practices, constituencies, religions, and so forth. Deleuze's political theory expresses a more experimental, radical sensibility than Rawls's, which seeks to actualize the values already agreed upon by most reasonable citizens. Rawlsian and Deleuzian political theories both contribute to forging lenses to help contemporary progressives navigate the political universe.

Yet the process of constructivism must be renewed again. The reason is this: Constructivism begins with a certain conception of the person. Kant's moral doctrine, as I have demonstrated, employs a transhistorical conception of the person, but Rawls and Deleuze think that any adequate conception of self-identity must contextualize the person in a historical milieu. Political constructivism, then, must take account of the population if it is to construct lenses that both reflect and shape our aspirations. Today, the demographics of Western democracies are changing rapidly, including but not limited to an increasing Muslim percentage of the population. One of the great tasks of the contemporary Enlightenment is to construct new terms of political pluralism that welcome Muslims. In the next chapter, I take a step in this direction by considering how Rawls, Deleuze, and the Muslim political reformer Tariq Ramadan have already begun to do this.

Engaging Islam

One of the most common—and still-illuminating—observations about Kant's practical philosophy is that it attempts to secularize Christianity.[1] Kant clearly wanted his philosophy to resonate with the predominantly Christian audience that his work addressed. An emblematic statement, from the *Religion within the Boundaries of Mere Reason*, is that Christianity is the first doctrine of faith to expound "the true morality of a people of God" and that a universal history of religious faith—culminating in a pure rational religion—must commence with Christianity.[2] According to Gordon E. Michalson Jr. in *Kant and the Problem of God*, Kant is "a way station between Luther and Marx," that is, he opens the door to atheistic ways of thinking that depart more or less from the spirit of Christianity.[3] Yet for many commentators up to the present, Kant's practical philosophy substantively overlaps with Christian ideals.[4]

What is the relevance of Kant's practical philosophy, then, for contemporary pluralistic societies? A naturalized Kantianism, we saw in Chapter 2, proceeds with open eyes, and a political philosopher working today cannot help but notice that Islam may be becoming Europe's "second religion."[5] Numerous political commentators today—often explicitly appealing to Enlightenment values—worry that Muslim immigrants and their descendants are undermining the political, intellectual, and cultural traditions of the historical homeland of the Enlightenment. Christopher Caldwell, in *Reflections on the Revolution in Europe: Immigration, Islam, and the West*, observes: "Since its arrival half a century ago, Islam has broken . . . a good many of the European customs, received ideas, and state structures with which it has come into contact."[6] Europeans and Americans have a legitimate right to worry about the future of the Enlightenment in the face of certain militant groups—such as al-Qaeda and Hizb ut-Tahrir—committed to its demise.[7] Yet the Enlightenment as a living tradition must be willing to keep its ears, mind, and heart open as it charts its own future, and this may mean learning and respecting the viewpoints of Muslims in Europe, the United States, and around the world. As Kant himself reiterates through his work, part of being broad-minded is thinking from the vantage point of other people—real people whom one learns about through (though not exclusively) intellectual exchanges in the public sphere.[8] According to Andrew F. March in *Islam and Liberal Citizenship: The Search for an Overlapping Consensus*, contemporary Euro-American political theorists may not reasonably expect Muslims to situate themselves in a "common post-Reformation or post-Enlightenment shared tradition of secularism and political liberties."[9] To be sure, it is unfair to demand that Muslims learn the exact same lessons about religion and politics as Euro-American philosophers did in the eighteenth-century. Yet a future Enlightenment may take up the Enlightenment's flag of cultivating civic peace among diverse religious faiths. Muslims may phrase this commitment in different ways—for example, as a revival of the mid–nineteenth- to mid–twentieth-century Arab cultural movement known as the *Nahda* (literally: "rising")[10]—but the Enlightenment should be capacious enough to reach out to constituencies emerging out of different religious, political, cultural, and linguistic traditions.

The chapter proceeds by considering how Kantians may reconstruct their conceptual toolbox, so to speak, to foster religious-political alliances in pluralistic societies. Initially, I consider Kant's idea of the ethical community as a way to hoist a banner of virtue that diverse religious faiths may endorse. Then, I consider Rawls's idea of an overlapping consensus that widens the range of religious faiths that may congregate in an ethico-political body; Deleuze's idea of an assemblage that presses us to see political-religious bodies as protean, permeable, and multilayered; and Tariq Ramadan's idea of the space of testimony (*dar al-shahada*) that contributes to the contemporary Enlightenment from an Islamic (and yet partly Kantian) perspective. Finally, I consider the future of Kantian political theory. Though many Kantians today seek to recover Kant's vision as a bulwark against religious (including Islamic) militancy,[11] I argue instead that the Enlightenment tradition must generate new concepts and principles to facilitate beneficial political-religious alliances.

THE IDEA OF THE ETHICAL COMMUNITY

One of the remarkable features of Kant's *Religion within the Boundaries of Mere Reason* is the intercalation of philosophical and historical elements. Consider, for example, the third essay, "The victory of the good principle over the evil principle, and the founding of a kingdom of God on earth." The essay proceeds in two manners. The first division presents a "philosophical representation of the victory of the good principle in the founding of a Kingdom of God on earth." Here, Kant offers a highly abstract argument that proposes to "follow up the leading thread" of the moral need to presuppose "a higher moral being through whose universal organization the forces of single individuals, insufficient on their own, are united for a common effect."[12] In this approach, Kant formulates an *a priori* argument that aims to uncover the pure religion of reason at the basis of any "alleged revelation or other."[13] The second division—"historical representation of the gradual establishment of the dominion of the good principle on earth"—reverses course and explicitly reinterprets the history of Christianity as containing the seeds of a rational religion. Kant's historically reflective argument for the ethical community contributes to the post-Westphalian search for civil peace among contending confessional faiths.

One of the themes of the *Religion* is a historical verdict on the type of religions that precipitated such conflicts as the Thirty Years War. "The so-called religious struggles, which have so often shaken the world and spattered it with blood, have never been anything but squabbles over ecclesiastical faiths."[14] Religious strife between contending orthodoxies have "split the Christian world into bitter parties over opinions in matters of faith," to the point where many ethical people wonder if, with Lucretius, the world might be better off without the evil deeds that religion prompts.[15] Religious militancy also made possible the Crusades, which "would depopulate another portion of the world."[16] Religious orthodoxy and dogmatism, for Kant, signal close-mindedness and a threat to the physical, political, cultural, and moral well-being of people around the world.[17] An age of enlightenment must simply leave the medieval types of religious faith in the past.

And yet religion plays a vital historical role in flying a "banner of virtue" that may rally people to supersede the principle of political right.[18] Kant emphasizes that the coercive power of the state should not be deployed to enforce a religious morality. "A state has only a *negative* right to prevent public teachers from exercising an influence on the *visible* political community that might be prejudicial to public peace."[19] To this extent at least, Kant agrees with Hobbes that the modern state plays a vital role in brokering peace between clashing religious orthodoxies. For Kant, political soulcraft both defeats the purpose of morality (which must be freely chosen to qualify as moral) and tends to precipitate intractable political-religious conflicts. Yet Kant thinks that religion is necessary to help people leave the "ethical state of nature" in which each individual must combat by himself the radical propensity to evil within the will that tends to favor sensual inclinations over moral commands. The attainment of the highest moral good—"a universal republic based on the laws of virtue"—requires "a union of such persons into a whole toward that very end."[20] One sees, here, why Kant's *Religion* is an essential part of his political thought. Kant, one might say, articulates a left-wing political ethos that views human beings as members of the same family equally deserving of respect.[21] For Kant's religious politics, it is not enough that the state enforce the minimal principle of right that limits the freedom of each to the condition under which it can coexist with the freedom of everyone else[22]; rather, people must collaborate outside of the official pronouncements of the state to honor human dignity and practice human autonomy.

The first feature of the ethical community is that it houses numerous ecclesiastical faiths. "There is only *one* (true) *religion*, but there can be several different kinds of *faith*."[23] A pure rational religion concerns the moral dispositions within the soul, whereas an ecclesiastical faith blends religion with empirical elements to lodge itself in sensuous (*sinnliche*) human nature.[24] Kant points to the "Jewish, Mohammaden, Christian, Catholic, [and] Lutheran" faiths.[25] Ideally, human reason will be able to discard the historical shell of ecclesiastical faiths and express the pure religion of reason. Only "the pure faith of religion, based entirely on reason, can be recognized as necessary and hence as the one which exclusively marks out the *true* church."[26]

Kant's faith is that "in the end religion will gradually be freed of all empirical grounds of determination, of all statutes that rest on history and unite human beings provisionally for the promotion of the good through the intermediary of an ecclesiastical faith."[27] Even though this may be an ideal for human reason (like a world republic[28]), in practice, as far as human beings can see, we will always be divided by historical faiths. Human beings demand for "even the highest concepts and grounds of reason something that *the senses can hold on to*," and these sensual elements will always differ among human beings scattered across the globe.[29] In the face of what we might call, paraphrasing Rawls, the fact of reasonable religious pluralism, human beings have a choice. They may be catholics (including arch-catholic protestants) who claim that their "ecclesiastical faith is universally binding"; or they may be protestants (including protestant catholics) who object to the militant universalism of another's faith.[30] One purpose of the ethical community is to unite "protestants" who embrace an ecclesiastical faith and deny the "catholic" effort to deploy the state to make one faith official.

A second feature of the ethical community is that it searches for common ground that may be shared by diverse ecclesiastical faiths. Kant holds that inter-ecclesiastical disputes can never be truly settled: "For a statutory legislation (which presupposes a revelation) can be regarded only as contingent, as something that cannot have reached, nor can reach, every human being."[31] There are limits to how far philosophers can persuade others of the superiority of the Torah, the New Testament, or the Qur'an; Moses, Jesus, or Mohammed; or Judaism, Christianity, or Islam—in all cases, we are inevitably affected by our historical and geographical milieu. Below, we speculate more about Kant's deepest intentions in the *Religion*. But, here, we can see how Kant proposes a collective ethical agent that may appeal to diverse ecclesiastical faiths. One key is to focus on worldly reform that concerns all human beings, regardless of ecclesiastical faith. According to pure religious faith, whenever human beings "fulfill their duties toward human beings (themselves and others), by that very fact they also conform to God's commands."[32] Analogously, pure religious faith minimizes references to God that inevitably complicate human being's allegiance to worldly action. According to Michalson, God plays a much smaller role in the *Religion* than he did even in the *Critique of Practical Reason*. No longer an active God proportioning virtue and happiness, "God becomes a spectator or even a placeholder, serving . . . as a kind of background metaphysical premise guaranteeing a rational result for genuinely moral endeavors."[33] Regardless of how one interprets the robustness of Kant's late theology, Kant's religious politics drops many of the most controversial dogmas that divide Catholics, Lutherans, and Calvinists to focus attention on improving the ethical quality of political life.

A third feature of the ethical community is its principled commitment to divesting ecclesiastical faiths of political power. Establishing a state, Kant famously declares in *Toward Perpetual Peace*, "is a problem that may be solved even for a nation of devils."[34] The principle of right, Kant elaborates in the *Metaphysics of Morals*, originates simply by thinking through the coordination problem for imperfectly rational beings such as humans. The state itself, then, is not a moral agent. Yet the state may dictate the terms of political cooperation, within moral limits, to historical churches: "The proposition, 'We ought to obey God rather than men [Acts 5:29],' means only that when human beings command something that is evil in itself (directly opposed to the ethical law), we may not, and ought not, obey them. But, conversely, if an alleged divine statutory law is opposed to a positive civil law not in itself immoral, there is then cause to consider the alleged divine law as spurious."[35] Ecclesiastical churches may not command or advise the state to commit or omit any action based on divine revelation alone. At the same time, the state may not promulgate any particular form of ecclesiastical faith, for, besides not improving anybody's moral disposition, this policy can "hardly produce good citizens for the state."[36] This is an early and influential account of modern secularism—the argument for the separation of church and state.[37] However, the idea of the ethical community also reconfigures the Augustinian-Lutheran distinction between the kingdom of God and the kingdom of man.[38] In formulating his political-religious vision, Kant may have had no choice but to work with the philosophical vocabulary at his disposal that was largely permeated by Christian concepts.[39]

Kant's political vision, for better or worse, was formulated to address the post-Westphalia condition of numerous ecclesiastical faiths humbled by the wars of religion but still committed to advocating their faith. Commentators disagree on Kant's intention in the *Religion*. For some, Kant follows in the footsteps of Leibniz in trying to envision a new type of *respublica Christiana* to unite peoples and churches, laws and politics, in post-Reformation Europe. On this account, Kant merely provides a modern veneer on medieval *Schulmetaphysik* committed to resacralizing politics.[40] Alternatively, Kant may have been trying nothing less than to establish a new Enlightenment religion.[41] Given that human beings corrupt each other's moral disposition and make each other evil, and that reason prescribes the formation of ethical communities to overcome radical evil, and that current churches actually contribute to the problem by perpetuating superstition and enthusiasm, then Kant may have wanted to capture the religious establishment.[42] A third option is that Kant may have been grappling towards the insight—taken up by Hegel, Feuerbach, and Marx—that humanity is responsible, through individual and collective effort, to reshape history to achieve our highest aspirations.[43] Kant may have made a crucial step in transforming theology into anthropology and all his talk about God may ultimately be about our own rational capacities for self-legislation.[44] Finally, there is a chance that different themes jostle in Kant's writings and that there are elements that look back towards Luther and Leibniz and others that point to a range of new possibilities (perhaps some not even appreciated yet). The advantage of this last approach is that it enables us to view Kant's philosophy of religion as a toolbox from which we may take what we want and put aside what we do not.

In light of my analysis in Chapter 2, I venture three critiques of Kant's idea of the ethical community. First, Kant's initial presentation of the idea from "mere principles *a priori*" assumes that any rational agent, by following the leading thread of moral reflection, will arrive at the exact same principles. Consider, for example, Kant's claim that a true church will have an unchangeable constitution—"primordial laws publicly laid down for instruction once and for all"—even if its administration may change according to time and circumstances.[45] Kant presents his description of the true church as "an interpretation of the traditional attributes of the Church: one, holy, catholic, apostolic."[46] It may, of course, be the case that rational reflection necessarily leads to the idea of a catholic church with an unalterable constitution. Yet it is worth considering Konrad Lorenz's description of how Kant's account of *a priori* reasoning must be adjusted in light of contemporary biology: "If the '*a priori*' apparatus of possible experience with all its forms of intuition and categories is not something immutably determined by factors extraneous to nature but rather something that mirrors the natural law in contact with which it has evolved in the closest reciprocal interaction, then the boundaries of the transcendental begin to shift."[47] What does this mean for our current discussion? It means that Kant's *a priori* reasoning is historically inflected (but not necessarily historically determined) and that subsequent Kantians may rework Kant's transcendental categories. For instance, we may anticipate that there are many ways to leave the "ethical state of nature" to form collective bodies to advance ethical ideals (themselves open to reconstruction).

Next, Kant provides a philosophic veneer to the Christian common sense of eighteenth-century Prussia. Numerous studies have documented Kant's deep debt to Christian theology in his religious philosophy, including in the reinterpretation of original sin as radical evil. There is nothing, in itself, wrong with Kant's reappropriation of Christian theology or contemporary Kantians endorsing Kant's religious philosophy (however interpreted). The issue is formulating a political theory out of Kant's *Religion*, and Kant's attempt to reconcile contending Christian faiths may not suffice for contemporary pluralistic societies.

Finally, Kant's idea excludes too many faiths that seem to be necessary for any ethico-political coalition in the twenty-first century. One of the defining features of pure rational religion is its concern with the inner disposition of the human being rather than external behavior (which may be regulated by the state). Throughout the *Religion*, Kant excoriates faiths that emphasize orthopraxy rather than a free faith "founded on pure dispositions of the heart (*fides ingenua*)."[48] In addition to disparaging Judaism[49], Kant turns for one moment to consider whether Islamic practices relate to practical concepts and dispositions.

> [Of] the five great commands of the Mohammaden faith—washing, praying, fasting, almsgiving, and the pilgrimage to Mecca—almsgiving alone would deserve to be excepted, if it occurred from a truly virtuous and at the same time religious disposition to human duty, and would thus also truly deserve to be regarded as a means of grace; but in fact, since in this faith almsgiving can well coexist with the extortion from others of things which are offered to God in the person of the poor, it does not deserve to be thus exempted.[50]

Islam, like Judaism, is a "*fetish-faith*" (*Fetishglaube*) that tries to please God through public practices rather than exhort "*service of the heart* (in spirit and truth)."[51] Kant, here, confronts a real dilemma. Any vision of pluralism must draw lines between acceptable and unacceptable moral, political, philosophical, and religious doctrines. In his time and place, Kant tried to broker peace between Catholics and Protestants—and within Protestantism, between Lutheranism and Calvinism—through formulating a religion of reason that different ecclesiastical faiths could honor in their own ways. But Kant's vision of an ethical community does not include the faiths, or visible churches, of Judaism and Islam.

Allen W. Wood describes the insight behind Kant's idea of the ethical community as follows:

> Kant's model . . . is obviously an idealized Enlightenment version of the Christian church, with its evangelical mission one day to unite the whole human race into a single "Kingdom of God." Kant's historical hope is obviously that existing religious communities throughout the world, both Christian and non-Christian, will gradually purify their doctrines and practices through the progress of culture and the influence of enlightened reason. As they do so, they will loosen their attachment to practices, beliefs, doctrines, and authorities whose foundation is parochial and exclusive. They will become less sectarian, more ecumenical, more cosmopolitan. Kant expects them to preserve their traditional cultural identities, but reason will require them to distinguish between the "historical shell" of each limited ecclesiastical faith and the "rational kernel" of pure moral religion—which alone can be the basis for a universal moral community. Each ecclesiastical faith will come to regard itself not as the one true path to salvation, but as one possible historical vehicle (along with others) of the pure rational religion by which humanity will be united in the collective fulfillment of its moral vocation.[52]

With the benefit of over two hundred years' hindsight, how may we evaluate Kant's hope for the purification and unification of religions? Despite the controversy with the Prussian censors over the publication of his late theology writings, Kant does seem to strive to place the core tenets of Christian ethics on a more secure, rational philosophical foundation. By itself, this does not discredit Kant's moral religion, but it does parochialize it. For many Muslims, Euro-American secularism, though in principle neutral between religions, in fact favors Christian—or more precisely, Protestant—expressions of religiosity.[53] Kantians would do well to recognize the Christian elements within Kant's philosophy as they think about how it may be recast for political theories for pluralistic societies. Furthermore, the urgency for this project becomes apparent as Kant's expectation of the demise of historical faiths has not transpired—on the contrary! As José Casanova details in *Public Religions in the Modern World*, many religious traditions today refuse to be marginalized by theories and practices of secularism.[54] These traditions seek to repoliticize the religious and moral spheres and to renormativize the economic and political spheres.[55] Few public religions today say that they are merely historical shells expressing a common human reason, and one of the few that may—mainline Protestantism—has seen a precipitous decline in membership.[56] None of this implies that Kantians should abandon Kant's call for a "banner of virtue" that may unite diverse faiths to communicate and collaborate on pressing ethical projects.[57] The challenge today, rather, is how to renovate the Enlightenment's commitment to interfaith respect and cooperation.

NEW IDEAS OF POLITICAL-RELIGIOUS PLURALISM

How should contemporary heirs of the Enlightenment forge concepts to facilitate beneficial pluralism in the face of an ever-present possibility of sectarian warfare? The minimal definition of a Kantian political theory is an embrace of the central claim of Kant's Copernican revolution that the task of philosophy is to create (or construct), rather than to discover (or find), the concepts that make possible experience and practice.[58] Philosophers have always created concepts; but the *Critique of Pure Reason* legitimated announcing this fact publicly rather than esoterically. In the face of the widespread belief (particularly after the publication of Thomas Kuhn's *The Structure of Scientific Revolutions*[59]) that human beings construct the paradigms through which we perceive the world, one might be tempted to say that we are all Kantians now.[60] Yet numerous contemporary philosophers think that Kant's account of reason is incoherent and many Kantians respond to this charge by offering a metaethical realist account of Kant's philosophy that makes the difference between Kantianism and Platonism almost semantic.[61] Furthermore, billions of people around the world simply embrace a variant or moral realism and think that constructivism signals a fall away from the Truth. And yet the contemporary Enlightenment requires an infusion of Kantian courage to forge concepts to help people around the world envision ways to live together respectfully (even if sometimes agonistically) across deep religious, philosophical, and political differences.[62] In particular, forging mutually satisfactory terms of ethical and political co-operation among Muslims and non-Muslims is one of the most pressing problems of our time.[63]

In this section, I consider how Rawls, Deleuze, and Ramadan exercise Kantian courage to construct new terms of political-religious pluralism. In

Chapters 2 and 3, I describe how Rawls and Deleuze recast Kant's meta-ethics to build their political theories. In this chapter, I will not go through the details of how Rawls or Deleuze employ constructivist procedures to build the concepts under consideration. However, I will note why Rawls and Deleuze construct concepts that depart so far from Kant's in the *Metaphysics of Morals* or the *Religion*. The key element in a Kantian political theory is its conception of the person, and today, we increasingly recognize that persons in contemporary pluralistic societies disagree with one another about some of the most important existential questions. In the *Metaphysics of Morals*, for instance, Kant claims to derive "a system of *a priori* cognition alone" that is then applied to the particular nature of human beings.[64] And yet philosophic candor demands that we see that Kant's practical philosophy is largely (though not entirely) generated from within its historical milieu and meant to be applied to it. Kant himself did not see the need to learn much about Islam or Muslim politics.[65] In our increasingly interconnected world, however, heirs of the Enlightenment must think about how to engage constituencies largely absent from Europe and North America in the eighteenth century. This is a security issue, but it is also an opportunity to think about new forms of democratic pluralism at home and abroad. I now turn to showing how Rawls, Deleuze, and Ramadan exercise Kantian courage to generate new terms of political pluralism.

Overlapping Consensus

Rawls invents the concept of overlapping consensus as part of his project of political liberalism. Enlightenment liberalism, on Rawls's account, aspires to replace Christianity's religious and political authority with a comprehensive secular moral doctrine that addresses all, or nearly all, the great metaphysical questions.[66] In Chapter 2, I considered three reasons why Rawls does not think that Kant's metaphysics of morals is an adequate political theory today: It relies upon an ontology rendered highly contestable by Darwin's *Origin of Species*; it codifies a different common sense than the one present in contemporary liberal democracies; and it ignores the fact that thoughtful people may disagree on the supreme principle of morality. In this section, I explain why Rawls invents the concept of overlapping consensus to fill a lacuna in Kantian political theory. First, political liberals, in formulating a foreign policy, need to reach out to (Muslim) peoples who can be global allies in matters of common concern. Furthermore, political liberals need to be alive to the possibility that considered convictions may change as (Muslim) immigrants and native-born populations change the public political culture.

Rawls opens *The Law of Peoples* by highlighting the difficulty of applying his political conception of justice—justice as fairness—to the globe. The purpose of the book is to "work out the ideals and principles of the *foreign policy* of a reasonably just *liberal* people."[67] Rawls writes the book as a liberal addressing fellow liberals, that is, people who believe in certain fundamental rights and liberties and society's role in providing the minimum all-purpose means to exercise those rights and liberties. We may not assume that most peoples around the world share the same considered convictions as citizens of advanced industrial liberal democracies. So what principles should liberals advocate in the international arena and how? It is incumbent upon liberals to prioritize central foreign policy objectives from those that are more peripheral. Among the more central concerns are stopping genocides, combating aggressive states, helping burdened peoples (for the partially self-interested reason of preventing a negative domino effect on neighboring peoples), and addressing collective action problems such as protecting the natural environment. At the same time, liberals cannot realistically or reasonably expect other peoples to endorse the exact same liberal political principles and policy objectives. Bellicose liberalism overlooks the "great importance of maintaining mutual respect between peoples and of each people maintaining its self-respect, not lapsing into contempt for the other, on one side, and bitterness and resentment, on the other."[68] Rawls's hope is that by setting a good example, liberal peoples can inspire other, decent peoples to honor liberal ideals. But for the foreseeable future, liberals will need to forge alliances with peoples with whom we have only a partial overlap in values.

Rawls's example of a decent people on the global stage is Kazanistan. Kazanistan is an "idealized Islamic people" that organizes itself politically as a decent consultation hierarchy. Rawls models his conception of Kazanistan on the historical Ottoman Empire, but its idealized nature allows it to apply, more or less precisely, to contemporary peoples such as Pakistan and Turkey.[69] Rawls identifies two criteria that qualify Kazanistan as a decent people—that is, as one sufficiently close to liberals to forge international agreements and coalitions. First, Kazanistan is nonaggressive: It may seek to influence other peoples, but it only uses noncoercive means such as diplomacy and commerce. Thus, Kazanistan does not replicate the behavior of "the leading European states during the religious wars of the sixteenth and seventeenth centuries."[70] Second, Kazanistan's political system contains the rudiments of a liberal democratic society even if it is not itself one. Kazanistan extols a "common good idea of justice" that honors human rights for all its citizens; it imposes "*bona fide* moral duties and obligations" on all persons within its territory; and it possesses an independent judiciary that guarantees the possibility of dissent and reform movements.[71] In a lengthy footnote, Rawls argues that Kazanistan actually possesses a political system analogous to the one that Hegel advocated in the *Philosophy of Right*. Rawls's point is that liberal democratic societies do not miraculously appear fully formed, but rather that they evolve gradually and that we liberals should be patient—within limits, for instance, by retaining the right and obligation to intervene in the case of mass human rights abuses—as other peoples find their own ways to democratic constitutionalism.

At the same time, Rawls emphasizes that decent peoples will not necessarily share or even aspire to liberal ideals. In Kazanistan, there is no separation of church and state, Islam is the favored religion, and only Muslims may hold the highest positions of governmental authority.[72] Liberal political systems treat citizens as individuals first and foremost, whereas Kazanistan treats citizens as members of groups—some more favored than others. Why, in principle, should liberals treat Kazanistan as a fully equal member of a Society of Peoples? Why, in other words, should liberals tolerate sexual or religious discrimination in other peoples when it is strictly prohibited at home? If Kazanistan oppresses women, John Tasioulas asks: "Why . . . should we concede, and why should our Kazanistani woman join us in conceding, that 'Kazanistan is the best we can realistically—and coherently—hope for.' After all . . . a present-day Islamic society such as Iran has much in common with 17th century England. There is no obviously insuperable empirical barrier to an Islamic society, whether decent or not, undergoing a comparable transformation in regard to, say, respecting equal freedom of conscience."[73] It is theoretically possible that Muslim-majority societies may transform themselves in analogous ways to seventeenth-century England. Some Muslims themselves argue that Muslims should mine their own reformist resources to move out of Kazanistan in the direction of liberal democratic pluralism.[74] Yet, Rawls insists, the human pursuit of goodness and justice manifests itself in myriad ways, and it is hubris to imagine that every society around the globe will institutionalize the will of the people, or protect human dignity, in exactly the same way. Some peoples may not, upon reflection and with ample evidence, choose liberalism. Liberals should not despair at this fact;

rather, they should try to forge international agreements on the most important topics (while still trying to influence other countries peacefully through just, generous, and admirable behavior). "Enlightenment about the limits of liberalism recommends trying to conceive a reasonably just Law of Peoples that liberal and nonliberal peoples could endorse together."[75]

Rawls coins the term "overlapping consensus" to describe political-religious coalitions that coalesce around certain principles even as the parties may arrive at or conceptualize those principles differently. In the international arena, this means that all liberal and decent peoples can agree to certain principles of global justice even if the peoples "start from within their own comprehensive view and draw on the religious, philosophical, and moral grounds it provides."[76] How do we, global citizens, create an overlapping consensus? By articulating theories of global justice that may garner the principled support of a wide array of liberal and decent peoples.[77] As a political constructivist, Rawls thinks that it is the responsibility of people, here and now, to make those theories. What this means is that an overlapping consensus shifts over time as new ideas appear, as new constituencies emerge and raise their voices, as established constituencies respond to philosophical and historical developments, and so on. Liberals should not view the provisional nature of an overlapping consensus as a forced compromise; rather, liberals should recognize that any political view must adjust to the general conditions of a "normal and human social world" characterized by deep doctrinal differences.[78]

One benefit of the concept of the overlapping consensus is that it welcomes a broader array of faiths than Kant's ethical community, including Jews and Muslims. Importantly, for the thesis of this book, Rawls presents this development as an extension of the Enlightenment spirit.[79] Catholics and Protestants in the sixteenth century did not form an overlapping consensus on the principle of toleration: "Both faiths held that it was the duty of the ruler to uphold the true religion and to repress the spread of heresy and false doctrine."[80] To forestall the possibility of religious warfare, Enlightenment philosophers such as Kant and Hume "hoped to establish a basis of moral knowledge independent of ecclesiastical authority and available to the ordinary reasonable and conscientious person."[81] Alas, Kant and Hume overlooked the possibility that thoughtful citizens of faith might profoundly disagree with their ostensibly rational or scientific practical philosophies. According to Rawls, contemporary heirs of the Enlightenment should apply the principle of toleration to philosophy itself and allow mul-

tiple faiths to flourish in constitutional democracies. Yet citizens should exercise self-restraint when advancing arguments in the public sphere lest it
spark sectarianism. That is why political liberals "do not put forward more
of our comprehensive view than we think needed or useful for the political
aim of consensus."[82] Many Muslims—including conservative ones—may
appreciate political liberalism precisely because it refrains from metaphysical
claims and allows Muslims to frame the ideals of constitutional democracy
in Islamic terms.[83]

A second benefit of the concept of the overlapping consensus is a foundation for international institutions to address global problems. In *Toward
Perpetual Peace*, Kant allows that though a world republic might be the ideal
for rational beings, humanity's imperfections (our "crooked wood") virtually guarantees that the best we may realistically hope for is a pacific federa-
tion that prevents the outbreak of war.[84] How, though, do human beings
advance shared ethical ends without either going through the political route
(limited to states forestalling warfare) or the religious route (of participating
in visible churches recognized by the ethical community)? Rawls's response
is to argue that a Society of Peoples may form cooperative organizations to
address shared ethical ends such as ensuring fair trade among peoples, forming a cooperative banking system, and building international organizations,
such as the United Nations, to facilitate dialogue and collaboration among
the world's peoples.[85] Rawls drops Kant's talk of an "invisible church"; rather,
he addresses urgent practical problems facing global citizens.

A third benefit of the concept of an overlapping consensus is that its
principles are open to revision as convictions change. Here, one might consider how Rawls constructs concepts such as overlapping consensus using
the method of reflective equilibrium: "Since we seek an agreed basis of public justification in matters of justice, and since no political agreement on
those disputed questions can reasonably be expected, we turn instead to
the fundamental ideas we seem to share through the public political culture. From these ideas we try to work out a political conception of justice
congruent with our considered convictions on due reflection."[86] The first
step in concept creation is to research the fundamental ideas of the public
political culture; the second step is to reconstruct them to make them more
internally consistent and less vulnerable to outside objects. The content of
an overlapping consensus may not merely be a *modus vivendi* among competing factions present in a domestic or international order—that would
simply postpone the inevitable strife once power relations shift among con-

stituencies. Yet the content of an overlapping consensus is partly empirical since it draws upon the shared realm of civic experiences for the political body in question. That is why a political liberal foreign policy will appeal to the shared tenets of liberal and decent peoples rather than to the considered convictions of a liberal democratic polity considered in isolation. That is also why Rawls leaves open the possibility that justice as fairness is but one of "a family of reasonable liberal political conceptions of justice."[87] A simple fact about families is that they grow. If Muslims constitute an increasingly important presence in the public political cultures of Europe and North America, then political liberals have to leave open the theoretical possibility that cherished ideals may have to undergo dramatic revision. This is not merely a pragmatic necessity; it also reflects the democratic aspiration to honor the will of the people.[88]

Is political liberalism synonymous with relativism or nihilism? Robert S. Taylor says yes, and argues that the idea of the overlapping consensus (OC) opens the door for the Taliban to enter the international community in good standing.

> Suppose that a nonaggressive but malevolent absolutism wishes to be admitted into a duly expanded society of peoples and thereby secured against invasion, embargoes, etc. Afghanistan under the Taliban— had they not been *indirectly* aggressive by harboring international terrorists—would have provided a splendid real-world example: the Taliban effected a complete exclusion of women from employment and education, the destruction of non-Islamic religious sites, the implementation of cruel forms of criminal punishment, even against apostates, etc. *Should a society of well-ordered peoples try to impose human rights on such a people—by force if needed—or . . . should the scope of toleration and the width of the international OC be expanded to bring this people within a framework of (very limited) international cooperation on peace, trade, etc.?*[89]

Taylor thinks that Rawlsian political theory needs to go back to its Kantian roots in order to formulate a fighting liberalism to oppose injustice around the world. There are at least two problems with this strategy, however. Philosophically, Kant ultimately justifies his practical philosophy by appealing to a "fact of reason" that many Euro-American philosophers (much less non-philosophically trained people around the world) find exceedingly dubious; and politically, the idea of trying to impose a reconstructed Kantian political theory on a domestic or an international political body seems highly unlikely to gain many supporters or much political power. Taylor should encourage the formation of political bodies to work for a more humane future for Afghanistan. The world needs more fighting liberals. The question, though, is whether they should try to go it alone, so to speak, confident in the apodicticity of their arguments, or whether they should reach out to "decent" peoples around the world. Plenty of Muslims think that the Taliban maintains a perverse vision of Islam—read Khaled Hosseini's novels, *The Kite Runner* and *A Thousand Splendid Suns*. An overlapping consensus is a work in progress; the task for liberals is to present terms—from within their own, often Kantian backgrounds—that may resonate with other peoples.

Assemblage

One of Deleuze's great conceptual inventions in *A Thousand Plateaus* is assemblage (*agencement*). In this section, I consider how this concept may enrich liberal efforts to rethink the terms of political alliance with Muslims around the world. The concept of assemblage illuminates the fluidity of identities, the multilayered nature of pluralism, and the decentered form of political networks in the contemporary world. In this instance, we can see how the radical Enlightenment (or the postmodern Left) may help the moderate Enlightenment (or liberal democrats) formulate more ethical and effective political principles and policies.

Deleuze presents the concept of assemblage as part of a Spinozist ontology that views reality as a single substance: "a single phylogenetic lineage, a single machinic phylum, ideally continuous."[90] On this account, there is "a unity of human beings and Nature," every being swimming in the same "flow of matter-movement, the flow of matter in continuous variation."[91] Yet this description of reality risks descending into chaos that combines bodies and attributes at infinite speed. How does reality segment itself into livable parts? There is something like Platonic ideas that pilot the formation of physical bodies. Deleuze calls these incorporeal but effective entities "abstract machines." An abstract machine is sometimes defined by the name and date of an author and book in which it first becomes manifest. Political theory and theorists thus matter, as the envelopes of the abstract machines that they express. Yet an abstract machine becomes effectual by coagulating into something concrete: an assemblage. "We will call an *assemblage* every constellation of singularities and traits deducted from the flow—selected, organized, stratified—in such a way as to converge (consistency) artificially and naturally; an assemblage, in this sense, is a veritable invention. Assemblages may group themselves into extremely vast constellations constituting 'cultures,' or even 'ages'; within these constellations, the assemblages still differentiate the phyla or the flow."[92] The first quality of an assemblage is coherence. An assemblage hangs together, persists, and interacts with other bodies. The content of an assemblage is the "actions and passions of bodies," that is, material parts that affect and are affected by other concrete entities.[93] The expression of an assemblage is "the set of incorporeal transformations," most commonly language, emanating from a body.[94] One quality of an assemblage, stated simply, is that it has a body and it communicates with other bodies. This feature of assemblages matches up with a common sense belief in concrete objects and meaningful words.

The second quality of an assemblage, however, is porosity. To survive in a complex world, human beings have to simplify reality so that they may quickly identify needs, such as food, and threats, such as lions. Human cognition, according to Henri Bergson and Friedrich Nietzsche, is subtractive, that is, the human mind subtracts data to identify patterns that may sustain the organism.[95] Yet philosophy—according to the minor tradition in which Deleuze inserts himself—illuminates the fuzzy borders that define corporeal and linguistic bodies. An assemblage holds a certain territory: but it is also always in the process of falling apart (deterritorialization) and reconstituting itself (reterritorialization), in the same way that a human body is constantly losing and generating cells. An assemblage possesses a certain code that governs its processes, but it is also always reinterpreting (decoding) its rules and producing new ones (over- or recoding). The key point is that assemblages always "open onto something else, assemblages of another type, the molecular, the cosmic."[96] Everything in the universe is, in principle, connected to everything else: every border is permeable.

The payoff to the concept of assemblage is that it widens our political aperture. Of course, political scientists and philosophers need to pay attention to bodies and identities. Despite a caricature of his work as "extra-worldly," Deleuze knows that political philosophy must address the real conditions of actual assemblages.[97] But *A Thousand Plateaus* seeks to construct a philosophical vocabulary to help us perceive the layers that, in John Protevi's words, are above, below, and alongside bodies politic.[98] That is, any political assemblage is part of a larger (meteorological, cosmological, political, cultural, economic) assemblage; constituted by micropolitical processes that often elude scientific observation; and affected by other political bodies with which it comes into contact. If a photograph captures the actual contours of a landscape, Cezanne's or Van Gogh's paintings express the energetic flows coursing through rocks and flowers. Analogously, if mainstream political science or theory describes the power relations between definable entities, Deleuzian political theory helps us perceive the virtual layer of politics that is real but not amenable to common sense or scientific representation. One does not have to be a Spinozist to take advantage of this insight.

In the context of envisioning the future of political-religious pluralism, the concept of assemblage contributes at least three things to political liberalism. First, it highlights the constructed nature of such terms as Catholicism, Protestantism, Islam, the West, peoples, or any other identity marker in contemporary political discourse. The point of Deleuzian political theory is not to abolish the fiction that our concepts correspond to real objects: we need such fictions to navigate the world.[99] And yet we also need to be alert to the fine-grain distinctions that exist in any political-religious body. An example might illustrate. In *Islam and Liberal Citizenship*, Andrew March's first principle of comparative ethics is to theorize from more orthodox sources to less: "Epistemic communities develop more and less authoritative bodies of doctrine, and outside interpreters should strive to conjecture first from within the more authoritative sources."[100] March's "canon first" principle is sensible: If political liberals are to conjecture Islamic arguments defending the principles of constitutional democracy, they ought to draw upon the sources that many if not most Muslims consider central to their religious way of life (*din*). The problem is March's statement that "there is no shortage of 'liberal' or 'moderate' Muslim intellectuals" alongside the recognition that "internal reformers face the danger of being shunned, ridiculed, or killed."[101] March, then, focuses on hegemonic arguments within Islam while dismissing liberals or moderates as peripheral to Muslim politics. One can see the hazard in March's position if one considers that a political liberal study of the seventeenth-century Dutch Jewish community would marginalize Benedict Spinoza. At the time, he was excommunicated; in the eyes of posterity, he is one of the great figures of the historical Enlightenment. Shouldn't we be alert to the possibility of Muslim Spinozas who stretch the borders of what it means to be a Muslim in the modern world? Consider, for example, Abdullahi Ahmed An-Na'im 2008 "Celebration of Heresy Conference."[102] March states in *Islam and Liberal Citizenship* that he prefers "exploring the possibility of an overlapping consensus with views less metaphysically and hermeneutically innovative than those of An-Na'im."[103] Deleuzian political theory may complement Rawlsian political liberalism by investigating the work of Muslim "heretics" in case the latter hold a key to the future of at least part of the Muslim community.

A second benefit of the concept of assemblage is that it discloses multiple layers of political-religious analysis. Late Rawls, once again, sought to find political conceptions of justice that could gain the support of an overlapping consensus of reasonable (and decent) comprehensive doctrines. Thus, in *Islam and Liberal Citizenship*, March theorizes an "ideal moral encounter" between "political liberalism as an ideal theory of social cooperation and Islamic doctrine as a tradition of systematic thought."[104] Political theory must pay attention to traditions of systematic doctrinal thought, just as political science must observe and systematize empirical evidence about political bodies. Yet there is a somatic or visceral level to political thinking not captured by focusing on the doctrinal level. Deleuze writes: "Take aggregates of the perception or feeling type: their molar organization, their rigid segmentarity, does not preclude the existence of an entire world of unconscious micropercepts, unconscious affects, fine segmentations that grasp or experience different things, are distributed and operate differently."[105] A political assemblage has a coherent identity (molar organization) and clearly delineated structure and parts (rigid segmentarity), but it also affects other bodies in ways that elude quantitative study (micropercepts), that transpire beneath the level of consciousness (unconscious affects) and that may even work against the explicit intentions of the assemblage (fine segmentations). The Al-Jazeera satellite news network, for instance, transmits information, but it also conveys images of Iraqi opposition figures debating their critics, feminists challenging Islamists on the issues of women's rights, and Kurds challenging Al-Jazeera itself for its silence concerning Saddam Hussein's atrocities.[106] In Deleuzian terms, Al-Jazeera transmits doctrinal content as well as images and sounds that help constitute a transversal subjectivity—a new Arab public sphere—with cognitive and affective layers. Rawlsian political theory does not necessarily reject this type of political analysis. But Deleuzian concepts may help flesh out political liberalism by highlighting how micropolitical forces can impact macropolitical events.

A third benefit of the concept of assemblage is that it presents a possibility of political coalitions without a center. A persistent assumption of Euro-American political theory is that political bodies need a common ideology, or religion, to sustain disagreements on peripheral issues.[107] Thus Kant holds out hope for one true religion, and Rawls envisions political liberalism (or the Law of Peoples) constituting the center circle in the Venn Diagram of society's reasonable (and decent) comprehensive moral doctrines. Politics sometimes does need centralized institutions and ideologies, such as the United Nations and the UN Charter on Human Rights. Yet sometimes political bodies need to assemble protean and provisional coalitions to address pressing common problems among people(s) who disagree at a profound level.

Take, for instance, the twenty-first–century need to fashion an assemblage to combat the al-Qaeda war machine. This assemblage will have consistency insofar as it has the stated goal of destroying an organization committed to draining the global political garden of diversity. Yet this assemblage will necessarily be profoundly complex, combining British, French, German, and Spanish intelligence agencies sharing information on militant Islamist groups in Europe; Afghani, Pakistani, Saudi Arabian, and Turkish governments combating militants while still proclaiming Islamic ideals; ordinary people throughout the world alerting authorities of potential terror attacks and protesting abuses committed in the name of preventing terror; religious believers throughout the world condemning militant extremists; and so on. This assemblage will bring together people who may strongly dislike each other about other issues: a Deleuzian political theory points out the futility and unethical consequences of employing the language of "with us or against us." This assemblage will require elites, politicians, and statesmen, as well as celebrities, entertainers, intellectuals, newscasters, restaurateurs, sports planners, and others to participate in the micropolitical battles that cultivate the soil on which political pluralism can flourish. Finally, hopefully, someday this assemblage will no longer need to exist.

Space of Testimony

In the eighteenth-century, Kant set himself the task of philosophically unifying different sects of Christianity; the task of the contemporary Enlightenment is to broaden the spectrum of religions that may confidently participate in ethical assemblages. In the introduction, I argue that Tariq Ramadan advances a call for Muslims to reread their sources to enact an intellectual revolution along the lines of Kant's Copernican revolution. Here I consider how Ramadan embodies Kantian courage to create a new concept of political-religious pluralism: the space of testimony (*dar al-shahada*). Certain Kantians and liberals may never trust a political thinker who explicitly situates his argument so firmly in a religious tradition. Ramadan simply disagrees with Kant's moral philosophy that proceeds as if God's existence is a mere postulate that reason gives itself.[108] Yet Rawls's and Deleuze's political theory suggests why those who situate themselves in the Kantian, or Enlightenment, tradition may be willing to consider Ramadan a joint participant in a common venture. Ramadan enjoins Muslims to exercise "autonomous critical rationality" (*ijtihad*) in the realm of social affairs (*al-muamalat*) so that Muslims and non-Muslims may freely and respectfully testify to the truth of their ethical visions.[109] I shall consider in more detail how Ramadan presents his case and how the contemporary Enlightenment may respond to it.

Ramadan invents the concept of the space of testimony to highlight the theoretical and practical dangers of maintaining a distinction between the *dar al-islam* (abode of islam) and *dar al-harb* (abode of war). Sayyid Qutb, in the Islamist manifesto *Milestones*, articulates one influential account of this distinction: "There is only one place on earth which can be called the home of Islam (*dar al-islam*), and it is that place where the Islamic state is established and the *shari'ah* is the authority and God's limits are observed, and where all the Muslims administer the affairs of the state with mutual consultation. The rest of the world is the home of hostility (*dar-al-harb*)."[110] Qutb is not a robust political pluralist. Muslims may sign treaties with other countries, but these do not change the fact that Muslims must establish the Islamic state either through preaching or "striving through fighting" (*Jihaad bis saif*).[111] Muslims may permit other people of the book (*ahl al-kitab*), Jews and Christians, to practice their religion in the confines of their own homes, but the comprehensive teaching of Islam must penetrate every other aspect of life. Ironically, Qutb employs Kantian-sounding terms to explain why Muslims must not tolerate anything like Kant's principle of autonomy: "Only in the Islamic way of life do all men become free from the servitude of some men to others and devote themselves to the worship of God alone."[112] Numerous qualifiers are in order here: Qutb represents a small population of the Muslim world; many Muslims may hold these views explicitly while actually honoring pluralistic norms; we should not focus too much on (legitimate) threats lest we too harshly color our perceptions of real-world Muslim politics.[113] Yet Qutb's perspective is common enough among religious activists—as is the equally problematic English distinction between Islam and the West[114]—and the Prophetic tradition against innovation (*bida'*) in Islam has made many Muslim scholars ('*ulama*) hesitant to criticize a traditional political binary.[115] Although Ramadan is not the first Muslim political thinker to criticize imitation (*taqlid*) or call for a renewal of the spirit of philosophy (*falsafah*) among Muslims, Ramadan's reformist strategy of explicitly drawing upon Euro-American Enlightenment sources such as Kant's philosophy, as well as the pluralist political vision he articulates, makes a notable contribution to Islamic and Euro-American political thought.[116]

Ramadan constructs the concept of the space of testimony in his books, *To Be a European Muslim* and *Western Muslims and the Future of Islam*. Initially, Ramadan provides a genealogy to denaturalize the *dar al-Islam/dar al-harb* distinction. The terms do not occur in the Qur'an or the Prophetic tradition and thus "do not pertain to the fundamental sources of Islam whose principles are presented for the whole world (*lil-alamin*), over all time and beyond any geographical limitation."[117] Islamic scholars, rather, invented the concepts, during the first three centuries of Islam, to formulate a coherent foreign policy given the geopolitical reality of their time. The scholars studied the Prophet's attitude after the Peace of Hudaybiyya and identified four relevant criteria: the population, the ownership of the land, the nature of the government, and the laws governing the country. From the beginning, there have been ambiguities and tensions between the criteria. The Maliki school argues that Muslims must own the land and be governed by Islamic law for a place to qualify as *dar al-Islam*. The Hanafi school, by contrast, stipulates that *dar al-Islam* is wherever Muslims are protected and safe to practice their religion. Furthermore, Islamic scholars disagree among themselves on whether a Muslim-majority population suffices to call a place *dar al-Islam*. To apply old concepts to contemporary reality "as they were thought out more than ten centuries ago appears to be a methodological mistake."[118] Over the past thousand years, empires have risen and collapsed, Muslims have migrated throughout the world, and everybody has been affected by globalization. There is no good reason why Muslims must blindly follow the juridical categories of a by-gone era.[119]

According to Ramadan, Muslims need to reread the texts and contexts in light of historical developments. Ramadan asks: What elements permit the flourishing of the Muslim personality today?[120] Reworking Abu Hamid al-Ghazali's definition of the objectives of the law, Ramadan identifies five socio-political conditions that protect the public welfare: freedom to manifest faith and spirituality; freedom to worship individually and collectively; physical security; freedom to educate others about Islam; and freedom to participate in the social, political, and economic life of one's community.[121] Turning back to the context, Ramadan finds that Western societies by and large satisfy the objectives of the law, or, in Euro-American discourse, secure Muslims' fundamental rights. Western Muslims have the rights to practice Islam (declare their faith, pray, pay the purifying tax, fast, and make the pilgrimage to Mecca), to public education, to found organizations, to autonomous representation, and to appeal to the law.[122] Without minimizing the problems that Muslims face in Europe and North America, Ramadan thinks that Western Muslims "are at home and must consider the attainments of these societies as their own."[123]

Ramadan considers several possibilities offered by fellow Muslim intellectuals to describe this unique context where Muslims may flourish as religious minorities. Yusuf al-Qaradawi writes a book *On the Law and Jurisprudence of Muslim Minorities* with the subtitle: *The Life of Muslims in Other Societies.* Describing Europe or the United States as "other societies," however, means preserving antiquated notions of necessity (*darura*) and legal exemptions (*rukhas*).[124] Certain Shafi'i scholars speak of the Western countries as *dar al-ahd* (abode of treaty) or *dar al-amn* (abode of safety), but these concepts presuppose a matrix where communities in the *dar al-Islam* and the *dar al-harb* sign contracts.[125] Faysal al-Mawlawi calls the West the *dar al-dawa* (abode of invitation to God), but this implies that Muslims do not have a principled commitment to pluralism but rather aim to convert everyone to Islam.[126] Though these latter possibilities are better than the *dar al-Islam / dar al-harb* binary, the weight of the past weighs heavy on the present. Ramadan's Copernican revolution demands that Muslim political thinkers overturn old, simple, binary visions of reality and exert themselves to create concepts to grasp the distinct possibilities of our time and place.

Thus Ramadan proposes the term *space of testimony* (*dar al-shahada*).[127] Ramadan translates the Arabic *dar* into English space because it makes no sense, in a world of cell phones, jet planes, and the Internet, to divide the world into two abodes, or houses.[128] Space better captures the openness of the global religious-political landscape. The term *shahada*, for Ramadan, has two valences. Every Muslim, to be recognized as such, must pronounce before God and humanity: "There is no god but God and Muhammad is His messenger." Muslims must also bear testimony in their actions as well as their words. The space of testimony assigns Muslims "the responsibility to remind others of the presence of God and to act in such a way that our presence among them and with them is, in itself, a reminder of the Creator, spirituality, and ethics."[129] The space of testimony is a place where Muslims are free from government intrusion on their religious beliefs and practices and free to teach others about Islam and act politically on Islamic principles. This is a new development in human history and it deserves a new concept: the space of testimony.

Islamists disagree with Ramadan's contention that Western Muslims should not work to make a literal reading of *shar'ia* the supreme law of the land,[130] and even Muslims committed to a "middle way" may question whether Muslims should accept the persistence of un-Islamic activities on the grounds that they are not imposed on Muslims.[131] For Ramadan, though, it is ethically and practically imperative for Muslims to be loyal, active citizens alongside citizens of other faiths in European and North American societies. For Ramadan, Muslims must find a way to join something like Kant's ethical community, Rawls's overlapping consensus, or Deleuze's assemblage, even if Islamic concepts articulate the political universe in a different way.

And yet it is important to see that the concept of the space of testimony stretches the boundaries of contemporary Kantian political theory. In Rawls's overlapping consensus, citizens, speaking on constitutional essentials in a public forum, must sooner or later present "proper political reasons" that are acceptable to reasonable citizens of other faiths.[132] Ramadan thinks that European and North American Muslims tacitly accept the social contract underwriting the constitutional democratic structure and, unless directly ordered to violate their conscience, must exhibit "absolute faithfulness to agreements, contracts, and treaties that have been explicitly or silently entered into."[133] However, Ramadan maintains that Muslims must refuse the strong secular demand that faith and practice be confined to the private sphere. "Assertive and confident, [Muslims] have to remind the people around them of God, of spirituality and, regarding social affairs, to work for values and ethics, justice and solidarity."[134] For Ramadan, Islam is not just an abstract belief but also an ethics that infuses a Muslim's whole life. In this way, Ramadan shares a Deleuzian concern for cultivating all of the dimensions of rhizomatic democratic pluralism, as well as the Deleuzian effort to prevent any one religion from establishing the trunk within which pluralism may be sustained. Ramadan thinks, as a Muslim, about the concrete question of how Muslims and non-Muslims may mutually and beneficially transform their political and social life. Muslims must be free, individually and collectively, to embody Islam and educate others about its message—even forming, if necessary, what Nancy Fraser calls "subaltern counterpublics" that propose radical alternatives to the majority's perspective on particular issues.[135] Ramadan believes that other faiths must have the same rights to practice and express their values—as long as everyone accepts the tacit social contract with its prohibition on doctrinal enforcement—but that the secular conceit of a religiously neutral public sphere must be abandoned.

"If God had willed, He would have made you one community but things are as they are to test you in what He has given you. So compete with each other in doing good."[136] Ramadan interprets this famous verse of the Qur'an (5:48) to say that God has willed diversity and Muslims should appreciate that the world has hermitages, synagogues, and chapels as well as mosques. In *The Quest for Meaning*, Ramadan emphasizes the common values shared across religious, secular, and indigenous spiritual traditions. Yet Ramadan also thinks that Muslims may compete with adherents of other faiths in presenting and acting on ethical principles. Muslims have the right to assert their values in public discussions about drug and alcohol abuse, the disintegration of family and community life, the destruction of the natural environment, and the future of their communities. In *Islam, the West, and the Challenges of Modernity* Ramadan argues that Islam does not share the "tragic consciousness" that permeates European philosophy and Christianity.[137] "We are indeed dealing with two different universes of reference, two civilizations, and two cultures."[138] Ramadan disputes the clashing civilizations thesis, but he also believes that Muslims have a right to criticize, at a profound level, present-day Euro-American values.[139] The space of testimony, in sum, invites Muslims and non-Muslims to respectfully collaborate and compete with one another in presenting and acting on their ethical visions.

Ramadan, to be sure, is not a doctrinaire Kantian, and his vision of religious pluralism directly challenges Kant's dismissal of Islam as a "fetish-faith." As a Muslim who professes the *shahada*, Ramadan would refuse Wood's call for him to discard the "historical shell" of Islam and "accept the 'rational kernel' of pure moral religion." Ramadan may consider joining a Rawlsian overlapping consensus, but not if that means Muslims may not exercise critical loyalty in their societies and publicly proclaim a Muslim perspective on political issues.[140] Ramadan would join Deleuze's effort to broaden and deepen the pluralist imaginary to make room for ways of life that do not conform to the Christian majority, and he would insist that Muslims have a role in shaping Europe's and America's postsecular future. Ramadan, in sum, draws upon Kant's great contribution to the history of philosophy—the Copernican revolution that says that we are the legislators of our theoretical and practical concepts and principles—to broaden and challenge the Kantian and Enlightenment traditions. This does not mean that contemporary Kantians need to respect or agree with everything that Ramadan says—on the contrary! The Enlightenment thrives on debate between its moderate, radical, and (now) Muslim members. It is pure caprice to forbid Muslims to learn their own lessons from Kant and make their own contributions to the post-Kantian legacy.

FORESTALLING RELIGIOUS WARFARE

Contemporary political theorists face a choice: buttress the post-Westphalian secular order or reconstruct it to account for the new religious-political pluralism. Secularism—the doctrine of the separation of church and state instituted by Enlightenment philosophers such as Kant—has had some success in the past three or four centuries containing religious warfare (though much of this success was set back by the Holocaust). It would be a mistake to minimize this accomplishment and try to raze Kant's philosophy or its political analogues. There is still a lot to be gained from studying such notions as the ethical community, and though Kant's vision is constrained by its personal and historical limits, contemporary political actors and theorists ought to recover its guiding insight that we need a "banner of virtue" that may rally people from numerous faiths into overlapping consensuses, assemblages, or a space of testimony. And yet, as this last sentence illuminates, we—who identify with the Enlightenment more broadly or the Kantian tradition more specifically—need to drop Kant's doctrinal insistence of pure practical reason (at least in the political realm) and grasp the new political pluralism around us and invent concepts accordingly. In this section, I say a bit more about why heirs of the Enlightenment may follow the lead of Rawls, Deleuze, and Ramadan and exercise Kantian courage.

In contemporary Euro-American political theory, we are currently witnessing a widespread call for a return to the fundamental principles of the Enlightenment. Robert S. Taylor, in *Reconstructing Rawls*, articulates one powerful version of this thesis. In the face of resurgent religious fundamentalism around the globe, the notion that contemporary Kantians should make peace with "benevolent absolutisms" or "decent hierarchical societies" seems absurd. Far better to lock arms with other comprehensive Enlightenment liberals and stand up to religious fundamentalisms. "The lion's share of philosophical labor by analytic liberals should be devoted to perfecting, extending, as well as popularizing universalistic comprehensive liberalisms of *all* stripes—Lockean, Kantian, Millian—as part of a shared liberal philosophical project: to undermine ideological support for the illiberal political institutions and values that are still widespread in the world today."[141] Taylor's contribution to this project is to ground Rawls's early conception of justice as fairness on a more secure ground than the public political culture to which Rawls eventually turned. According to Taylor, Enlightenment liberals may rework Kant's argument in Section III of the *Groundwork* to advance the claim that human beings must presuppose themselves as free. Then, once this has been established, Taylor deduces a Kantian conception of the person that will find political fulfillment in justice as fairness as a universalistic Kantian liberalism. It is worth noting, however, that this argument brazenly alienates most Muslims.[142] In brief: after the Mihna—the Muslim community's civil war in the ninth century—most Muslims deny that human beings have the ability to choose their own destiny. The Ash'arite doctrine accepted by most mainstream Sunni theologians holds that "on earth there is neither good nor evil except what God wills, and that things come to be by the will of God."[143] This is the doctrine behind the common Arabic saying: *In shah Allah* ("God willing"). Taylor and other Kantians may dispute this doctrine. But liberals must decide whether they want the basis of their universalistic agenda to be one that roughly a billion Muslims around the world will reject out of hand. The question is not merely one of self-interest. The question is rather whether the Enlightenment may expand its self-conception to include self- and other-critical Muslims to address common ethical political problems. There is certainly a place for Lockeans, Kantians, and Millians in any contemporary Enlightenment; but there should also be room for Muslim reformers walking in the footsteps of Jamal al-Din al-Afghani, Muhammad 'Abduh, and Muhammad Iqbal.

Is there a realistic prospect for an Islamic Enlightenment? Consider the legacy of the Nahda.[144] For thinkers in this movement, Muslims could learn from the Europeans and Americans, particularly regarding science and technology, but also retain confidence in the truth and power of Islam. These thinkers valued the "spirit of philosophy" and often traveled abroad and read European authors.[145] Rifa'a al-Tahtawi (1801–73), for example, visited Paris in the early nineteenth century and, upon his return to Egypt, supervised the translation of books by Rousseau, Voltaire, and Montesquieu.[146] For certain Muslim intellectuals in the early nineteenth century, Europe presented "a path to be followed."[147] Yet the relationship between Europe and the

Muslim community deteriorated throughout the nineteenth century and twentieth century: for exogenous reasons, such as the presence of European armies in Egypt, Algeria, and Tunisia, the United States' recognition of the state of Israel, and the Arab defeat by Israel in 1967; and for endogenous reasons, such as the rise of Islamism. As Elizabeth Suzanne Kassab details in *Contemporary Arab Thought: Cultural Critique in Comparative Perspective*, Muslim intellectuals throughout the twentieth century have believed that "only genuine critical thinking can lead the way out of all the damage and the multiple forms of servitude."[148] Yet Kassab ends her book on a plaintiff note, observing that spaces for critical thinking (such as independent universities) are disappearing from the Muslim world and that we still await the rise of new Nahda impulses.[149] Political scientists, then, may be despondent about the probability of Islam going through an Enlightenment or another Nahda. And, in fact, many Muslims around the world resent the implication that they need to replicate the exact steps of the eighteenth-century Euro-American Enlightenment.[150]

Yet political theorists need not despair. "A key role of theory," William E. Connolly observes, "is to probe positive possibilities that might otherwise be overlooked" and to "inspire the pursuit of those possibilities."[151] Political theorists are visionaries that see things that other people do not (yet) and mobilize people to actualize them. Kant was a visionary: He identified ends (such as the ethical community) that have inspired progressive political thinkers and actors for over two centuries. Rawls, Deleuze, and Ramadan are also visionaries: They envision a world in which political constituencies, from multiple religious backgrounds, may dialogue and collaborate to advance common goals of actualizing human safety, freedom, and liberty. Rawls and Deleuze are rethinking the Euro-American Enlightenment to make it more welcoming to people from diverse religious faiths; Ramadan is renewing the Nahda to consider how Muslims may be loyal, critical citizens in pluralistic constitutional democracies; and together they exercise Kantian courage to create new concepts to facilitate interreligious cooperation. The great question of our time is whether they, and kindred spirits, may be able to inspire enough people in time to prevent future religious wars that may dwarf the scale of the Thirty Years War.

Conclusion:

The Battle for Autonomy

In *Kant and the Limits of Autonomy* Susan Meld Shell explains why she—and many other political philosophers and theorists—treat Kant's legacy so seriously. Kant's practical philosophy has inspired liberal democrats for over two centuries. The concept of autonomy, in particular, has served as the foundation for (American) progressive political thought from the time of Abraham Lincoln up to the War on Terror.[1] Religious fundamentalists attack Kantian philosophy from an external perspective—the notion of humans giving themselves the moral law strikes many people around the world as blasphemous. As troubling, however, is the recent trend within left academia—the natural home of the Enlightenment legacy—to historicize Kant's practical philosophy. "In my view, the historicism that pervades contemporary histories of philosophy is not unconnected to the weaknesses of most defense of liberalism today, both in and outside the academy."[2] Shell raises a legitimate problem. Heidegger, one of the most famous twentieth-century critics of Kant and the Enlightenment, notoriously endorsed the Nazis.[3] Furthermore, the events of 9/11 indicate that "a newly resurgent

Islam" may pose a threat to the stability of liberal democracies.[4] The Enlightenment legacy is under attack, intellectually and physically, and we, its self-identified heirs, must decide how to proceed in the twenty-first century. I view Enlightenment liberals—or those who think that we need to reclaim the great principles of the eighteenth-century Euro-American Enlightenment—as key participants in the twenty-first–century Enlightenment as I have tried to present it in this book. Yet strong, or dogmatic, Enlightenment liberalism may betray the Enlightenment's mission of cultivating fruitful pluralism among different societal and global constituencies. Kant scholars, in particular, may preserve Kant's legacy at the cost of making it just another militant universalism that thoughtful people around the globe must resist or contain. In the conclusion to this book, I pull together arguments from Rawls, Deleuze, and Ramadan to argue why progressives must exercise Kantian courage—or philosophical autonomy—to chart a new path for the twenty-first century Enlightenment.

LIMITING AUTONOMY

In *The Invention of Autonomy* J. B. Schneewind explains why most political theorists and actors on the left embrace the concept of autonomy. "The early modern moral philosophy in which the conception of morality as self-governance emerged . . . made a vital contribution to the rise of the Western liberal vision of the proper relations between individual and society."[5] The concept of autonomy expresses the moral foundation of democratic politics: The collective is the self (*auto*) that gives itself the law (*nomos*). Political autonomy challenges the idea that a king, elite, or church should govern the polity. Furthermore, the concept of autonomy expresses the key insight of modern moral philosophy that each person is capable of knowing and respecting the moral law (moral autonomy) or their own life plans (personal autonomy).[6] The vast majority of political theorists on the left thus embrace the concept of autonomy. Yet there is an ongoing effort to limit the excesses of autonomy, namely its potential implication that human beings may legislate any laws that they wish rather than the strict (or categorical) laws that morality seems to require. In this section, I consider Charles Larmore's critique of Kant's conception of autonomy as well as Allen W. Wood's defense of Kantian autonomy that, in effect, agrees with Larmore's fears about moral relativism and historicism. In the next and final section, I argue why contemporary heirs of the Enlightenment need courage to face these fears head on and make our way bravely in the post-Kantian philosophical landscape.

Charles Larmore has recently launched an attack against Kant and the Kantian tradition in the provocatively titled *The Autonomy of Morality*. Larmore writes from the perspective of a metaethical realist for whom "not all that exists is physical or psychological in character. Reasons, which are irreducibly normative, must also figure among what is real."[7] What Larmore is for is hard to glean from *The Autonomy of Morality*. He calls himself a lowercase platonist because he wants to distance himself from Plato's account of an extra-worldly realm of forms.[8] As an example of a moral truth that is woven into the nature of things, Larmore cites the biblical formula: "Love thy neighbor as thyself."[9] Yet Larmore does not flesh out a biblical morality nor does he, as a self-professed political liberal, want to make the Bible the law of the land.[10] Larmore aligns himself with the tradition of rational intuitionism that Rawls distances himself from in his *Lectures on the History of Moral Philosophy*, yet Larmore does not dedicate much of his book to explicating the rational intuitionist philosophies of Samuel Clarke, Leibniz, H. A. Prichard, or W. D. Ross.[11] Larmore may be on the path to explicating a systematic and coherent positive account of morality.[12] But in *The Autonomy of Morality*, Larmore makes perfectly clear what he is against: Kant's conception of autonomy as self-legislation.

Kant's conception of autonomy, according to Larmore, holds that the authority of moral principles arises from their origin in our own practical thinking. After the Scientific Revolution, Kant believed that human beings could no longer trust the natural world to supply moral principles. The Newtonian universe has no freedom and provides little moral guidance. The only way to rescue morality is to consider ourselves the legislators of the moral law. For many of Kant's critics, this notion seems sinful: a blatant call for human beings to pick the fruit of (or even plant) the tree of the knowledge of good and evil.[13] To Kantians who seek to downplay this element in his thought, Larmore emphasizes that Kant wrote in the *Groundwork*, "that reason is the 'author' or 'originator' (*Urheberin*) of its principles, a point confirmed by his frequent talk of reason giving (*geben*) itself its laws."[14]

Larmore appreciates some of Kant's insights, including the need to treat other human beings with respect and dignity. Larmore's problem is that Kant's account of moral autonomy is incoherent. Rational beings need reasons to make moral judgments. Human beings can identify or even make some reasons, but ultimately we must always appeal to reasons that we find or discover. "The idea of autonomy cannot provide a complete account of the 'normativity' that structures all our thought and action. . . . Self-legislation, when it does occur, is an activity that takes place in the light of reasons that we must antecedently recognize."[15] Larmore, in other words, accuses Kant of a performative contradiction: Kant denies the need for onto-logically grounded reasons at the same time as his moral philosophy tacitly appeals to them. Kant's moral philosophy explains some aspects of practical deliberation, but it denies the fundamental fact that "we take our moral bearings from an independent order of right and wrong."[16] Larmore aims to replace the Kantian tradition's thesis that we make or write the moral law with the thesis that morality exists and that the task of human reason is to find and respond to it.

Larmore calls himself a political liberal insofar as he agrees with Rawls that the government cannot reasonably enforce any one comprehensive moral doctrine.[17] Yet Larmore thinks that political liberals need to recognize that citizens must agree on a common moral ground that human reason can discover. "We as citizens do well to see that our political life is founded upon a principle, the principle of equal respect, whose authority does not derive from our collective will since it serves to define the democratic ideal itself."[18] The ontological foundation of democratic politics is equal human dignity; once this is recognized, then citizens may subsequently disagree on how they pursue their life plans, some going more in the direction of Kantian and Millian autonomy, others taking up the Romantic tradition's emphasis on belonging and custom.[19] At all costs, though, political liberals must renounce the idea of Kantian constructivism, that is, the notion that human beings can make out of their own practical reflections the funda-mental moral or political laws.[20] For Kant's conception of autonomy opens the door to less-responsible philosophers, such as Nietzsche, who have no hesitation "inventing" values that legitimate immoral acts. Far better, for Larmore, for political theorists to resuscitate the natural law tradition that holds that there are certain laws that no human being may abrogate.

Ironically, Wood, one of the most vocal defenders of Kantian ethics in contemporary political theory, agrees with Larmore's critique of autonomy as self-legislation. In *Kant's Ethical Thought*, Wood specifies how Kantians are to interpret Kant's advocacy of autonomy. Kant extols the idea of au-tonomy that "the moral law is binding on me only because it is regarded as proceeding from my own will."[21] Yet the will may not legislate anything that our animal desires and inclinations may wish: "I cannot loose myself from the moral law, because it is not up to me to make or unmake the idea of a rational will."[22] Practical reason, or the rational will, is real and, when we follow its progress of moral reflection—as Kant documents in Section II of the *Groundwork*—we necessarily arrive at the categorical imperative in all of its formulations. Kant, for Wood, is a metaethical realist and thus is not vulnerable to Larmore's charge of moral decisionism.

Wood presents the case for Kant as a realist—rather than a constructivist—through a careful tracking of Kant's terminology. In the *Groundwork*, for example, "we should be struck by the frequency with which Kant uses expressions conveying the thought that autonomy of the will is only a way of *considering* or *regarding* the objectively valid moral law."[23] Kant does not use the concept of autonomy to imply that we literally legislate, or decide, the moral law, but rather that we must "regard" (*ansehen*) or "consider" (*betrachten*) ourselves as the legislator. Furthermore, in the *Lectures on Ethics*, Kant states that the moral law is a natural, rather than an arbitrary or positive, law: "All laws are natural or arbitrary. If the obligation springs from the *lex naturalis*, and has this as the ground of the action, it is *obligatio naturalis*, but if it has arisen from *lex arbitraria*, and has its ground in the will of another, it is *obligatio positiva*."[24] For Kant, the moral law is a *lex naturalis*, and no human (or any other rational being, including God), may erase or change it. What is new about Kant's philosophy if he merely preserves the language of natural law? Kant locates the natural law in practical reason rather than entities inside or outside of the world: "If the content of the moral law 'lies in the nature' of something . . . the faculty of will or practical reason is precisely the sort of thing in whose nature you might have expected it to lie."[25] Kant places the moral law on a more secure foundation—practical reason—than any of the fluctuating or unknowable objects of heteronomous moralities. Autonomy, for Wood, means recognizing and obeying the one moral law that applies to rational beings such as humans.

What are the political consequences for saying that Kantian ethics is true? In *Kant's Ethical Thought*, Wood explains and defends "the final form of Kant's ethical theory," namely, the *Metaphysics of Morals* divided between a doctrine of right (*Rechtslehre*) and a doctrine of virtue (*Tugendslehre*). The doctrine of right addresses the permissible use of external coercion; the doctrine of virtue concerns the motivating grounds by which one wills a course of action. Wood acknowledges the Kantian stipulation against using political power to teach moral lessons. However, the doctrine of right gains legitimacy because of its foundation in Kant's metaphysics of morals: "Right and ethics are two distinct spheres of practical philosophy, or 'morals' (*Sitten*), but the values grounding ethics also show themselves in the system of right."[26] The political constitution, so to speak, must agree with Kant's principle of right, though citizens may endorse different comprehensive moralities (including Kant's, of which Wood is an unapologetic partisan). In an essay titled "The Supreme Principle of Morality" Wood explains how different faiths may agree with the core of Kantian morality: "It seems quite possible for the Stoic, mystical (or Platonic), and Christian ideals to be framed in terms that are compatible with understanding morality as grounded on a categorical imperative."[27] Ultimately, no political actor may legitimately propose constitutional principles that counter Kant's principle of right, and no religious faith may join the ethical community unless its principles may be framed as categorical imperatives.

In *Kantian Ethics*, Wood castigates the interpretation of autonomy as self-legislation. If Wood stresses the *nomos* side of the proper reading of Kant's conception of autonomy, Kant's early Romantic followers and critics embraced the *autos* side that seemingly empowered them to invent any "authentic" or "individualistic" morality that they pleased. For Wood, as for Larmore, this reading of Kant opens the door for immoralists such as Nietzsche and relativists such as Rawls. At the least, Wood argues that those who interpret Kant's conception of autonomy as self-legislation have no right to call themselves Kantians: "Kantian autonomy, once it is understood, will (and ought to) disappoint those shallow minds and immature souls who are attracted to the doctrine of autonomy for the wrong reasons."[28]

Larmore and Wood place limits on what type of principles Kantians—and by extension political theorists and actors—may reasonably propose. Both Larmore and Wood endorse the notion of autonomy as self-governance.[29] In the face of oppressive governments or immoral social pressure, moral actors need the mental fortitude and independence to stand up and do what is right.[30] Self-governance means obeying the moral law even when confronted by immoral desires and the radical propensity to evil that rationalizes subverting the law.[31] Self-governance is compatible with metaethical realism. For realists such as Wood and Larmore, what is completely unacceptable is the idea that human beings may invent any moral principle that they like. The difference over Kant interpretation pales in comparison to this substantive agreement on the task of philosophy: to articulate "*the fundamental truth about morality*"[32] and present "truths about how in general we ought to think and act."[33] Politically, Wood and Larmore may situate themselves on the left; but philosophically, they are conservatives: the task of philosophy is to identify moral truths that have already been discovered and ward off false theories.

Why should progressives open up the potential Pandora's box that is a Kantian conception of autonomy as self-legislation?

EXERCISING AUTONOMY

There are elements within Kant's practical philosophy that place limits on autonomy, that is, that maintain that the higher side of human nature, the will (*Wille*), may only endorse the moral law as categorical imperative, whatever the range of selections confronting the power of choice (*Willkür*).[34] Kant himself, it seems, anticipated and tried to prevent the relativistic and historicist appropriation of his Copernican revolution in philosophy. And, up to the present, many Kantians embrace Kantian morality precisely because it does seem to articulate universal and necessary moral standards by which to, say, condemn the Holocaust or fight against al-Qaeda. Yet, as P. F. Strawson famously observed in *The Bounds of Sense*, Kant's critical philosophy has two faces: one looking backward to the historical milieu from which it erupted, and the other looking forward to philosophical developments that it made possible.[35] The notion of autonomy as self-governance traces its lineage at least to Paul's declaration in the *Letter to the Romans* that the Gentiles are "a law unto themselves."[36] As Larmore notes, even rational intuitionists accept this conception of autonomy. Yet Kant's Copernican revolution, as well as Kant's presentation of it in exhortatory terms ("Have the courage to use your own understanding!"), suggests that autonomy is a project rather than a doctrine. That is, the Kantian ethos, as well as Kantian metaethics, provides the incentive and the means to build new Kantian political theories. The battle over the meaning of autonomy may not ultimately be decided by Kant exegesis, though that may be a valuable exercise to clarify many of the issues. Now, I wish to suggest why Kant's heirs should embody Kantian courage to construct new concepts through which to perceive and navigate the political universe.

First, Kant's conception of autonomy is embedded within a metaphysical framework—transcendental idealism—that has been rendered problematic by subsequent scientific and philosophical developments. According to Wood, Kant's conception of autonomy in Section II of the *Groundwork* has a reciprocal relationship with the account of supersensible freedom in Section III of the *Groundwork*. That is, Kant holds that only by transcending the natural world entirely may we be in a position to discern the moral law that always applies to the will. Yet Wood also holds that Kant's account of supersensible freedom evinces "insuperable difficulties" and that philosophers have not yet solved the problem of free will.[37] How, then, can Wood dogmatically advocate Kant's conception of autonomy when Kant fails to offer a viable account of the *autos* in question? Post-Kantian philosophers may study Kant's reflections on autonomy, but they should also be receptive to insights on how the *autos* is permeated by biological urges (Darwin), economic imperatives (Marx), unconscious structures (Freud), moral prejudices (Nietzsche), linguistic forms of life (Wittgenstein), societal background conditions (Rawls), micropercepts (Deleuze), Greek philosophical assumptions about the tragic nature of existence (Ramadan), and so forth.[38] Kant's assertion in the *Critique of Practical Reason*—that one choose either his account of transcendental freedom or fall prey to empiricist determinism—places a roadblock to philosophers who want to think about how some degree of freedom is possible for socially and materially embedded beings.[39] What happens if we let this paradox linger longer than Kant (or Wood) likes? Philosophically, it gives us confidence that we may experiment with new concepts confident that neither we nor anyone else is likely to have the last word on the concepts that structure our cognition, practice, aesthetic experience, and so on. That is the guiding insight behind Rawls placing Kant's conception of autonomy within an empirical framework; Deleuze inventing the notion of transcendental empiricism; and Ramadan (re-)interpreting the Islamic jurisprudential concept of *ijtihad* as "autonomous critical rationality." In each case, Rawls, Deleuze, and Ramadan appreciate Kant's insight that human beings construct their own philosophical lenses—but they also want to highlight how these lenses have an earthy or semicontingent nature that Kant himself denied. One meaning of Kantian courage, then, is making and using practical concepts even though we have no guarantee that they match up with the nature of reality.

The second reason to embrace the task of self-legislation is political. In *A Kant Dictionary*, Howard Caygill points out that Kant's conception of autonomy builds upon two early modern thinkers, Machiavelli and Luther. In the *Discourses* (1531), Machiavelli articulates the political conception of autonomy as a state's independence from other states as well as its power to make its own laws. In *The Freedom of a Christian* (1520), Luther described spiritual autonomy as freedom from the body's inclinations as well as the power to obey God's law. "Kant's account of autonomy in his practical philosophy in its turn makes a philosophical transposition and critique of Luther's religious autonomy into moral autonomy."[40] Kant transposes Luther's theology into practical philosophy by assigning human beings negative freedom (from natural determinants) as well as positive freedom (to determine the will's own law). Kant criticizes Luther's voluntaristic conception of autonomy by holding that all human beings may know the moral law (without the contingency of revelation) and obey it (without priests, ministers, or political authorities threatening sanctions). Kant's account of autonomy in the *Groundwork*, like Machiavelli's in the *Discourses*, may provide guidance for politicians charting the affairs of state. Unlike Machiavelli's account, Kant explicitly promises to help the moral politician, that is, the "one who interprets the principles of political prudence in such a way that they can co-exist with morality."[41] And in fact, that explains part of the enduring appeal of Kant's practical philosophy: It provides a compass for political theorists and actors even in the direst circumstances. And yet Kant's conception of moral autonomy may suppress political deliberation and judgment when old categories fail to make sense of the moment at hand.[42] In moments of great political transition, Kantians may need to tip the balance in their conceptions of autonomy from Luther to Machiavelli. In other words, contemporary Kantians may need to articulate new conceptions of political autonomy even if this means discarding claims to moral purity.

Today, I contend, we—heirs of the Enlightenment in pluralistic liberal democracies—urgently need to exercise autonomy to create new political theories. In the *Groundwork*, Kant claimed that he was thinking from the perspective of "a rational being in general" which just happened to be human,[43] yet, with two hundred years' hindsight, we see that Kant's practical philosophy was imbued with Christian concepts and themes—many of which Kant recognized, some of which he missed. In itself, there is nothing wrong with this: All philosophers are influenced by their historical and linguistic milieu. Yet we should address this situation unblinkingly and recognize that Kant's practical philosophy, in its original form, does not always serve our needs. In academia, Kant scholarship is thriving, and though this practice may serve as a kind of intellectual cross training, it can also turn into a form of scholasticism blind to the distinct challenges of our time. In politics, this attitude translates into a militant secularism that refuses to listen carefully to alien perspectives and critiques. Yet part of Kant's legacy is the belief that in a genuine age of Enlightenment, everything must submit to criticism. Non-Muslims have a right and a duty to criticize certain political appropriations of Islam.[44] Muslims have a right and a duty to criticize non-Islamic ideas and practices. In Chapter 4, I demonstrate how Rawls (overlapping consensus), Deleuze (assemblage), and Ramadan (space of testimony) exercised Kantian courage to envision political coalitions among people who agree on some issues and disagree profoundly on others. This is precisely the type of autonomy we need today: the intellectual courage to create concepts that may be shared by a wide array of global constituencies.

Notes

INTRODUCTION: ADVANCING THE ENLIGHTENMENT

In notes referring to Kant's work, I cite a short title, the volume and page numbers from the standard Preussischen Akademie edition (except for the "A" and "B" pages of the first and second editions of the *Critique of Pure Reason*), followed by the page number of the relevant English translation.

1. On the danger of Manichaean dualisms—such as between Islam and the West—see Roxanne L. Euben, "The New Manichaeans," *Theory & Event* 5, no. 4 (2001), http://tinyurl.com/new-manichaeans.

2. Roger Cohen, "After the War on Terror," *New York Times*, January 29, 2009. Alan Cowell, "U.S. is 'Not Your Enemy,' Obama Tells Islamic World," *New York Times*, January 28, 2009.

3. Marc Redfield, *The Rhetoric of Terror: Reflections on 9/11 and the War on Terror* (New York: Fordham University Press, 2009).

4. "The Haze Administration," *Wall Street Journal*, April 4, 2009.

5. This book complements several other recent studies of Kant's legacy in contemporary political theory. On Kant's appropriation by Rawls and Habermas, see Katrin Flikschuh, *Kant and Modern Political Philosophy* (Cambridge: Cambridge University Press, 2000); by Habermas, Arendt, Foucault, Lyotard, international relations theory, and feminist critical theory, see Kimberly Hutchings, *Kant, Critique and Politics* (New York: Routledge, 1996); by Habermas and Charles Taylor, see Paul Saurette, *The Kantian Imperative: Humiliation, Common Sense, Politics* (Toronto: University of Toronto Press, 2005); by Adorno, Horkheimer, Foucault, and Carol Gilligan, see Katerina Deligiorgi, *Kant and the Culture of Enlightenment* (Albany: State University of New York Press, 2000); by Heidegger, Gadamer, Adorno, Arendt, Leo Strauss, and John McDowell, see

Robert B. Pippin, *The Persistence of Subjectivity: On the Kantian Aftermath* (New York: Cambridge University Press, 2005); and by Thomas E. Hill Jr., Christine Korsgaard, Onora O'Neill, and Susan Neiman, see Ana Marta González, "John Rawls and the New Kantian Moral Theory," in *The Legacy of John Rawls*, ed. Thom Brooks and Fabian Freyenhagen (New York: Continuum, 2005), 152–76. I discuss several of these books in Nicholas Tampio, "Redefining Kant's Legacy," *Political Theory* 34, no. 6 (2006): 807–13. For an essay responding to my claim that contemporary Kantians (should) look beyond Kant's doctrine of the categorical imperative, see Shalini Pradeepa Satkunanandan, "The Extraordinary Categorical Imperative," *Political Theory* 39, no. 1 (2011): 234–60.

6. Sheldon S. Wolin, *Politics and Vision: Continuity and Innovation in Western Political Thought* (Princeton, NJ: Princeton University Press, 2004), 9–12.

7. On the history of the concept of the Enlightenment, see James Schmidt, "Inventing the Enlightenment: Anti-Jacobins, British Hegelians, and the Oxford English Dictionary," *Journal of the History of Ideas* 64, no. 3 (2003): 421–43.

8. On religious strife, rather than scientific developments, serving as the impetus for modern moral and political philosophy, see J. B. Schneewind, *The Invention of Autonomy: A History of Modern Moral Philosophy* (New York: Cambridge University Press, 1998), 6–7. For the opposite view, see Alex Schulman, *The Secular Contract: On the Politics of Enlightenment* (New York: Continuum, 2011).

9. Peter H. Wilson, *The Thirty Years War: Europe's Tragedy* (Cambridge, MA: Harvard University Press, 2009), 787.

10. Ibid., 788.

11. Ibid., 795.

12. Ibid., 796, 800.

13. Ibid., 809.

14. Ibid., 810.

15. Ibid., 6.

16. The subtitle of ibid.

17. "In explaining the Thirty Years War, we should pay more attention to contingency and agency." Peter H. Wilson, "Dynasty, Constitution, and Confession: The Role of Religion in the Thirty Years War," *International History Review* 30, no. 3 (2008): 513.

18. Wilson, *The Thirty Years War*, 10–11, 851.

19. Ibid., 9.

20. Ibid., 10.

21. Ibid., 753.

22. Ibid., 760.

23. See John Rawls, *Lectures on the History of Moral Philosophy*, ed. Barbara Herman (Cambridge, MA: Harvard University Press, 2000), 8.

24. Jonathan Israel, *A Revolution of the Mind: Radical Enlightenment and the Intellectual Origins of Modern Democracy* (Princeton, NJ: Princeton University Press, 2010).

25. Ian Hunter, *Rival Enlightenments: Civil and Metaphysical Philosophy in Early Modern Germany* (New York: Cambridge University Press, 2001).

26. Michael L. Frazer, "John Rawls: Between Two Enlightenments," *Political Theory* 35, no. 6 (2007): 756–80.

27. Gertrude Himmelfarb, *The Roads to Modernity: The British, French, and American Enlightenments* (New York: Knopf, 2004).

28. James Schmidt points out that conservatives have often defined the terms of the Enlightenment project in "What Enlightenment Project?" *Political Theory* 28, no. 6 (2000): 734–57. Ironically, this may serve as a definition of the Enlightenment project: it refuses the political-religious models of the past. See Leo Strauss's definition of modern political philosophy in *Introduction to Political Philosophy: Ten Essays by Leo Strauss*, ed. Hilail Gildin (Detroit, MI: Wayne State Press, 1989), 60.

29. Mark Juergensmeyer, *Global Rebellion: Religious Challenges to the Secular State, from Christian Militias to al Qaeda* (Berkeley: University of California Press, 2008), 1.

30. "We are looking for a route that will connect critical discourses that have evolved in partial contexts, in order to make them useful for a yet-to-be-constituted, global, progressive Left." Susan Buck-Morss, *Thinking Past Terror: Islamism and Critical Theory on the Left* (New York: Verso, 2003), 101.

31. For one attempt to reclaim the Enlightenment for a multicultural future, see Sankar Muthu, *Enlightenment Against Empire* (Princeton, NJ: Princeton University Press, 2003).

32. Juergensmeyer, *Global Rebellion*, 17.

33. Ibid., 14.

34. Ibid.

35. Ibid., 3.

36. Ibid., 4.

37. Ibid., 252–53.

38. Ibid., 254–55.

39. Ibid., 255.

40. Ibid., 256–57.

41. On the chronology and interrelationship of Foucault's late essays, see James Schmidt and Thomas E. Wartenberg, "Foucault's Enlightenment: Critique, Revolution, and the Fashioning of the Self," in *Critique and Power: Re-*

casting the Foucault/Habermas Debate, ed. Michael Kelly (Cambridge, MA: MIT Press, 1994), 283–314.

42. Amy Allen, *The Politics of Our Selves: Power, Autonomy, and Gender in Contemporary Critical Theory* (New York: Columbia University Press, 2008), 24.

43. Alain Beaulieu, "Towards a Liberal Utopia: The Connection between Foucault's Reporting on the Iranian Revolution and the Ethical Turn," *Philosophy & Social Criticism* 36 (September 2010): 801–18.

44. Michel Foucault, "What is Critique?," in *The Essential Foucault: Selections from Essential Works of Foucault, 1954–1984* (New York: New Press, 2003), 272.

45. Ibid.

46. Michel Foucault, "Nietzsche, Genealogy, History," in *The Foucault Reader*, ed. Paul Rabinow (New York: Pantheon Books, 1984), 77, 76.

47. See the essays by Richard Bernstein, Nancy Frazer, Jürgen Habermas, and Thomas McCarthy in *Critique and Power: Recasting the Foucault/Habermas Debate*, ed. Michael Kelly (Cambridge, MA: MIT Press, 1994).

48. Christina Hendricks, "Foucault's Kantian Critique: Philosophy and the Present," *Philosophy and Social Criticism* 34, no. 4 (2008): 369.

49. Michel Foucault, "What is Enlightenment?," in *Ethics: Subjectivity and Truth*, ed. Paul Rabinow (New York: New Press, 1997), 312.

50. Stephen K. White, *The Ethos of a Late-Modern Citizen* (Cambridge, MA: Harvard University Press, 2009), 2.

51. See Immanuel Kant, *Groundwork for the Metaphysics of Morals*, ed. and trans. Allen W. Wood (New Haven, CT: Yale University Press, 2002), 4:452, 68.

52. Foucault, "What is Critique?," 264.

53. Ibid., 264–65.

54. Allen, *The Politics of Our Selves*, 68.

55. Foucault, "What is Critique?," 266.

56. Foucault, "What is Enlightenment?," 315.

57. Ibid., 316.

58. Foucault, "What is Enlightenment?," 314, 317.

59. For an attempt to free Kant's political theory of its "teleological blinders," see Elisabeth Ellis, *Kant's Politics: Provisional Theory for an Uncertain World* (New Haven, CT: Yale University Press, 2005).

60. Foucault, "What is Enlightenment?," 305.

61. Foucault, "What is Critique?," 272.

62. Allen, *The Politics of Our Selves*, chapter 3.

63. Michel Foucault, "The Art of Telling the Truth," in *Critique and Power: Recasting the Foucault/Habermas Debate*, ed. Michael Kelly (Cambridge, MA: MIT Press, 1994), 147.

64. Foucault, "What is Enlightenment?," 305–6.

65. On locutionary and perlocutionary speech acts, see J. L. Austin, *How to do Things with Words* (Oxford: Clarendon Press, 1975).

66. Foucault, *The Essential Foucault*, 244.

67. Foucault, "The Art of Telling the Truth," 147.

68. Beaulieu, "Towards a Liberal Utopia."

69. Foucault, "The Art of Telling the Truth," 142–43.

70. Foucault, "What is Critique?," 271. Emphasis added.

71. Charles Taylor, *Sources of the Self: The Making of the Modern Identity* (Cambridge, MA: Harvard University Press, 1989), 27.

72. Paul Rabinow, "Foucault's Untimely Struggle Toward a Form of Spirituality," *Theory, Culture & Society* 26, no. 6 (2009): 25–44.

73. Ibid., 41.

74. On how Foucault's analysis of neo-liberal governmentality may enrich and complicate Rawls's conception of public reason, see Paul Patton, "Foucault and Normative Political Philosophy," in *Foucault and Philosophy*, ed. Timothy O'Leary and Christopher Falzon (Malden, MA: Wiley-Blackwell, 2010), 204–21.

75. James Schmidt, "Civility, Enlightenment, and Society: Conceptual Confusions and Kantian Remedies," *American Political Science Review* 92, no. 2 (1998): 419–27.

76. See Richard Rorty, "Kant Vs. Dewey: The Current Situation of Moral Philosophy," in *Philosophy as Cultural Politics* (New York: Cambridge University Press, 2007), 183–202.

77. Tom Rockmore, *In Kant's Wake: Philosophy in the Twentieth Century* (Malden, MA: Blackwell Pub., 2006), 19.

78. Foucault, "What is Critique?," 267.

79. Hannah Arendt, *Lectures on Kant's Political Philosophy*, ed. Ronald Beiner (Chicago: University of Chicago Press, 1982), 22.

80. On the argument that Hume took the decisive philosophical step in the Copernican revolution, see Robert Paul Wolff, "Hume's Theory of Mental Activity," *Philosophical Review* 69, no. 3 (1960): 289–310.

81. On Kant's metaethical strategy in the *Groundwork*, see Paul Guyer, *Kant on Freedom, Law, and Happiness* (New York: Cambridge University Press, 2000), chapter 6.

82. Tom Rockmore, *On Constructivist Epistemology* (Lanham: Rowman & Littlefield, 2005).

83. Recent writings on the *Rechslehre* include B. Sharon Byrd and Joachim Hruschka, *Kant's Doctrine of Right: A Commentary* (Cambridge: Cambridge University Press, 2010); Arthur Ripstein, *Force and Freedom: Kant's Legal and Political Philosophy* (Cambridge, MA: Harvard University Press, 2009); and

Mark Timmons, ed., *Kant's Metaphysics of Morals: Interpretative Essays* (New York: Oxford University Press, 2002).

84. See note 5 above.

85. See William Galston, "What is Living and what is Dead in Kant's Practical Philosophy?," in *Kant & Political Philosophy: The Contemporary Legacy*, ed. Ronald Beiner and William James Booth (New Haven, CT: Yale University Press, 1993), 207–23.

86. "Most Cited Authors in the Humanities, 2007," *Times Higher Education*, March 26, 2009.

87. Allen W. Wood, *Kant's Ethical Thought* (New York: Cambridge University Press, 1999), 14.

88. See also Robert B. Louden, *The World We Want: How and Why the Ideals of the Enlightenment Still Elude Us* (New York: Oxford University Press, 2007), 9.

89. John Rawls, *Political Liberalism* (New York: Columbia University Press, 2005), 438–39.

90. John Rawls, "The Independence of Moral Theory," in *Collected Papers*, ed. Samuel Freeman (Cambridge, MA: Harvard University Press, 1999), 302.

91. I read Deleuze's coauthored books through the prism of his philosophical writings, and thus drop mention of Félix Guattari in this book without wishing to deny his contribution to their joint endeavors. On how Deleuze and Guattari differed in their interpretations of key concepts in their coauthored books (of which Deleuze always wrote the final version), see Daniel W. Smith, "Inside Out: Guattari's Anti-Oedipus Papers," *Radical Philosophy* 140 (2006): 35–39. Though Deleuze writes in a different style than virtually any other canonical author in the history of political philosophy or contemporary political theory, he pursues the goal of political philosophy and theory: to "fashion a political cosmos out of political chaos." Wolin, *Politics and Vision*, 9.

92. On Deleuze's relationship to Kant and the Kantian tradition, see Constantin V. Boundas, "The Art of Begetting Monsters: The Unnatural Nuptials of Deleuze and Kant," in *Current Continental Theory and Modern Philosophy*, ed. Stephen H. Daniel (Evanston, IL: Northwestern University Press, 2005), 254–79; Levi R. Bryant, *Difference and Givenness: Deleuze's Transcendental Empiricism and the Ontology of Immanence* (Evanston, IL: Northwestern University Press, 2008); Melissa McMahon, "Immanuel Kant," in *Deleuze's Philosophical Lineage*, eds. Graham Jones and Jon Roffe (Edinburgh: Edinburgh University Press, 2009), 87–103; Steven Shaviro, *Without Criteria: Kant, Whitehead, Deleuze, and Aesthetics* (Cambridge, MA: MIT Press, 2009); Daniel W. Smith, "Deleuze, Kant, and the Theory of Immanent Ideas," in *Deleuze and Philosophy*, ed. Constantin V. Boundas (Edinburgh: Edinburgh University Press, 2006), 43–61; Edward Willatt, *Kant, Deleuze and Architectonics* (New York: Contin-

uum, 2010); and James Williams, *Gilles Deleuze's 'Difference and Repetition': A Critical Introduction and Guide* (Edinburgh: Edinburgh University Press, 2003).

93. On Deleuze's place in a minor Kantian tradition, including such figures as Salomon Maimön, Hoëne Wronski, and Francis Warrain, see Christian Kerslake, *Immanence and the Vertigo of Philosophy: From Kant to Deleuze* (Edinburgh: Edinburgh University Press, 2009).

94. On the Left's debt to the Enlightenment, see Stephen Eric Bronner, *Reclaiming the Enlightenment: Toward a Politics of Radical Engagement* (New York: Columbia University Press, 2004).

95. See Paul Berman, *The Flight of the Intellectuals* (Brooklyn, NY: Melville House, 2010); Christopher Caldwell, *Reflections on the Revolution in Europe: Immigration, Islam, and the West* (New York: Doubleday, 2009); and Caroline Fourest, *Brother Tariq: The Doublespeak of Tariq Ramadan* (New York: Encounter Books, 2008).

96. Tariq Ramadan, *Western Muslims and the Future of Islam* (New York: Oxford University Press, 2004), 53.

97. On the need for Muslim Voltaires, see Ayaan Hirsi Ali, *The Caged Virgin: An Emancipation Proclamation for Women and Islam* (New York: Free Press, 2006), 27–34. On the need for Muslim John Lockes, see Nader Hashemi, *Islam, Secularism, and Liberal Democracy: Toward a Democratic Theory for Muslim Societies* (New York: Oxford University Press, 2009), 67–102.

98. Ramadan, *The Quest for Meaning: Developing a Philosophy of Pluralism* (New York: Allen Lane, 2010), 187, 25, 33, 208.

99. On the amalgamative nature of political theory in general, and Islamic political theory in particular, see Roxanne L. Euben, "Contingent Borders, Syncretic Perspectives: Globalization, Political Theory, and Islamizing Knowledge," *International Studies Review* 4, no. 1 (2002).

100. Ramadan, *The Quest for Meaning*, 5, 97–98.

101. Judith Butler, "The Sensibility of Critique: Response to Asad and Mahmood," in *Is Critique Secular?: Blasphemy, Injury, and Free Speech*, ed. Talal Asad (Berkeley: University of California Press, 2009), 114.

102. Ramadan, *The Quest for Meaning*, 159. Emphasis in original.

103. On how Kant scholarship may be used as a means to bring diverse authors into conversation—such as Habermas, Adorno, and Bernice Johnson Reagon—see Romand Coles, *Rethinking Generosity: Critical Theory and the Politics of Caritas* (Ithaca, NY: Cornell University Press, 1997).

1. KANTIAN COURAGE

1. Ernst Cassirer, *The Philosophy of the Enlightenment*, ed. Peter Gay (Princeton, NJ: Princeton University Press, 2009), xi.

2. For a critique of Enlightenment rhetoric conjoined with the use of torture and prohibition of dissent—in the case of Mubarak's Egypt—see Mona Abaza, "The Trafficking with *Tanwir* (Enlightenment)," *Comparative Studies of South Asia, Africa and the Middle East* 30, no. 1 (2010): 32–46.

3. Max Horkheimer and Theodor W. Adorno, *Dialectic of Enlightenment* (New York: Continuum, 1997), 3.

4. For many liberals, "courage is politically obsolete, a relic of an unenlightened age, when either might made right or nothing did." Jason A. Scorza, *Strong Liberalism: Habits of Mind for Democratic Citizenship* (Hanover, NH: University Press of New England, 2008), 116. Karl Rove provides an example of the delusions perpetrated by the veneer of courage in *Courage and Consequence: My Life as a Conservative in the Fight* (New York: Threshold, 2010).

5. Immanuel Kant, "An Answer to the Question: What is Enlightenment?," in *Practical Philosophy*, ed. and trans. Mary J. Gregor (New York: Cambridge University Press, 1996), 8:35, 17.

6. On the Enlightenment's relationship to Aristotle, see Alasdair MacIntyre, *After Virtue: A Study in Moral Theory* (Notre Dame, IN: University of Notre Dame Press, 1984) and Peter Gay, *The Enlightenment: The Rise of Modern Paganism* (New York: Knopf, 1966).

7. Kant, *Groundwork*, 4:393, 9.

8. Aristotle, *Nicomachean Ethics*, ed. Roger Crisp (Cambridge: Cambridge University Press, 2000), 1115b, 9.

9. Ibid., 1103a, 23.

10. Ibid., 1115a, 48.

11. Ibid., 1117a, 53–54.

12. Hannah Arendt, *The Human Condition* (Chicago: University of Chicago Press, 1958), 33.

13. Aristotle, *Nicomachean Ethics* 1115a, 49.

14. Kant, *Groundwork*, 4:397, 13; 4:411, 27.

15. Taylor, *Sources of the Self*, part 3.

16. Kant, "Groundwork," in *Practical Philosophy*, 4:462, 108.

17. Kant, "Critique of Practical Reason," in *Practical Philosophy*, 5:84, 208.

18. See Mika LaVaque-Manty, "Dueling for Equality: Masculine Honor and the Modern Politics of Dignity," *Political Theory* 34, no. 6 (2006): 715–40.

19. Douglas N. Walton, *Courage: A Philosophical Investigation* (Berkeley: University of California Press, 1985), 18.

20. Lewis White Beck, *A Commentary on Kant's Critique of Practical Reason* (Chicago: University of Chicago Press, 1960), 102–8.

21. Kant, "The Metaphysics of Morals," in *Practical Philosophy*, 6:207, 366.

22. Kant, "What is Enlightenment?," 8:36, 18.

23. J. B. Schneewind, *Essays on the History of Moral Philosophy* (New York: Oxford University Press, 2010), 309.

24. On Kant's imagery of teaching children to walk as a metaphor for inculcating autonomy, see Mika LaVaque-Manty, "Kant's Children," *Social Theory and Practice* 32, no. 3 (July 2006): 365–88.

25. Kant, "What is Enlightenment?," 8:39, 20.

26. "The most important political problem" of Kant's time was "the transition from absolutism without revolutionary violence." Ellis, *Kant's Politics*, 30. Today, and perhaps in Kant's time as well, this transition requires a confrontation with religious orthodoxy. On how Kantian provisional politics can bend hard-and-fast rules, for instance, to accommodate devout Sikhs who wish to wear turbans on the job as Canadian Mounted Police, see Elisabeth Ellis, *Provisional Politics: Kantian Arguments in Policy Context* (New Haven, CT: Yale University Press, 2008), 94. This case points the way to big questions: What other rules may liberals bend? How may liberals construct new rules? What might these rules look like?

27. On the two valences of the word critique, see Dieter Henrich, "The Deduction of the Moral Law: The Reasons for the Obscurity of the Final Section of Kant's *Groundwork of the Metaphysics of Morals*" In *Kant's Groundwork of the Metaphysics of Morals: Critical Essays*, ed. Paul Guyer (Lanham, MD: Rowman & Littlefield, 1998), 308–9.

28. On Kant's conception of publicity, see John Christian Laursen, "The Subversive Kant: The Vocabulary of 'Public' and 'Publicity,'" in *What is Enlightenment? Eighteenth-Century Answers and Twentieth-Century Questions*, ed. James Schmidt (Berkeley: University of California Press, 1996), 253–69.

29. Kant, "What is Enlightenment?," 8:38, 19. Emphasis added.

30. Ibid., 8:37, 19.

31. See *Critique of Pure Reason*, Bxiii, 109.

32. See Alan Ryan, "Intellectual Courage," *Social Research* 71, no. 1 (2004): 13–28.

33. Kant, "What is Enlightenment?," 8:36, 18.

34. Immanuel Kant, "Public Declaration Concerning Fichte's *Wissenschaftslehre*, August 7, 1799," in *Correspondence*, ed. and trans. Arnulf Zweig (New York: Cambridge University Press, 1999), 560.

35. Kant, "What is Enlightenment?," 8:39, 21.

36. Immanuel Kant, *Critique of Pure Reason*, eds. and trans. Paul Guyer and Allen W. Wood, Axi, 100–1.

37. See G. Felicitas Munzel, *Kant's Conception of Moral Character: The "Critical" Link of Morality, Anthropology, and Reflective Judgment* (Chicago: University of Chicago Press, 1999), xv–xviii.

38. Immanuel Kant, "Anthropology from a Pragmatic Point of View," in *Anthropology, History, and Education*, ed. Günter Zöller and Robert B. Louden, trans. Robert B. Louden (New York: Cambridge University Press, 2007), 7:256, 358.

39. Ibid., 7:256, 358.

40. Kant, *The Metaphysics of Morals*, 6:405, 533.

41. Ibid., 6:399–403, 528–31.

42. Kant, *Anthropology from a Pragmatic Point of View*, 7:257, 359.

43. Ibid., 7:256, 358.

44. Ibid., 7:257, 359.

45. Immanuel Kant, "Observations on the Feeling of the Beautiful and Sublime," in *Anthropology, History, and Education*, ed. Günter Zöller and Robert B. Louden, trans. Paul Guyer (New York: Cambridge University Press, 2007), 2:218, 32.

46. Ibid., 2:218, 32.

47. Kant, *The Metaphysics of Morals*, 6:380, 513.

48. See Rawls, *Lectures on the History of Moral Philosophy*, 303–6.

49. Immanuel Kant, "Religion within the Boundaries of Mere Reason," in *Religion and Rational Theology*, ed. and trans. Allen W. Wood and George Di Giovanni (New York: Cambridge University Press, 1996), 6:30, 78.

50. Schneewind, *Essays on the History of Moral Philosophy*, 318.

51. See Hutchings, *Kant, Critique and Politics*, 11.

52. Allen W. Wood, "Philosophy: Enlightenment Apology, Enlightenment Critique," in *What is Philosophy?*, ed. C. P. Ragland and Sarah Heidt (New Haven, CT: Yale University Press, 2001), 101.

53. Wood, *Kant's Ethical Thought*, 335.

54. Wood, "Enlightenment Apology," 102.

55. Allen W. Wood, "What is Kantian Ethics?," in *Groundwork for the Metaphysics of Morals*, ed. Allen W. Wood (New Haven, CT: Yale University Press, 2002), 157.

56. Ibid., 157.

57. Allen W. Wood, *Kantian Ethics*, 6.

58. Wood, "What is Kantian Ethics?," 172–73. See also Allen W. Wood, *Hegel's Ethical Thought* (New York: Cambridge University Press, 1990).

59. Wood, "Enlightenment Apology," 111.

60. Ibid., 106. Wood attributes the quote to César Chesnau Dumarsais.

61. Wood, *Kantian Ethics*, 2.

62. Wood, "Enlightenment Apology," 102.

63. Wood, *Kantian Ethics*, x.

64. Ibid., 45.

65. Ibid., 51.

66. Wood, "Enlightenment Apology," 115.

67. Ibid., 103.

68. Ibid., 116.

69. Wood, *Kantian Ethics*, 43.

70. Wood, "Enlightenment Apology," 117.

71. Rawls, *Political Liberalism*, xviii.

72. Ibid., 438.

73. Rawls, *Lectures on the History of Moral Philosophy*, 18.

74. Ibid., 329.

75. Ibid., 17–18.

76. John Rawls, *A Theory of Justice,* rev. ed. (Cambridge, MA: Harvard University Press, 1999), 226. All other citations to *A Theory of Justice*, unless otherwise mentioned, are to the revised edition.

77. See Robert S. Taylor, *Reconstructing Rawls.* I discuss this book in "Rawls, Constructivism, and the Tragic," *H-Net: Humanities and Social Sciences*, 2011, and "A Defense of Political Constructivism," *Contemporary Political Theory* 11, no. 3 (August 2012).

78. Rawls, *Lectures on the History of Moral Philosophy*, xvii.

79. Kant, *Critique of Pure Reason* A836/B864, 693.

80. Rawls, "The Independence of Moral Theory," 302.

81. Taylor, *Reconstructing Rawls*, xxiii.

82. Samuel Freeman, *Rawls* (New York: Routledge, 2007), 21–22.

83. Rawls, *Lectures on the History of Moral Philosophy*, 330.

84. See Sibyl A. Schwarzenbach, "Rawls, Hegel, and Communitarianism," *Political Theory* 19, no. 4 (1991): 539–71.

85. Rawls, *Lectures on the History of Moral Philosophy*, 332.

86. Rawls, *Political Liberalism*, 285–88.

87. John Rawls, *Lectures on the History of Political Philosophy*, ed. Samuel Freeman (Cambridge, MA: Harvard University Press, 2007), 10.

88. Rawls, *Lectures on the History of Moral Philosophy*, 330.

89. John Rawls, "Kantian Constructivism in Moral Theory," in *Collected Papers*, ed. Samuel Freeman (Cambridge, MA: Harvard University Press, 1999), 303–4.

90. Rawls, *Lectures on the History of Moral Philosophy*, 369.

91. Rawls, *Political Liberalism*, 225.

92. Rawls, *Lectures on the History of Moral Philosophy*, 5.

93. Richard Rorty, "The Priority of Democracy to Philosophy," in *Objectivity, Relativism, and Truth* (New York: Cambridge University Press, 1991), 179.

94. Rawls, *Political Liberalism*, 249–51.

95. Ibid., li.

96. Rorty, "The Priority of Democracy to Philosophy," 180, 189.

97. Michael J. Sandel, *Liberalism and the Limits of Justice* (New York: Cambridge University Press, 1998), 2.

98. See Allan David Bloom, "Justice: John Rawls Versus the Tradition of Political Philosophy," *American Political Science Review* 69 (1975): 648–62.

99. Bonnie Honig argues that the "Rawlsian supplement" does not politicize citizens, call on them to amend or augment the constitution, or protest the consolidation of their institutions, identities, or public or private practices. Bonnie Honig, *Political Theory and the Displacement of Politics* (Ithaca, NY: Cornell University Press, 1993), 195–99. Rawls, on my reading, both tempers Enlightenment dogmatism and opens the door to more experimental thinkers—such as Deleuze—to participate in the Enlightenment tradition.

100. Rawls, *Political Liberalism*, liii.

101. Kant, *Critique of Pure Reason*, Axi–Axii, 101.

102. Rawls, *Political Liberalism*, 236.

103. Ibid. 237.

104. Ibid. 236.

105. Ibid. 234.

106. Ibid., 236.

107. Determining judgment subsumes the particular under a universal; reflecting judgment occurs when "only the particular is given, for which the universal is to be found." Immanuel Kant, *Critique of the Power of Judgment*, ed. Paul Guyer, trans. Paul Guyer and Eric Matthews (New York: Cambridge University Press, 2000), 5:179, 67. On the notion of reflecting judgment as the key to unlocking Kant's political theory, see Arendt, *Lectures on Kant's Political Philosophy*.

108. Rawls, *Political Liberalism*, 254.

109. Rawls, *Lectures on the History of Moral Philosophy*, xvii–xviii.

110. Gilles Deleuze, *Negotiations, 1972–1990* (New York: Columbia University Press, 1995), 6.

111. Gilles Deleuze, *Nietzsche and Philosophy* (New York: Columbia University Press, 2006), 52.

112. On the Nietzschean Enlightenment, see Laurence Lampert, *Leo Strauss and Nietzsche* (Chicago: University of Chicago Press, 1996), chapter 5. On the notion that Deleuze seeks to revive *a* Kantian Enlightenment, see James Williams, *The Transversal Thought of Gilles Deleuze: Encounters and Influences* (Manchester, UK: Clinamen Press, 2005), 27, and Christopher R. Groves, "Deleuze's Kant: Enlightenment and Education," *Philosophy Today* 45, no. 1 (2001): 77.

113. Deleuze, *Nietzsche and Philosophy*, 91.

114. Daniel Mendelsohn, "Nailed!" *New York Review of Books* 51, no. 12 (2004): 43–46.

115. See Douglas Burnham, *An Introduction to Kant's* Critique of Judgement (Edinburgh: Edinburgh University Press, 2000), 7–8.

116. Deleuze, *Nietzsche and Philosophy*, 89.

117. Kant, *Critique of Pure Reason*, Axi, 100–1.

118. Cited in Arendt, *Lectures on Kant's Political Philosophy*, 34.

119. "Of all philosophers, Kant is the one who discovers the prodigious domain of the transcendental. He is the analogue of a great explorer—not of another world, but of the upper or lower reaches of this one." Gilles Deleuze, *Difference and Repetition* (New York: Columbia University Press, 1994), 135.

120. Gilles Deleuze, "On Four Poetic Formulas that might Summarize the Kantian Philosophy," in *Essays Critical and Clinical*, trans. Daniel W. Smith and Michael A. Greco (Minneapolis: University of Minnesota Press, 1997), 32.

121. Ibid., 33.

122. Christian Kerslake, "Deleuze, Kant, and the Question of Metacritique," *Southern Journal of Philosophy* 42, no. 4 (2004): 482.

123. Deleuze, *Difference and Repetition*, 303. Gilles Deleuze and Félix Guattari, *What is Philosophy?* (New York: Columbia University Press, 1994), chapter 2. Christian Kerslake argues that Deleuze offers a strong justification for his ontological vision in *Difference and Repetition*; otherwise, reading Deleuze means " merely taking a possible, somewhat aesthetic, perspective on the world, in which case one would have already secretly surrendered to our pragmatist, pluralist episteme." Christian Kerslake, "Copernican Deleuzeanism," *Radical Philosophy: A Journal of Socialist and Feminist Philosophy* 114 (2002): 33. Deleuze and Guattari's concept of the rhizome, in *A Thousand Plateaus*, enables diverse constituencies to form political alliances without subscribing to the same understanding of the absolute. That book also explicitly appeals to aesthetic criteria such as loving, beautiful, and political. Deleuze's thinking, then, shifts over time, and his later work, from my perspective, makes a more profound contribution to democratic theory.

124. Friedrich Nietzsche, *Untimely Meditations*, ed. Daniel Breazeale, trans. R. J. Hollingdale (New York: Cambridge University Press, 1997), 60. On the shift from the revolutionary *Anti-Oedipus* to the reformist *A Thousand Plateaus*, see Ian Buchanan, *Deleuze and Guattari's Anti-Oedipus: A Reader's Guide* (London: Continuum, 2008), 138–39.

125. Kant, *Critique of Pure Reason*, A841/B869, 696.

126. Deleuze, *Nietzsche and Philosophy*, 89.

127. Ibid., 75.

128. Friedrich Nietzsche, *On the Genealogy of Morality*, ed. Keith Ansell-Pearson, trans. Carol Diethe (New York: Cambridge University Press, 2007), 76.

129. Friedrich Nietzsche, *The Anti-Christ, Ecce Homo, Twilight of the Idols, and Other Writings*, ed. Aaron Ridley and Judith Norman, trans. Judith Norman (New York: Cambridge University Press, 2005), 170.

130. For a defense of Nietzsche's aristocratic—but not racist or fascist—philosophical politics, see Laurence Lampert, *Nietzsche's Task: An Interpretation of Beyond Good and Evil* (New Haven, CT: Yale University Press, 2001).

131. See Deleuze, "On Four Poetic Formulas"

132. Friedrich Nietzsche, *Beyond Good and Evil*, ed. Rolf-Peter Horstmann and Judith Norman, trans. Judith Norman (New York: Cambridge University Press, 2002), 164.

133. William E. Connolly, *Neuropolitics: Thinking, Culture, Speed* (Minneapolis: University of Minnesota Press, 2002), 154.

134. See Mohamed Zayani, "The Nietzschean Temptation: Gilles Deleuze and the Exuberance of Philosophy," *Comparative Literature Studies* 36, no. 4 (1999): 320–40.

135. Deleuze, *Nietzsche and Philosophy*, 40.

136. Ian Donaldson, "Hierarchy and Ontological Dualism: Rethinking Gilles Deleuze's Nietzsche for Political Philosophy," *History of Political Thought* 23, no. 4 (2002): 666, 669.

137. Deleuze, *Negotiations*, 6.

138. See, for example, Michael Hardt, *Gilles Deleuze: An Apprenticeship in Philosophy* (Minneapolis: University of Minnesota Press, 1993).

139. Deleuze, *Nietzsche and Philosophy*, 107.

140. See Patricia Farrell, "The Philosopher-Monkey: Learning and the Discordant Harmony of the Faculties," in *Thinking between Deleuze and Kant*, 11–27.

141. See Gilles Deleuze, "Kant: Synthesis and Time."

142. Michel Foucault, *Language, Counter-Memory, Practice: Selected Essays and Interviews* (Ithaca, NY: Cornell University Press, 1977), 205.

143. Ibid., 208.

144. See Buchanan, *Deleuze and Guattari's Anti-Oedipus*, 7–12; François Dosse, *Gilles Deleuze and Félix Guattari: Intersecting Lives* (New York: Columbia University Press, 2010), 170–222.

145. Gilles Deleuze, *Two Regimes of Madness: Texts and Interviews 1975–1995*, ed. David Lapoujade, trans. Ames Hodges and Mike Taormina (Cambridge, MA: Semiotexte, 2006), 233–34.

146. Deleuze and Guattari, *What is Philosophy?*, 159.

147. Gilles Deleuze and Félix Guattari, *Anti-Oedipus: Capitalism and Schizophrenia* (Minneapolis: University of Minnesota Press, 1983), xiii.

148. Gilles Deleuze and Félix Guattari, *A Thousand Plateaus*, trans. Brian Massumi (Minneapolis: University of Minnesota Press, 1987), 215.

149. Nietzsche, *The Anti-Christ*, 82.

150. Deleuze, *Nietzsche and Philosophy*, 86–87.

151. Ibid., 3.

152. See Nathan Widder, *Reflections on Time and Politics* (University Park: Pennsylvania State University Press, 2008), 63–75, 108–14.

153. Deleuze, *Nietzsche and Philosophy*, 176–77.

154. Kant, *Critique of Pure Reason*, Aix–xi, 99–101.

155. See Sidney Axinn, "The First Western Pragmatist, Immanuel Kant," *Journal of Chinese Philosophy* 33, no. 1 (2006): 83–94.

156. Paul Patton, "Redescriptive Philosophy: Deleuze and Guattari's Critical Pragmatism" In *Micropolitics of Media Culture: Reading the Rhizomes of Deleuze and Guattari*, ed. Patricia Pisters (Amsterdam: Amsterdam University Press, 2001), 40–42.

157. On the role of sensibility in philosophy, see William E. Connolly, *Politics and Ambiguity* (Madison: University of Wisconsin Press, 1987), 123–26.

158. On the conflicting moments of Kant's legacy, from a Deleuzian perspective, see John Protevi, *Political Physics: Deleuze, Derrida, and the Body Politic* (New York: Athlone Press, 2001), chapter 7.

159. See John Tasioulas, "From Utopia to Kazanistan: John Rawls and the Law of Peoples," *Oxford Journal of Legal Studies* 22, no. 2 (2002), and Onora O'Neill, *Towards Justice and Virtue: A Constructive Account of Practical Reasoning* (New York: Cambridge University Press, 1996).

160. See Alexandre Lefebvre, *The Image of Law: Deleuze, Bergson, Spinoza* (Stanford, CA: Stanford University Press, 2008).

161. See Juergensmeyer, *Global Rebellion*.

162. Wood, *Kantian Ethics*, 18.

163. See William J. Clinton, "Remarks on Presenting the Arts and Humanities Awards," *Weekly Compilation of Presidential Documents*, 35, no. 39 (1999): 1847–53.

164. Rawls, *Political Liberalism*, 239.

165. See Jane Bennett, *Vibrant Matter: A Political Ecology of Things* (Durham, NC: Duke University Press, 2010).

166. On the need for democrats to balance establishing and resisting power, see Jane Mansbridge, "Using Power, Fighting Power," *Constellations* 1, no. 1 (1994): 53–73.

2. FORMULATING PROBLEMS

1. Borradori, *Philosophy in a Time of Terror*, 1.

2. Kant, *Groundwork*, 4:392, 7–8.

3. Allen W. Wood, "The Supreme Principle of Morality," in *The Cambridge Companion to Kant and Modern Philosophy*, ed. Paul Guyer (New York: Cambridge University Press, 2006).

212 Notes to pages 73–75

4. On Kant's account of the origin of the faculty of reason, see Immanuel Kant, "Conjectural Beginning of Human History," in *Anthropology, History, and Education*, eds. Günter Zöller and Robert B. Louden, trans. Allen W. Wood (New York: Cambridge University Press, 2007), 176–81.

5. John Dewey, "The Influence of Darwinism on Philosophy," in *Philosophy After Darwin: Classic and Contemporary Readings*, ed. Michael Ruse (Princeton, NJ: Princeton University Press, 2009), 58.

6. Ibid., 59.

7. Ibid., 60.

8. Ibid.

9. Ibid.

10. Rorty, "Kant Vs. Dewey," 188.

11. One of the most famous efforts in contemporary political theory to de-transcendentalize Kant's practical philosophy is by Jürgen Habermas. According to Habermas, it is possible to find a middle point between Kant's other-worldly and Hegel's thisworldly conceptions of practical reason by attending to the universal pragmatic presuppositions of communicative action. That is, Habermas defends "a weak and transitory unity of reason" that holds that people may criticize one another precisely because they share a common linguistic framework that makes possible and contains a drive towards consensus. See Jürgen Habermas, *Postmetaphysical Thinking*, trans. William Mark Hohengarten (Cambridge, MA: MIT Press, 1992). On the points of contact between Habermas and Rawls, see Todd Hedrick, *Rawls and Habermas: Reason, Pluralism, and the Claims of Political Philosophy* (Stanford, CA: Stanford University Press, 2010); for a Deleuzian critique of Habermas, see Alexandre Lefebvre, *The Image of Law: Deleuze, Bergson, Spinoza* (Stanford, CA: Stanford University Press, 2008), chapter 3.

12. Ira Katznelson, *Desolation and Enlightenment: Political Knowledge After Total War, Totalitarianism, and the Holocaust* (New York: Columbia University Press, 2003), 28.

13. Ibid., 30.

14. Hannah Arendt, *Eichmann in Jerusalem: A Report on the Banality of Evil* (New York: Penguin Books, 2006).

15. On Machiavelli—the founder of modern political philosophy—being one of the only non-Jews to protest the Inquisition, see Leo Strauss, *An Introduction to Political Philosophy*, ed. Hilail Gildin (Detroit, MI: Wayne State University Press, 1989), 44.

16. Susan Meld Shell, *Kant and the Limits of Autonomy* (Cambridge, MA: Harvard University Press, 2009), 313.

17. Cited in ibid., 325.

18. Ibid., 328.

19. Hunter, *Rival Enlightenments*, 277.

20. Malise Ruthven, *Historical Atlas of Islam* (Cambridge, MA: Harvard University Press, 2004), 168.

21. Shireen Hunter, ed., *Islam, Europe's Second Religion: The New Social, Cultural, and Political Landscape* (Westport, CT: Praeger, 2002).

22. For a provocative account of how Kant's practical philosophy forms the backdrop to atrocities committed in the war on terror, see Saurette, *The Kantian Imperative*, Epilogue.

23. Shibley Telhami, "Of Power and Compassion," in *The Philosophical Challenge of September 11*, eds. Tom Rockmore, Joseph Margolis, and Armen Marsoobian (Malden, MA: Blackwell, 2005), 77.

24. Deleuze and Guattari, *What is Philosophy?*, 96.

25. Christine M. Korsgaard, *The Sources of Normativity*, ed. Onora O'Neill (New York: Cambridge University Press, 1996).

26. Wood, *Kantian Ethics*, 14.

27. See Michael L. Frazer, *The Enlightenment of Sympathy: Justice and the Moral Sentiments in the Eighteenth Century and Today* (New York: Oxford University Press, 2010); Sharon R. Krause, *Civil Passions: Moral Sentiment and Democratic Deliberation* (Princeton, NJ: Princeton University Press, 2008); and Paul Guyer, "Naturalizing Kant," in *Kant Verstehen / Understanding Kant*, ed. Dieter Schönecker and Thomas Zwenger (Darmstadt, Ger.: Wissenschaftliche Buchgesellschaft, 2001), 59–84.

28. Hume, *A Treatise of Human Nature*, 266.

29. Ibid., 295.

30. Ibid., 174, 81.

31. Ibid., 120. Emphasis added.

32. "Any harm or uneasiness has a natural tendency to excite our hatred, and . . . afterwards we seek for reasons upon which we may justify and establish the passion." Hume, *A Treatise of Human Nature*, 227.

33. See Paul Guyer, *Knowledge, Reason, and Taste: Kant's Response to Hume* (Princeton, NJ: Princeton University Press, 2008).

34. Kant, *Groundwork*, 4:389, 5.

35. Ibid., 4:389, 5.

36. Schneewind, *The Invention of Autonomy*, 513.

37. See, in particular, Frazer, *The Enlightenment of Sympathy*, chapter 2; Krause, *Civil Passions*, chapter 3.

38. Hume, *A Treatise of Human Nature*, 234.

39. Ibid., 368.

40. Rawls, *Lectures on the History of Moral Philosophy*, 31–36.

41. Hume, *A Treatise of Human Nature*, 206.

42. See Elizabeth Radcliffe, "Kantian Tunes on a Humean Instrument: Why Hume Is Not Really a Skeptic about Practical Reasoning," *Canadian Journal of Philosophy* 27, no. 2 (1997): 247–70.

43. Hume, *A Treatise of Human Nature*, 185.

44. Ibid., 301.

45. Rawls, *Political Liberalism*, xxvi.

46. Ibid., xxvi.

47. Kant, *Groundwork*, 4:425, 43.

48. On the term *reflective autonomy*, see Frazer, *The Enlightenment of Sympathy*, 183.

49. See Hannah Arendt, *The Life of the Mind* (New York: Harcourt Brace Jovanovich, 1978).

50. Kant, *Groundwork*, 4:452, 68.

51. Hunter, *Rival Enlightenments*.

52. See Patricia Kitcher, "Changing the Name of the Game: Kant's Cognitivism Versus Hume's Psychologism," in *Immanuel Kant's Prolegomena to any Future Metaphysics: In Focus*, ed. Beryl Logan (New York: Routledge, 1996), 178–218.

53. Hume, *A Treatise of Human Nature*, 6.

54. On the role this distinction plays in Kant scholarship, see Sebastian Gardner, *Routledge Philosophy Guidebook to Kant and the* Critique of Pure Reason (New York: Routledge, 1999).

55. On Deleuze's early monographs transpiring within a Kantian and post-Kantian framework, see Kerslake, "Copernican Deleuzeanism," 32–33.

56. Humean themes that reappear in Deleuze's mature political theory include: a critique of negativity; the figure of the institution; the empiricist conviction that relations are external to their terms; the fluidity of thinking; the experiential genesis of the faculties; and subjectivity as a passive synthesis of experience. See Jon Roffe, "David Hume," in *Deleuze's Philosophical Lineage*, ed. Graham Jones and Jon Roffe (Edinburgh: Edinburgh University Press, 2009), 67–86.

57. Rawls, *A Theory of Justice*, 30.

58. Kant, *Critique of Pure Reason*, B9, 129.

59. White, *The Ethos of a Late-Modern Citizen*, 15.

60. Rawls, *Political Liberalism*, 50.

61. Rawls, *Lectures on the History of Moral Philosophy*, 27.

62. Rawls, *Political Liberalism*, 51.

63. Ibid., 49–51.

64. Ibid., 339.

65. Rawls, *Lectures on the History of Moral Philosophy*, 30.

66. Ibid., 96–98.

67. Frazer, "John Rawls."

68. Gilles Deleuze, *Empiricism and Subjectivity: An Essay on Hume's Theory of Human Nature* (New York: Columbia University Press, 1991), 87.

69. See Christian Kerslake, *Deleuze and the Unconscious* (New York: Continuum, 2007).

70. Deleuze, *Empiricism and Subjectivity*, 87. Emphasis added.

71. Hume, *A Treatise of Human Nature*, 171. Kant, *Critique of Practical Reason* 5:147, 258.

72. Connolly, *Neuropolitics*.

73. See Claire Colebrook, *Gilles Deleuze* (New York: Routledge, 2002), chapter 4.

74. Deleuze, *Empiricism and Subjectivity*, 23.

75. Hume, *A Treatise of Human Nature*, 137.

76. Deleuze, *Empiricism and Subjectivity*, 98.

77. Ibid., x.

78. Hume, *A Treatise of Human Nature*, 314.

79. Deleuze, *Empiricism and Subjectivity*, 43–44.

80. Hume appealed to Deleuze because he enabled "the creativity and inventiveness of the human species to shine forth." Jeffrey A. Bell, *Deleuze's Hume: Philosophy, Culture and the Scottish Enlightenment* (Edinburgh: Edinburgh University Press, 2009), 56.

81. Deleuze, *Empiricism and Subjectivity*, 64.

82. Ibid., 43.

83. Deleuze, *Difference and Repetition*, 248.

84. See Konrad Lorenz, "Kant's Doctrine of the *A Priori* in the Light of Contemporary Biology," in *Philosophy After Darwin: Classic and Contemporary Readings*, ed. Michael Ruse (Princeton, NJ: Princeton University Press, 2009).

85. Kant, *Critique of Practical Reason*, 5:9, 144.

86. Deleuze, *Empiricism and Subjectivity*, 132.

87. Ibid., 93.

88. Deleuze, *Difference and Repetition*, 262.

89. On Deleuze's conception of practical reason, see Paul Patton, *Deleuzian Concepts: Philosophy, Colonization, Politics* (Stanford, CA: Stanford University Press, 2010), 202–3.

90. Hilary Putnam, "Why Reason can't be Naturalized: Evolutionary Epistemology," in *Philosophy After Darwin*, ed. Michael Ruse (Princeton, NJ: Princeton University Press, 2009), 218.

91. The two-aspect reading of Kant's *Critique of Pure Reason* distinguishes "two ways of *considering* things (as they appear and as they are in themselves) rather than . . . two ontologically distinct sets of entities (appearances and things in themselves)." Henry Allison, *Kant's Transcendental Idealism: An Interpretation and Defense: Revised and Enlarged Edition* (New Haven, CT: Yale University Press, 2004), 16. One problem with this reading is that it ignores Kant's immersion in the tradition of medieval metaphysics as well as his recurrent use of two-world terminology; see Hunter, *Rival Enlightenments* and Henrich, "The Deduction of the Moral Law." Allison also denies that philosophers may feasibly separate "Kant's fundamental claims in the *Critique* from transcendental idealism." *Kant's Transcendental Idealism*, 4. Allison's thesis, however, downplays the fact that Kant's philosophy went through myriad permutations and invites future philosophers to make their own conceptual frameworks. In this book I aim to show the benefits of treating the Kantian, or Enlightenment, tradition as an ongoing project rather than as a settled body of doctrines.

92. For a diagnosis of modern nihilism from a Nietzschean perspective, see William E. Connolly, *Political Theory and Modernity* (Ithaca, NY: Cornell University Press, 1993).

93. See Daniel Jonah Goldhagen, *Hitler's Willing Executioners: Ordinary Germans and the Holocaust* (New York: Knopf, 1996). Goldhagen condemns the German common sense of the 1930s without recognizing the danger inherent in common sense as such. Hannah Arendt offers a more complex and interesting account of the banality of common sense and its possible recuperation as a *sensus communis* that is, alas, beyond the scope of this book.

94. On the historical context of Kant's reflections on common sense, see Manfred Kuehn, *Scottish Common Sense in Germany, 1768–1800: A Contribution to the History of Critical Philosophy* (Kingston, QC: McGill-Queen's University Press, 1987).

95. Kant, *Critique of Practical Reason*, 5:8, 143.

96. Kant, *Groundwork*, 4:405, 20–21.

97. Ibid., 4:404, 20.

98. Schneewind, *Essays on the History of Moral Philosophy*, 7.

99. Kant, *Groundwork*, 4:407, 23

100. See Gilles Deleuze, *Kant's Critical Philosophy: The Doctrine of the Faculties*, trans. Hugh Tomlinson and Barbara Habberjam (Minneapolis: University of Minnesota Press, 1984).

101. Schneewind, *Essays on the History of Moral Philosophy*, 255.

102. On radical evil as the source of common sense's natural dialectic, see ibid., 296–318.

103. Rawls, *Political Liberalism*, 14.

104. John Rawls, *Justice as Fairness: A Restatement*, ed. Erin Kelly (Cambridge, MA: Harvard University Press, 2001), 29.

105. Bloom, "Justice," 648.

106. Rawls, *Justice as Fairness*, 31.

107. Rawls, *Political Liberalism*, 9.

108. Friedrich Nietzsche, *The Gay Science*, trans. Walter Kaufmann (New York: Vintage Books, 1974), 264.

109. Deleuze, *Kant's Critical Philosophy*, 14.

110. Deleuze, *Nietzsche and Philosophy*, 89.

111. Deleuze and Guattari, *What is Philosophy?*, 112.

112. Deleuze, *Kant's Critical Philosophy*, 22.

113. Deleuze, *Kant: Synthesis and Time.*

114. Deleuze, *Kant's Critical Philosophy*, 23.

115. Deleuze, "On Four Poetic Formulas," 35. On Deleuze's relationship to the *Critique of Judgment*, see Daniel W. Smith, "Deleuze's Theory of Sensation: Overcoming the Kantian Duality," in *Deleuze: A Critical Reader*, ed. Paul Patton (Cambridge, MA: Blackwell, 1996), 29–56.

116. Deleuze, *Difference and Repetition*, 143–44.

117. See Keith Ansell-Pearson, *Germinal Life: The Difference and Repetition of Deleuze* (New York: Routledge, 1999).

118. Philippe Mengue, "The Absent People and the Void of Democracy," *Contemporary Political Theory* 4, no. 4 (2005), 386–499.

119. Deleuze and Guattari, *What is Philosophy?*, 107.

120. Patton, *Deleuzian Concepts*, 139.

121. Deleuze and Guattari, *What is Philosophy?*, 111.

122. Ibid., 104.

123. Patton, *Deleuzian Concepts*, 191.

124. Schneewind, *The Invention of Autonomy*, Epilogue.

125. John Rawls, *A Brief Inquiry into the Meaning of Sin and Faith: With "On My Religion,"* ed. Thomas Nagel (Cambridge, MA: Harvard University Press, 2009).

126. On Rawls's attempt to address the problems of his historical milieu, see Paul Weithman, "John Rawls and the Task of Political Philosophy," *Review of Politics* 71, no. 1 (2009): 113–25.

127. Rawls, *Political Liberalism*, lix.

128. On Rawls's early exposure to Nietzsche's ideas—as a graduate student indexing Walter Kaufmann's *Nietzsche: Philosophy, Psychologist and Anti-Christ*—see Thomas Pogge, *John Rawls*, trans. Michelle Kosch (New York: Oxford University Press, 2007), 15.

129. Rawls, *Political Liberalism*, lx.

130. Ibid., 44.

131. Deleuze, *Difference and Repetition*, 135.

132. David Reggio, "The Deleuzian Legacy," *History of the Human Sciences* 20, no. 1 (2007): 148.

133. See Patton, *Deleuzian Concepts*, 193–98.

134. Connolly, *Neuropolitics*, 172.

135. John Stuart Mill, *On Liberty*, ed. David Bromwich and George Kateb (New Haven, CT: Yale University Press, 2003), 114.

136. See Daniel W. Smith, "Deleuze and the Liberal Tradition: Normativity, Freedom, and Judgment," *Economy and Society* 32, no. 2 (May, 2003): 299–324.

137. Kant, *Groundwork*, 4:392, 7–8.

138. Kant, *The Metaphysics of Morals*, 6:219, 383.

139. Ibid., 6:230, 387.

140. Thomas W. Pogge, "Is Kant's Rechtslehre a 'Comprehensive Liberalism?'" In *Kant's* Metaphysics of Morals: *Interpretative Essays*, ed. Mark Timmons (New York: Oxford University Press, 2002), 145.

141. Hunter, *Rival Enlightenments*, 362–63.

142. Rawls, *Political Liberalism*, 58.

143. David Lewis Schaefer, *Illiberal Justice: John Rawls Vs. the American Political Tradition* (Columbia: University of Missouri Press, 2007).

144. Rawls, *Political Liberalism*, 37.

145. See Isaiah Berlin, "The Pursuit of the Ideal," in *The Crooked Timber of Humanity: Chapters in the History of Ideas* (Princeton, NJ: Princeton University Press, 1990), 1–18.

146. Rawls, *Political Liberalism*, 4.

147. Deleuze and Guattari, *A Thousand Plateaus*, 376.

148. On the need to fill out Deleuze's political philosophy—both by drawing upon the entire range of Deleuze's writings as well as other philosophers and contemporary states of affairs—see Patton, *Deleuzian Concepts*.

149. Deleuze and Guattari, *A Thousand Plateaus*, 17.

150. Ibid., 7.

151. Ibid., 9.

152. Ibid., 7.

153. Ibid., 12.

154. See Nicholas Tampio, "Assemblages and the Multitude: Deleuze, Hardt, Negri, and the Postmodern Left," *European Journal of Political Theory* 8, no. 3 (2009): 383–400.

155. See Rawls, *Political Liberalism*, 151.

156. Deleuze and Guattari, *A Thousand Plateaus*, 20.

157. On the idea of rhizomatic pluralism, see William E. Connolly, "Assembling the Left," *Boundary 2* 26, no. 3 (1999): 47–54.

158. For a Deleuzian critique of Rawls's intellectualism, see Connolly, *Why I Am Not a Secularist.*

159. See William E. Connolly, *Neuropolitics.*

160. Lorenz, "Kant's Doctrine," 236.

161. Deleuze and Guattari, *A Thousand Plateaus,* 15.

162. One of the greatest advocates of comparative political theory today, Fred Dallmayr, began as a scholar of the Frankfurt school of critical theory. See his *Integral Pluralism: Beyond Culture Wars* (Lexington: University Press of Kentucky, 2010).

163. David Hackett Fischer, *Liberty and Freedom: A Visual History of America's Founding Ideas* (New York: Oxford University Press, 2005), 5–6.

164. Ibid., 6.

165. Ibid., 15.

166. Rawls, *Justice as Fairness,* 199.

167. Ibid., 135–38.

168. Mill, *On Liberty,* 70. The quote is from Wilhelm von Humboldt, *Sphere and Duties of Government.*

169. Deleuze and Guattari, *A Thousand Plateaus,* 291.

170. Ibid., 470–71.

171. Ibid., 471.

172. Nicholas Thoburn, "Vacuoles of Noncommunication," in *Deleuze and the Contemporary World,* ed. Ian Buchanan and Adrian Parr (Edinburgh: Edinburgh University Press, 2006), 42–56.

173. On the preference of Deleuzian ethics and politics for lines of flight over rigid lines, or experimentation over solidification, see Paul Patton, *Deleuzian Concepts* and *Deleuze and the Political* (New York: Routledge, 2000).

3. CONSTRUCTING THEORIES

1. Talal Asad, "Free Speech, Blasphemy, and Secular Criticism," in *Is Critique Secular? Blasphemy, Injury, and Free Speech,* ed. Talal Asad (Berkeley: University of California Press, 2009), 48.

2. Ibid., 53.

3. Butler, "The Sensibility of Critique: Response to Asad and Mahmood," in *Is Critique Secular?,* 113.

4. Ibid., 115.

5. Kant, *Critique of Pure Reason,* Bxvi, 113.

6. Tom Rockmore, *Kant and Idealism* (New Haven, CT: Yale University Press, 2007), 9.

7. Kant, *Critique of Pure Reason,* A13/B27, 134.

8. Rockmore, *In Kant's Wake*; Rockmore, *On Constructivist Epistemology.*

9. John Rawls, "Themes in Kant's Moral Philosophy," in *Collected Papers*, ed. Samuel Freeman (Cambridge, MA: Harvard University Press, 1999), 511.

10. Ibid.

11. Constructivism looks "at how Kant seems to reason when he presents his various examples and we try to lay out in procedural form all the conditions he seems to rely on." Ibid., 514.

12. Deleuze and Guattari, *What is Philosophy?*, 5.

13. Kant, *Critique of Pure Reason*, A313/B370, 395.

14. Deleuze and Guattari, *What is Philosophy?*, 2.

15. Rockmore, *On Constructivist Epistemology*, 23–25.

16. Deleuze and Guattari, *What is Philosophy?*, 85.

17. Deleuze, *Kant's Critical Philosophy*, 3–4.

18. Deleuze and Guattari, *A Thousand Plateaus*, 40.

19. See Hardt, *Gilles Deleuze*, 29.

20. Rawls, *Political Liberalism*, 97.

21. Ibid., 100.

22. Deleuze and Guattari, *What is Philosophy?*, 106.

23. Ibid., 97.

24. Ibid., 107.

25. On Deleuze's conception of democracy, see Patton, *Deleuzian Concepts*, 161–84.

26. Deleuze and Guattari, *What is Philosophy?*, 110.

27. Onora O'Neill levels the charge of impurity, or relativism, against Rawls in "Constructivism in Rawls and Kant," in *The Cambridge Companion to Rawls*, ed. Samuel Freeman (New York: Cambridge University Press, 2003). On the idea that Deleuze's version of constructivism is too imbricated in the phenomena it wants to critique, see Iain Mackenzie, *The Idea of Pure Critique* (New York: Continuum, 2004).

28. Rawls, *Political Liberalism*, 120.

29. Ibid., 100.

30. Ibid., 121.

31. Deleuze and Guattari, *What is Philosophy?*, 105.

32. Ibid., 105.

33. Friedrich Nietzsche, *Philosophy and Truth: Selections from Nietzsche's Notebooks of the Early 1870's*, ed. Daniel Breazeale (Amherst, MA: Humanity Books, 1979), 28.

34. Kant, *Critique of Pure Reason*, A58/B82, 197.

35. Ibid., A35/B51, 164.

36. Ibid., A371, 427.

37. Ibid., A379–80, 431.

38. Deleuze, *Nietzsche and Philosophy*, 36.

39. See Sheldon S. Wolin, "Political Theory as a Vocation," *The American Political Science Review* 63, no. 4 (1969): 1062–82.

40. Ibid., 1074.

41. Rawls, *Lectures on the History of Moral Philosophy*, xvii.

42. On the mechanics of Rawlsian constructivism, see Taylor, *Reconstructing Rawls*, chapter 1.

43. Immanuel Kant, *Lectures on Logic*, ed. and trans. J. Michael Young (New York: Cambridge University Press, 1992), 538.

44. On the distinction between human nature, which defines us as "an *animal creature*," and personality, "in which the moral law reveals to me a life independent of animality," see Kant, *Critique of Practical Reason*, 5:162, 269–70.

45. Christine M. Korsgaard, *Self-Constitution: Agency, Identity, and Integrity* (New York: Oxford University Press, 2009).

46. Kant, *Groundwork*, 4:412, 28.

47. Schneewind, *The Invention of Autonomy*, 509–13.

48. Kant, *Religion within the Boundaries of Mere Reason*, 6:27–28, 76.

49. Rawls, *Political Liberalism*, 104, 14

50. Rawls, *A Theory of Justice*, 227.

51. Rawls, *Political Liberalism*, 18.

52. Bloom, "Justice."

53. George Klosko, "Political Constructivism in Rawls's Political Liberalism," *American Political Science Review* 91, no. 3 (1997): 641.

54. Rawls, *Political Liberalism*, 87.

55. Ibid., 49.

56. Deleuze and Guattari, *What is Philosophy?*, 70.

57. Ibid., 67.

58. Ibid., 69.

59. Ibid.

60. Deleuze and Guattari, *A Thousand Plateaus*, 150.

61. Ibid.

62. Rawls, *Political Liberalism*, 159.

63. Kerslake, *Immanence and the Vertigo of Philosophy*, 10.

64. Rawls, *Political Liberalism*, 15.

65. See Patton, *Deleuze and the Political*, 85.

66. Rawls, *Political Liberalism*, 51.

67. Ibid., 339.

68. Ibid. 23.

69. Immanuel Kant, "On the Common Saying: This May Be True in Theory, but It Does Not Hold in Practice," in *Toward Perpetual Peace and Other*

Writings on Politics, Peace, and History, ed. Pauline Kleingeld, trans. David L. Colclasure (New Haven, CT: Yale University Press, 2006), 8:297, 51.

70. Rawls, *A Theory of Justice*, 225.

71. See Rawls, *Lectures in the History of Political Philosophy*, 159–73.

72. Rawls, *Political Liberalism*, 27.

73. Jürgen Habermas argues that the original position predetermines too many political issues in advance: "The form of political autonomy granted virtual existence in the original position . . . does not fully unfold in the heart of the justly constituted society. For the higher the veil of ignorance is raised and the more Rawls's citizens themselves take on real flesh and blood, the more deeply they find themselves subject to principles and norms that have been anticipated in theory." "Reconciliation Through the Public Use of Reason: Remarks on John Rawls's Political Liberalism," *Journal of Philosophy* 92, no. 3 (1995): 128. Rawls denies the charge: "No (human) theory could possibly anticipate all the requisite considerations bearing on these problems under existing circumstances. . . . The ideal of a just constitution is always something to be worked toward." *Political Liberalism*, 401. On the one hand, Rawls wants to leave open the theoretical possibility that reflective citizens may wish to change the framework of the original position, the conception of the actors within it, and the principles of justice chosen. Rawls also acknowledges that citizens exercising public reason may transcend their partiality in multiple ways. On the other hand, Rawls denies that principles of justice may be too plastic, lest that they equate political liberalism with majoritarianism. Rather than try to adjudicate between Rawls and Habermas, I merely note that both confront a profound problem facing post-Kantian political theorists, namely, how to formulate practical principles for an unfathomable universe. See James Gordon Finlayson and Fabian Freyenhagen, eds. *Habermas and Rawls: Disputing the Political* (New York: Routledge, 2010).

74. Rawls, *Political Liberalism*, 26.

75. George Armstrong Kelly, "Veils: The Poetics of John Rawls," *Journal of the History of Ideas* 57, no. 2 (1996): 346.

76. Deleuze and Guattari, *What is Philosophy?*, 41.

77. Ibid.

78. Ibid., 42.

79. Ibid., 50.

80. In this paragraph, I assume that Deleuze means roughly the same thing by plane of consistency, plane of immanence, and field of immanence. See Adrian Parr, "Plane of Consistency," in *The Deleuze Dictionary* (New York: Columbia University Press, 2005).

81. Deleuze and Guattari, *A Thousand Plateaus*, 157.

82. Deleuze and Guattari, *What is Philosophy?*, 12.

83. In this book, I apply a Deleuzian analysis primarily to think about religious pluralism; for a Deleuzian analysis of late-modern capitalism, see William E. Connolly, *Capitalism and Christianity, American Style* (Durham, NC: Duke University Press, 2008).

84. Rawls, *Political Liberalism*, 273.

85. Rawls, "Themes," 498.

86. Ibid.

87. Ibid.

88. Kant, *Groundwork*, 4:412, 28–29.

89. John Rawls, *Collected Papers*, ed. Samuel Freeman (Cambridge, MA: Harvard University Press, 1999), 291.

90. Rawls, *Justice as Fairness*, 42.

91. Ibid.

92. Ibid., 43.

93. Rawls, *Political Liberalism*, xlvi.

94. Ibid.

95. See Charles Beitz, *Political Theory and International Relations* (Princeton, NJ: Princeton University Press, 1979).

96. Rawls, *Political Liberalism*, 161.

97. On the vitalism informing Deleuze's political ethics, see Claire Colebrook, *Deleuze and the Meaning of Life* (New York: Continuum, 2010).

98. Rawls, "Kantian Constructivism," 354.

99. Deleuze and Guattari, *What is Philosophy?*, 76.

100. Ibid.

101. The novelist Stephen King offers an intuitive explanation of the constructivist procedure: "I want to put a group of characters . . . in some sort of predicament and then watch them try to work themselves free. My job isn't to *help* them work their way free . . . but to watch what happens and then write it down." Stephen King, *On Writing* (New York: Scribner, 2000), 161.

102. John Rawls, *A Theory of Justice* (Cambridge, MA: Harvard University Press, 1971), 253.

103. Rawls, *Political Liberalism*, 165.

104. Ibid.

105. On the *Groundwork*, see Henrich, "The Deduction of the Moral Law." On the *Critique of Practical Reason*, see Dieter Henrich, *The Unity of Reason: Essays on Kant's Philosophy* (Cambridge, MA: Harvard University Press, 1994), chapter 2.

106. Kant, *Groundwork*, 4:457, 73.

107. Ibid., 4:463, 79.

108. Kant, *Critique of Practical Reason*, 5:4, 140.

109. Ibid., 5:47, 177.

110. Rawls, "Themes," 517.

111. Ibid., 523.

112. Rawls, *Political Liberalism*, 8–9.

113. Rawls, *Justice as Fairness*, 30.

114. Ibid., 29.

115. Ibid., 31. Emphasis added.

116. See Patton, *Deleuze and the Political*, 22.

117. Rawls, *Collected Papers*, 289.

118. Deleuze, *Kant's Critical Philosophy*, 11, 28.

119. Deleuze, *Difference and Repetition*, 135.

120. Ibid.

121. Ibid., 137.

122. Gilles Deleuze, *Essays Critical and Clinical* (Minneapolis: University of Minnesota Press, 1997), 135.

123. See William E. Connolly, *The Ethos of Pluralization* (Minneapolis: University of Minnesota Press, 1995).

124. On the theme of evaluation in Nietzsche's philosophy, see Deleuze, *Nietzsche and Philosophy*.

125. Rawls, *Political Liberalism*, 151. Emphasis added.

126. Gilles Deleuze, *Spinoza: Practical Philosophy* (San Francisco: City Lights Books, 1988), 19.

127. Nietzsche, *On the Genealogy of Morality*, 67.

128. Deleuze and Guattari, *A Thousand Plateaus*, 160.

129. On translating *Vernunft* as "thought" rather than "reason," see Arendt, *Lectures on Kant's Political Philosophy*.

130. Deleuze, *Spinoza: Practical Philosophy*, 108.

131. Kant, *Anthropology from a Pragmatic Point of View*, 7:119, 231.

132. Kant, *Critique of Practical Reason*, 5:78–79, 203–4. For a critique of the doctrine of the fact of reason, see Connolly, *Why I am not a Secularist*, chapter 7.

133. Deleuze and Guattari, *What is Philosophy?*, 78–79.

134. Ibid.

135. Ibid., 82.

136. Rawls, *Political Liberalism*, 43–46.

137. Jonathan Israel, *Radical Enlightenment: Philosophy and the Making of Modernity, 1650–1750* (New York: Oxford University Press, 2001), vi.

138. Ibid., 11.

139. Rawls, *A Brief Inquiry*, 264.

140. Ibid.

141. Hilary Putnam, "John Rawls, 21 February 1921–24 November 2002," *Proceedings of the American Philosophical Society* 149, no. 1 (2005): 113–17.

142. Rawls, *A Brief Inquiry*, 266–67.

143. John Rawls, "*Commonweal* Interview with John Rawls" In *Collected Papers*, ed. Samuel Freeman (Cambridge, MA: Harvard University Press, 1999), 622.

144. Micah Schwartzman, "The Relevance of Locke's Religious Arguments for Toleration," *Political Theory* 33, no. 5 (2005): 678–705.

145. Israel, *Radical Enlightenment*, 11.

146. Deleuze and Guattari, *What is Philosophy?*, 48.

147. Ibid., 44.

148. Ibid., 45.

149. Ibid., 46.

150. Ibid., 48.

151. Jonathan I. Israel, "Introduction," Spinoza, *Theological-Political Treatise*, xxviii.

152. Ibid.

153. Deleuze and Guattari, *What is Philosophy?*, 50.

154. William E. Connolly, "The Radical Enlightenment: Faith, Power, Theory," *Theory & Event* 7, no. 3 (2004), http://muse.jhu.edu/journals/theory_and_event/v007/7.3connolly.html.

4. ENGAGING ISLAM

1. For an early version of this thesis, see G. W. F. Hegel, *Early Theological Writings*, trans. T. M. Knox (Chicago: University of Chicago Press, 1948).

2. Kant, *Religion within the Boundaries of Mere Reason*, 6:141, 166; 6:127, 156.

3. Gordon E. Michalson, *Kant and the Problem of God* (Malden, MA: Blackwell, 1999), 126.

4. Wood, "The Supreme Principle of Morality," 372. See also Chris L. Firestone and Nathan Jacobs, *In Defense of Kant's Religion* (Bloomington: Indiana University Press, 2008).

5. Hunter, *Islam, Europe's Second Religion*.

6. Caldwell, *Reflections on the Revolution in Europe*, 13. See also Ian Buruma, *Murder in Amsterdam: The Death of Theo Van Gogh and the Limits of Tolerance* (New York: Penguin Press, 2006) and Paul M. Sniderman and A. Hagendoorn, *When Ways of Life Collide: Multiculturalism and its Discontents in the Netherlands* (Princeton, NJ: Princeton University Press, 2007).

7. On the Hizb ut-Tahrir (the "Islamic Liberation Party") and its policy of gradually, nonviolently laying the foundation for a global caliphate, see Peter G. Mandaville, *Global Political Islam* (New York: Routledge, 2007), 265–71.

8. Kant, *Critique of the Power of Judgment*, 5:294, 174.

9. Andrew F. March, *Islam and Liberal Citizenship: The Search for an Overlapping Consensus* (New York: Oxford University Press, 2009), 12.

10. The classic history of the Nahda is Albert Hourani, *Arabic Thought in the Liberal Age, 1798–1939* (New York: Cambridge University Press, 1983). On the appropriation of the Nahda legacy, see Elizabeth Suzanne Kassab, *Contemporary Arab Thought: Cultural Critique in Comparative Perspective* (New York: Columbia University Press, 2010).

11. See Alex Schulman, *The Secular Contract*.

12. Kant, *Religion within the Boundaries of Mere Reason*, 6:98, 133.

13. Ibid., 6:12, 64.

14. Ibid., 6:108, 141.

15. Ibid., 6:130–31, 158–59.

16. Ibid., 6:131, 159.

17. For a highly qualified defense of war and religious schisms, see "Towards Perpetual Peace," 8:360–368, 85–92.

18. Ibid., 6:94, 130.

19. Kant, *The Metaphysics of Morals*, 6:237, 469.

20. Kant, *Religion within the Boundaries of Mere Reason*, 6:97, 133.

21. Ibid., 6:102, 136.

22. Ibid., 6:98, 133.

23. Ibid., 6:10 –8, 140.

24. Ibid., 6:108, 141.

25. Ibid., 6:108, 140.

26. Ibid., 6:115, 146.

27. Ibid., 6:121, 151.

28. See Immanuel Kant, "Toward Perpetual Peace," 8:357, 81.

29. Kant, *Religion within the Boundaries of Mere Reason*, 6:109, 142. On parallels between political and religious schisms, see Ibid., 6:123, 153.

30. Ibid., 6:109, 141.

31. Ibid., 6:104, 138.

32. Ibid., 6:103, 137.

33. Michalson, *Kant and the Problem of God*, 117.

34. Kant, "Toward Perpetual Peace," 8:366, 90.

35. Kant, *Religion within the Boundaries of Mere Reason*, 6:99, 134.

36. Ibid., 6:134, 160–61.

37. Talal Asad, *Formations of the Secular: Christianity, Islam, Modernity* (Stanford, CA: Stanford University Press, 2003), 245.

38. Philip Rossi, "Kant's Philosophy of Religion," in *The Stanford Encyclopedia of Philosophy*, ed. Edward N. Zalta (2009), http://plato.stanford.edu/archives/win2009/entries/kant-religion/.

39. Michalson, *Kant and the Problem of God*, 126.

40. Hunter, *Rival Enlightenments*.

41. Wood, *Kant's Ethical Thought*, 411.

42. Shell, *Kant and the Limits of Autonomy*, 315.

43. Yirmiahu Yovel, *Kant and the Philosophy of History* (Princeton, NJ: Princeton University Press, 1980).

44. Michalson, *Kant and the Problem of God*, 123–28.

45. Kant, *Religion within the Boundaries of Mere Reason*, 6:102, 136.

46. Ibid., 463.

47. Lorenz, "Kant's Doctrine," 232.

48. Kant, *Religion within the Boundaries of Mere Reason*, 6:115, 146.

49. On "Kant's Jewish Problem," see Shell, *Kant and the Limits of Autonomy*, chapter 6.

50. Kant, *Religion within the Boundaries of Mere Reason*, 6:193–94, 209.

51. Ibid., 6:193, 209, 6:192, 208.

52. Wood, *Kant's Ethical Thought*, 316–17.

53. Saba Mahmood, "Religious Reason and Secular Affect: An Incommensurable Divide?," in *Is Critique Secular?: Blasphemy, Injury, and Free Speech*, ed. Talal Asad (Berkeley: University of California Press, 2009), 64–100.

54. José Casanova, *Public Religions in the Modern World* (Chicago: University of Chicago Press, 1994), 5.

55. Ibid., 5–6.

56. Robert D. Putnam, David E. Campbell and Shaylin Romney Garrett, *American Grace: How Religion Divides and Unites Us* (New York: Simon & Schuster, 2010), 17.

57. See Casanova, *Public Religions*, 39.

58. See Rockmore, *In Kant's Wake*, 43.

59. See Peter Lipton, "Kant on Wheels," *Social Epistemology* 17, no. 2 (2003): 215–19.

60. Quentin Meillassoux challenges Kant's doctrine of transcendental idealism in the name of a speculative materialism whose most urgent question is "how is thought able to think what there can be when there is no thought?" or "how is empirical knowledge of a world anterior to all experience possible?" *After Finitude: An Essay on the Necessity of Contingency*, trans. Ray Brassier (New York: Continuum, 2008), 121, 123. Meillassoux poses these questions at the end of his essay and does not answer them. Are they the right questions? Post-Kantian philosophers may hold that transcendental categories "allow of that indefinite refinement, correction, and extension which accompany the advance of science and the development of social forms." Strawson, *The Bounds of Sense*, 21. Here, I think, is a much more sensible proposal: Human beings can only perceive the world through their conceptual lenses, but these lenses are capable of change and

improvement (though there is no single scale to determine that quality). Perhaps Meillassoux advances the quest for speculative materialism because, like Alain Badiou, he sees a Platonic "originary alliance" between mathematics and philosophy (104). Or, perhaps like Badiou again, he holds a Maoist-Leninist view of politics that seeks to enforce absolutes. On the connection between scientific and political images of thought, see Deleuze and Guattari, *A Thousand Plateaus*, 361–74.

61. On the constitutive model of the soul common to Plato and Kant, see Christine Korsgaard, *The Constitution of Agency: Essays on Practical Reason and Moral Psychology* (New York: Oxford University Press, 2008), chapter 3.

62. On the virtue of agonistic respect, see Connolly, *The Ethos of Pluralization*.

63. Nader Hashemi, *Islam, Secularism, and Liberal Democracy*, 5.

64. Kant, *The Metaphysics of Morals*, 6:216–17, 371–72.

65. See Ian Almond, *History of Islam in German Thought from Leibniz to Nietzsche* (New York: Routledge, 2010), chapter 2.

66. Rawls, *Political Liberalism*, xvii.

67. John Rawls, *The Law of Peoples* (Cambridge, MA: Harvard University Press, 1999), 10.

68. Ibid., 122.

69. See Arif A. Jamal, "Moving Out of Kazanistan: Liberal Theory and Muslim Contexts," in *Muslim Societies and the Challenge of Secularization: An Interdisciplinary Approach*, ed. Gabriele Marranci (Dordrecht, Ger.: Springer, 2010), 83–98.

70. Rawls, *The Law of Peoples*, 64.

71. Ibid., 64–67.

72. Ibid., 75.

73. John Tasioulas, "From Utopia to Kazanistan," 384.

74. Jamal, "Moving Out of Kazanistan" and Hashemi, *Islam, Secularism, and Liberal Democracy*.

75. Rawls, *The Law of Peoples*, 78.

76. Rawls, *Political Liberalism*, 147.

77. Ibid., 171.

78. Ibid.

79. Ibid., 154.

80. Ibid., 148.

81. Ibid., xxvi.

82. Ibid., 153.

83. March, *Islam and Liberal Citizenship*, 15.

84. Kant, *Toward Perpetual Peace*, 8:354–57, 78–81.

85. Rawls, *The Law of Peoples*, 42.

86. Rawls, *Political Liberalism*, 150–51.

87. Ibid., xlvi.

88. On how the concept of the "will of the people" is both an elusive and yet necessary concept for democratic politics, see Jason A. Frank, *Constituent Moments: Enacting the People in Postrevolutionary America* (Durham, NC: Duke University Press, 2010).

89. Taylor, *Reconstructing Rawls*, 292. Emphasis in original.

90. Deleuze and Guattari, *A Thousand Plateaus*, 406.

91. Ibid.

92. Ibid.

93. Ibid., 85–86.

94. Ibid.

95. See Nicholas Tampio, "Multiplicity," in *Encyclopedia of Political Theory*, ed. Mark Bevir (Thousand Oaks, CA: Sage Publications, 2010), 911–12.

96. Deleuze and Guattari, *A Thousand Plateaus*, 510.

97. Tampio, "Assemblages and the Multitude."

98. Protevi, *Political Affect*, chapter 1.

99. Consider the analogous point that though Deleuzian jurisprudence prizes innovation for singular cases, "Deleuze is not recommending flux and destabilization in law." Lefebvre, *The Image of Law*, 58.

100. March, *Islam and Liberal Citizenship*, 73–74.

101. Ibid., 73, 75.

102. For a description, see http://www.youtube.com/user/muslimheretics.

103. March, *Islam and Liberal Citizenship*, 291.

104. Ibid., 7.

105. Deleuze and Guattari, *A Thousand Plateaus*, 213.

106. Marc Lynch, *Voices of the New Arab Public: Iraq, Al-Jazeera, and Middle East Politics Today* (New York: Columbia University Press, 2006), 9.

107. See Protevi, *Political Affect*, chapter 3, and Protevi, *Political Physics*, chapters 5 and 7.

108. See Tariq Ramadan, *Islam, the West and the Challenges of Modernity* (Leicester: The Islamic Foundation, 2001), 88, 128.

109. On how Ramadan extracts lessons from the life of the Prophet, the Islamic legal schools, and the Nahda, see Nicholas Tampio, "Constructing the Space of Testimony: Tariq Ramadan's Copernican Revolution," *Political Theory*, 39, no. 5 (2011): 600–29.

110. Sayyid Qutb, *Milestones* (Cedar Rapids: Mother Mosque Foundation, 1995), 118. On Qutb's influence, see Lawrence Wright, *The Looming Tower: Al-Qaeda and the Road to 9/11* (New York: Knopf, 2006), chapter 1.

111. Qutb, *Milestones*, 61.

112. Ibid., 11.

113. See John L. Esposito, *The Future of Islam* (New York: Oxford University Press, 2010).

114. Samuel P. Huntington, *The Clash of Civilizations and the Remaking of World Order* (New York: Touchstone, 1997).

115. See Tariq Ramadan, *Radical Reform: Islamic Ethics and Liberation* (New York: Oxford University Press, 2009) and Andrew F. March, "The Post-Legal Ethics of Tariq Ramadan: Persuasion and Performance in *Radical Reform: Islamic Ethics and Liberation*," *Middle East Law & Governance* 2, no. 2 (2010): 253–73.

116. On Ramadan's debts to earlier Nahda intellectuals such as Jamal al-din al-Afghani and Muhammad 'Abduh, see Tariq Ramadan, *Aux Sources Du Renouveau Musulman: D'Al-Afghani à Hassan Al-Banna, Un Siècle De Réformisme Islamique* (Paris: Bayard éditions/Centurion, 1998).

117. Tariq Ramadan, *To Be a European Muslim* (Markfield UK: Islamic Foundation, 1999), 123.

118. Ibid., 127.

119. Ibid., 129–30.

120. Ibid., 132.

121. Ibid., 132–34.

122. Ibid., 135–37.

123. Tariq Ramadan, *Western Muslims*, 5.

124. Ibid., 53–54.

125. Ramadan, *To Be a European Muslim*, 141–42, and *Western Muslims*, 71–72.

126. Ramadan, *To Be a European Muslim*, 142–43, and *Western Muslims*, 76.

127. On the concept of the space of testimony, see Andrew F. March, "Reading Tariq Ramadan: Political Liberalism, Islam, and 'Overlapping Consensus,'" *Ethics & International Affairs* 21, no. 4 (2007): 399–413; Peter G. Mandaville, "Sufis and Salafis: The Political Discourse of Transnational Islam," in *Remaking Muslim Politics: Pluralism, Contestation, Democratization*, ed. Robert W. Hefner (Princeton, NJ: Princeton University Press, 2005), 318–20; and Roxanne L. Euben, *Journeys to the Other Shore: Muslim and Western Travelers in Search of Knowledge* (Princeton, NJ: Princeton University Press, 2006), 187.

128. Ramadan, *Western Muslims*, 75.

129. Ibid., 74.

130. See Abu'l-A'la Mawdudi, "The Islamic Law," in *Princeton Readings in Islamist Thought*, 79–106.

131. Ramadan, *To Be a European Muslim*, 139.

132. Rawls, *Political Liberalism*, 462.

133. Ramadan, *Western Muslims*, 74.

134. Ramadan, *To Be a European Muslim*, 145.

135. Nancy Fraser, "Rethinking the Public Sphere," *Social Text* 25/26 (1990): 56–80.

136. Ramadan, *Western Muslims*, 202.

137. Ramadan, *Islam, the West and the Challenges of Modernity*, 201–18.

138. Ibid., 218.

139. On the possibility that long-standing liberal commitments might change in a thoughtful encounter with Muslims, see Roxanne L. Euben, "Making the World Safe for Compatibility," *Political Theory* 38, no. 3 (2010): 437.

140. On critical loyalty, see Ramadan, *The Quest for Meaning*, 108–10.

141. Taylor, *Reconstructing Rawls*, 303.

142. According to Taylor, "it is uncertain that even a reinterpreted Islam could accept doctrinal autonomy (as it sees Shari'ah as a binding—divine law)" and thus qualify as a Rawlsian reasonable comprehensive doctrine. Ibid., 263.

143. William Montgomery Watt, *Islamic Creeds: A Selection* (Edinburgh: Edinburgh University Press, 1994), 42.

144. Kassab, *Contemporary Arab Thought*.

145. See Nikki R. Keddie, *An Islamic Response to Imperialism: Political and Religious Writings of Sayyid Jamal Ad-Din "Al-Afghani"* (Berkeley: University of California Press, 1983). On Afghani's ambivalent relationship to European philosophy, see Roxanne L. Euben, *Enemy in the Mirror: Islamic Fundamentalism and the Limits of Modern Rationalism: A Work of Comparative Political Theory* (Princeton, NJ: Princeton University Press, 1999), 93–117.

146. Hourani, *Arabic Thought in the Liberal Age*, 71.

147. Ibid., vi.

148. Kassab, *Contemporary Arab Thought*, 8.

149. Ibid., 363.

150. See Ibrahim Kalin, "Does Islam Need Enlightenment?" *Today's Zaman*, August 27, 2009; Akeel Bilgrami, "Occidentalism, the Very Idea: An Essay on Enlightenment and Enchantment," *Critical Inquiry* 32, no. 3 (2006): 381–411; Saba Mahmood, "Secularism, Hermeneutics, and Empire: The Politics of Islamic Reformation," *Public Culture* 18, no. 2 (2006): 323–47.

151. Connolly, *Neuropolitics*, 215.

CONCLUSION: THE BATTLE FOR AUTONOMY

1. Shell, *Kant and the Limits of Autonomy*, 335.

2. Ibid., 14.

3. Ibid., 340.

4. Ibid., 14.

5. Schneewind, *The Invention of Autonomy*, 5.

6. See Robert S. Taylor, "Kantian Personal Autonomy," *Political Theory* 33, no. 5 (2005): 602–28.

7. Larmore, *The Autonomy of Morality* (New York: Cambridge University Press, 2008), 9.

8. Ibid.

9. Ibid., 89.

10. Larmore, "Political Liberalism," *Political Theory* 18, no. 3 (1990): 339–60.

11. Larmore, *The Autonomy of Morality*, 77.

12. See Charles Larmore, "Reflection and Morality," *Social Philosophy and Policy* 27, no. 2 (2010): 1–28.

13. "It is not such a very long step from Kant to Nietzsche, and from Nietzsche to existentialism and the Anglo-Saxon ethical doctrines that in some way resemble it. In fact, Kant's man had already received a glorious incarnation earlier in the work of Milton. His name is Lucifer." Iris Murdoch, *The Sovereignty of Good* (New York: Schocken Books, 1970), 80.

14. Larmore, *The Autonomy of Morality*, 46.

15. Ibid., 463–44.

16. Ibid., 84.

17. Larmore, "Political Liberalism."

18. Larmore, *The Autonomy of Morality*, 14.

19. Larmore, "Political Liberalism."

20. Charles Larmore, "Behind the Veil," *New Republic* 238, no. 3 (February 27, 2008): 43–47.

21. Wood, *Kantian Ethics*, 106.

22. Ibid., 108.

23. Ibid., 111.

24. Cited in ibid., 113.

25. Ibid., 116.

26. Wood, *Kant's Ethical Thought*, 321–22.

27. Wood, "The Supreme Principle of Morality," 372.

28. Wood, *Kantian Ethics*, 122.

29. On the historical roots of the idea of self-governance, see Schneewind, *The Invention of Autonomy*.

30. Larmore, *The Autonomy of Morality*, 6.

31. Wood, *Kantian Ethics*, 119.

32. Ibid., 51. Emphasis in original.

33. Larmore, *The Autonomy of Morality*, 12.

34. On the *Wille/ Willkür* distinction, see Wood, *Kantian Ethics*, 121.

35. Strawson, P. F. *The Bounds of Sense: An Essay on Kant's* Critique of Pure Reason (London: Routledge, 1966).

36. Romans 2:14–15, cited in Schneewind, *The Invention of Autonomy*, 18.

37. Wood, *Kantian Ethics*, 124.

38. On the Greek conception of the tragic permeating Western culture, see Ramadan, *Islam, the West and the Challenges of Modernity*, 210–27.

39. Kant, *Critique of Practical Reason*, 5:89–106, 211–25.

40. Howard Caygill, *A Kant Dictionary* (Oxford: Blackwell, 2002), 88.

41. Kant, *Toward Perpetual Peace*, 8:372, 96.

42. See Honig, *Political Theory and the Displacement of Politics*, chapter 2.

43. Kant, *Groundwork*, 4:412, 28. Lewis White Beck argues that Kant articulates at least five "degrees of purity" in his practical philosophy but wonders, "Just how 'pure' can moral philosophy be?" *A Commentary on Kant's Critique of Practical Reason*, 53.

44. According to Christian Rostbøll, a Kantian conception of autonomy must balance freedom of expression with the belief that "people should be able equally to live according to their deepest beliefs and commitments." Christian F. Rostbøll, "Autonomy, Respect, and Arrogance in the Danish Cartoon Controversy," *Political Theory* 37, no. 5 (2009): 623–48. I agree that political prudence, or the desire to cultivate civic friendship, often recommends respecting other ways of life that you do not share. Yet pluralistic democracies need to cultivate a culture of critique where people feel free to challenge others' ideas and beliefs. As Kant observes in the *Critique of Pure Reason*, "Religion through its holiness and legislation through its majesty commonly seek to exempt themselves from it. But in this way they excite a just suspicion against themselves, and cannot lay claim to that unfeigned respect that reason grants only to that which has been able to withstand its free and public examination." Kant, *Critique of Pure Reason*, Axi, 101.

Bibliography

"The Haze Administration." *Wall Street Journal,* April 4, 2009.

"Most Cited Authors in the Humanities," 2007. *Times Higher Education,* March 26, 2009.

Abaza, Mona. "The Trafficking with Tanwir (Enlightenment)." *Comparative Studies of South Asia, Africa and the Middle East* 30, no. 1 (2010): 32–46.

Allen, Amy. *The Politics of our Selves: Power, Autonomy, and Gender in Contemporary Critical Theory.* New York: Columbia University Press, 2008.

Ali, Ayaan Hirsi. *The Caged Virgin: An Emancipation Proclamation for Women and Islam.* New York: Free Press, 2006.

Allison, Henry. *Kant's Transcendental Idealism: An Interpretation and Defense: Revised and Enlarged Edition.* New Haven, CT: Yale University Press, 2004.

Almond, Ian. *History of Islam in German Thought from Leibniz to Nietzsche.* New York: Routledge, 2010.

Ansell-Pearson, Keith. *Germinal Life: The Difference and Repetition of Deleuze.* New York: Routledge, 1999.

Arendt, Hannah. *Eichmann in Jerusalem: A Report on the Banality of Evil.* New York: Penguin Books, 2006.

———. *The Human Condition.* Chicago: University of Chicago Press, 1958.

———. *Lectures on Kant's Political Philosophy.* Edited by Ronald Beiner. Chicago: University of Chicago Press, 1982.

———. *The Life of the Mind.* New York: Harcourt Brace Jovanovich, 1978.

Aristotle. *Nicomachean Ethics.* Edited by Roger Crisp. Cambridge: Cambridge University Press, 2000.

Asad, Talal. *Formations of the Secular: Christianity, Islam, Modernity.* Stanford, CA: Stanford University Press, 2003.

———. "Free Speech, Blasphemy, and Secular Criticism." In *Is Critique Secular?: Blasphemy, Injury, and Free Speech*, edited by Talal Asad, 20–63. Berkeley: University of California Press, 2009.

Austin, J. L. *How to do Things with Words*. Oxford: Clarendon Press, 1975.

Axinn, Sidney. "The First Western Pragmatist, Immanuel Kant." *Journal of Chinese Philosophy* 33, no. 1 (2006): 83–94.

Beaulieu, Alain. "Towards a Liberal Utopia: The Connection between Foucault's Reporting on the Iranian Revolution and the Ethical Turn." *Philosophy & Social Criticism* 36 (2010): 801–18.

Beck, Lewis White. *A Commentary on Kant's Critique of Practical Reason*. Chicago: University of Chicago Press, 1960.

Beitz, Charles R. *Political Theory and International Relations*. Princeton, NJ: Princeton University Press, 1999.

Bell, Jeffrey A. *Deleuze's Hume: Philosophy, Culture and the Scottish Enlightenment*. Edinburgh: Edinburgh University Press, 2009.

Bennett, Jane. *Vibrant Matter: A Political Ecology of Things*. Durham, NC: Duke University Press, 2010.

Berlin, Isaiah. *The Crooked Timber of Humanity: Chapters in the History of Ideas*. Princeton, NJ: Princeton University Press, 1990.

Berman, Paul. *The Flight of the Intellectuals*. Brooklyn, NY: Melville House, 2010.

Bilgrami, Akeel. "Occidentalism, the Very Idea: An Essay on Enlightenment and Enchantment." *Critical Inquiry* 32, no. 3 (2006): 381–411.

Bloom, Allan David. "Justice: John Rawls Versus the Tradition of Political Philosophy." *American Political Science Review* 69 (1975): 648–62.

Borradori, Giovanna. *Philosophy in a Time of Terror: Dialogues with Jürgen Habermas and Jacques Derrida*. Chicago: University of Chicago Press, 2003.

Boundas, Constantin V. "The Art of Begetting Monsters: The Unnatural Nuptials of Deleuze and Kant." In *Current Continental Theory and Modern Philosophy*, edited by Stephen H. Daniel, 254–79. Evanston, IL: Northwestern University Press, 2005.

Bronner, Stephen Eric. *Reclaiming the Enlightenment: Toward a Politics of Radical Engagement*. New York: Columbia University Press, 2004.

Bryant, Levi R. *Difference and Givenness: Deleuze's Transcendental Empiricism and the Ontology of Immanence*. Evanston, IL: Northwestern University Press, 2008.

Buchanan, Ian. *Deleuze and Guattari's Anti-Oedipus: A Reader's Guide*. London: Continuum, 2008.

Buck-Morss, Susan. *Thinking Past Terror: Islamism and Critical Theory on the Left*. New York: Verso, 2003.

Burnham, Douglas. *An Introduction to Kant's* Critique of Judgement. Edinburgh: Edinburgh University Press, 2000.

Buruma, Ian. *Murder in Amsterdam: The Death of Theo Van Gogh and the Limits of Tolerance*. New York: Penguin Press, 2006.

Butler, Judith. "The Sensibility of Critique: Response to Asad and Mahmood." In *Is Critique Secular?: Blasphemy, Injury, and Free Speech*, edited by Talal Asad, 101–36. Berkeley: University of California Press, 2009.

Byrd, B. Sharon, and Joachim Hruschka. *Kant's* Doctrine of Right: *A Commentary*. Cambridge: Cambridge University Press, 2010.

Caldwell, Christopher. *Reflections on the Revolution in Europe: Immigration, Islam, and the West*. New York: Doubleday, 2009.

Casanova, José. *Public Religions in the Modern World*. Chicago: University of Chicago Press, 1994.

Cassirer, Ernst. *The Philosophy of the Enlightenment*. Edited by Peter Gay. Princeton, NJ: Princeton University Press, 2009.

Caygill, Howard. *A Kant Dictionary*. Oxford: Blackwell, 2002.

Clinton, William J. "Remarks on Presenting the Arts and Humanities Awards," *Weekly Compilation of Presidential Documents* 35, no. 39 (1999): 1847–53.

Cohen, Roger. "After the War on Terror." *New York Times*, January 29, 2009.

Colebrook, Claire. *Deleuze and the Meaning of Life*. New York: Continuum, 2010.

———. *Gilles Deleuze*. New York: Routledge, 2002.

Coles, Romand. *Rethinking Generosity: Critical Theory and the Politics of Caritas*. Ithaca, NY: Cornell University Press, 1997.

Connolly, William E. "Assembling the Left." *Boundary 2* 26, no. 3 (1999): 47–54.

———. *Capitalism and Christianity, American Style*. Durham, NC: Duke University Press, 2008.

———. *The Ethos of Pluralization*. Minneapolis: University of Minnesota Press, 1995.

———. *Neuropolitics: Thinking, Culture, Speed*. Minneapolis: University of Minnesota Press, 2002.

———. *Political Theory and Modernity*. Ithaca, NY: Cornell University Press, 1993.

———. *Politics and Ambiguity*. Madison: University of Wisconsin Press, 1987.

———. "The Radical Enlightenment: Faith, Power, Theory." *Theory & Event* 7, no. 3 (2004). http://muse.jhu.edu/journals/theory_and_event/v007/7.3connolly.html.

———. *Why I Am Not a Secularist*. Minneapolis: University of Minnesota Press, 1999.

Cowell, Alan. "U.S. is 'Not Your Enemy,' Obama Tells Islamic World." *New York Times*, January 28, 2009.

Dallmayr, Fred. *Integral Pluralism: Beyond Culture Wars*. Lexington: University Press of Kentucky, 2010.

Deleuze, Gilles. *Difference and Repetition*. Translated by Paul Patton. New York: Columbia University Press, 1994.

———. *Empiricism and Subjectivity: An Essay on Hume's Theory of Human Nature*. Translated by Constantin Boundas. New York: Columbia University Press, 1991.

———. *Essays Critical and Clinical*. Translated by Daniel W. Smith. Minneapolis: University of Minnesota Press, 1997.

———. "Kant: Synthesis and Time." Lectures of March 1978, translated by Melissa McMahon. http://www.webdeleuze.com/php/sommaire.html.

———. *Kant's Critical Philosophy: The Doctrine of the Faculties*. Translated by Hugh Tomlinson and Barbara Habberjam. Minneapolis: University of Minnesota Press, 1984.

———. *Negotiations, 1972–1990*. Translated by Martin Joughin. New York: Columbia University Press, 1995.

———. *Nietzsche and Philosophy*. Translated by Hugh Tomlinson. New York: Columbia University Press, 2006.

———. "On Four Poetic Formulas that might Summarize the Kantian Philosophy." In *Essays Critical and Clinical*. Translated by Daniel W. Smith and Michael A. Greco. Minneapolis: University of Minnesota Press, 1997.

———. *Spinoza: Practical Philosophy*. Translated by Robert Hurley. San Francisco: City Lights Books, 1988.

———. *Two Regimes of Madness: Texts and Interviews 1975–1995*. Translated by Ames Hodges and Mike Taormina. Edited by David Lapoujade. Cambridge, MA: Semiotexte, 2006.

Deleuze, Gilles, and Félix Guattari. *Anti-Oedipus: Capitalism and Schizophrenia*. Translated by Robert Hurley, Mark Seem, and Helen R. Lane. Minneapolis: University of Minnesota Press, 1983.

———. *A Thousand Plateaus: Capitalism and Schizophrenia*. Translated by Brian Massumi. Minneapolis: University of Minnesota Press, 1987.

———. *What Is Philosophy?*. Translated by Hugh Tomlinson and Graham Burchell. New York: Columbia University Press, 1994.

Deligiorgi, Katerina. *Kant and the Culture of Enlightenment*. Albany: State University of New York Press, 2005.

Dewey, John. "The Influence of Darwinism on Philosophy." In *Philosophy After Darwin: Classic and Contemporary Readings*, edited by Michael Ruse, 55–62. Princeton, NJ: Princeton University Press, 2009.

Donaldson, Ian. "Hierarchy and Ontological Dualism: Rethinking Gilles Deleuze's Nietzsche for Political Philosophy." *History of Political Thought* 23, no. 4 (2002): 654–69.

Dosse, François. *Gilles Deleuze and Félix Guattari: Intersecting Lives*. Translated by Deborah Glassman. New York: Columbia University Press, 2010.

Ellis, Elisabeth. *Kant's Politics: Provisional Theory for an Uncertain World*. New Haven, CT: Yale University Press, 2005.

———. *Provisional Politics: Kantian Arguments in Policy Context*. New Haven, CT: Yale University Press, 2008.

Esposito, John L. *The Future of Islam*. New York: Oxford University Press, 2010.

Euben, Roxanne L. *Enemy in the Mirror: Islamic Fundamentalism and the Limits of Modern Rationalism: A Work of Comparative Political Theory*. Princeton, NJ: Princeton University Press, 1999.

———. *Journeys to the Other Shore: Muslim and Western Travelers in Search of Knowledge*. Princeton, NJ: Princeton University Press, 2006.

———. "Making the World Safe for Compatibility." *Political Theory* 38, no. 3 (2010): 424–41.

———. "The New Manichaeans." *Theory & Event* 5, no. 4 (2001). http://muse .jhu.edu/login?auth=0&type=summary&url=/journals/theory_and_event/ v005/5.4euben.html.

Farrell, Patricia. "The Philosopher-Monkey: Learning and the Discordant Harmony of the Faculties." In *Thinking between Deleuze and Kant: A Strange Encounter*, edited by Edward Willatt and Matt Lee, 11–27. New York: Continuum, 2009.

Finlayson, James Gordon, and Fabian Freyenhagen, eds. *Habermas and Rawls: Disputing the Political*. New York: Routledge, 2010.

Firestone, Chris L., and Nathan Jacobs. *In Defense of Kant's Religion*. Bloomington: Indiana University Press, 2008.

Fischer, David Hackett. *Liberty and Freedom: A Visual History of America's Founding Ideas*. New York: Oxford University Press, 2005.

Flikschuh, Katrin. *Kant and Modern Political Philosophy*. Cambridge: Cambridge University Press, 2000.

Foucault, Michel. "The Art of Telling the Truth." In *Critique and Power: Recasting the Foucault/Habermas Debate*, edited by Michael Kelly, 139–48. Cambridge, MA: MIT Press, 1994.

———. *The Essential Foucault: Selections from Essential Works of Foucault, 1954– 1984*. Edited by Paul Rabinow and Nikolas S. Rose. New York: New Press, 2003.

———. *Language, Counter-Memory, Practice: Selected Essays and Interviews*. Ithaca, NY: Cornell University Press, 1977.

———. "Nietzsche, Genealogy, History." In *The Foucault Reader*, edited by Paul Rabinow, 76–100. New York: Pantheon Books, 1984.

———. "What is Critique?" In *The Essential Foucault: Selections from Essential Works of Foucault, 1954–1984*, edited by Paul Rabinow and Nikolas S. Rose, 263–78. New York: New Press, 2003.

———. "What is Enlightenment?" In *Ethics: Subjectivity and Truth*, edited by Paul Rabinow, 303–19. New York: New Press, 1997.

Foucault, Michel, and Jürgen Habermas. *Critique and Power: Recasting the Foucault/Habermas Debate*, edited by Michael Kelly. Cambridge, MA: MIT Press, 1994.

Fourest, Caroline. *Brother Tariq: The Doublespeak of Tariq Ramadan*. New York: Encounter Books, 2008.

Frank, Jason A. *Constituent Moments: Enacting the People in Postrevolutionary America*. Durham, NC: Duke University Press, 2010.

Fraser, Nancy. "Rethinking the Public Sphere." *Social Text* 25/26 (1990): 56–80.

Frazer, Michael L. *The Enlightenment of Sympathy: Justice and the Moral Sentiments in the Eighteenth Century and Today*. New York: Oxford University Press, 2010.

———. "John Rawls: Between Two Enlightenments." *Political Theory* 35, no. 6 (2007): 756–80.

Galston, William. "What Is Living and What Is Dead in Kant's Practical Philosophy?" In *Kant & Political Philosophy: The Contemporary Legacy*, edited by Ronald Beiner and William James Booth, 207–23. New Haven, CT: Yale University Press, 1993.

Gardner, Sebastian. *Routledge Philosophy Guidebook to Kant and the* Critique of Pure Reason. New York: Routledge, 1999.

Gay, Peter. *The Enlightenment: The Rise of Modern Paganism*. New York: Knopf, 1966.

Goldhagen, Daniel Jonah. *Hitler's Willing Executioners: Ordinary Germans and the Holocaust*. New York: Knopf, 1996.

González, Ana Marta. "John Rawls and the New Kantian Moral Theory." In *The Legacy of John Rawls*, edited by Thom Brooks and Fabian Freyenhagen, 152–76. New York: Continuum, 2005.

Groves, Christopher R. "Deleuze's Kant: Enlightenment and Education." *Philosophy Today* 45, no. 1 (2001): 77–94.

Guyer, Paul. *Kant on Freedom, Law, and Happiness*. New York: Cambridge University Press, 2000.

———. *Knowledge, Reason, and Taste: Kant's Response to Hume*. Princeton, NJ: Princeton University Press, 2008.

———. "Naturalizing Kant." In *Kant Verstehen / Understanding Kant*, edited by Dieter Schönecker and Thomas Zwenger, 59–84. Darmstadt, Ger.: Wissenschaftliche Buchgesellschaft, 2001.

Habermas, Jürgen. "Reconciliation Through the Public Use of Reason: Remarks on John Rawls's Political Liberalism," *Journal of Philosophy* 92, no. 3 (1995): 109–31.

———. *Postmetaphysical Thinking*. Translated by William Mark Hohengarten. Cambridge, MA: MIT Press, 1992.

Hardt, Michael. *Gilles Deleuze: An Apprenticeship in Philosophy*. Minneapolis: University of Minnesota Press, 1993.

Hashemi, Nader. *Islam, Secularism, and Liberal Democracy: Toward a Democratic Theory for Muslim Societies*. New York: Oxford University Press, 2009.

Hedrick, Todd. *Rawls and Habermas: Reason, Pluralism, and the Claims of Political Philosophy*. Stanford, CA: Stanford University Press, 2010.

Hegel, Georg Wilhelm Friedrich. *Early Theological Writings*. Translated by T. M. Knox. Chicago: University of Chicago Press, 1948.

Hendricks, Christina. "Foucault's Kantian Critique: Philosophy and the Present." *Philosophy and Social Criticism* 34, no. 4 (2008): 357–82.

Henrich, Dieter. "The Deduction of the Moral Law: The Reasons for the Obscurity of the Final Section of Kant's *Groundwork of the Metaphysics of Morals*." In *Kant's Groundwork of the Metaphysics of Morals: Critical Essays*, edited by Paul Guyer, 303–42. Lanham, MD: Rowman & Littlefield, 1998.

Henrich, Dieter, and Richard L. Velkley. *The Unity of Reason: Essays on Kant's Philosophy*. Cambridge, MA: Harvard University Press, 1994.

Himmelfarb, Gertrude. *The Roads to Modernity: The British, French, and American Enlightenments*. New York: Knopf, 2004.

Honig, Bonnie. *Political Theory and the Displacement of Politics*. Ithaca, NY: Cornell University Press, 1993.

Horkheimer, Max, and Theodor W. Adorno. *Dialectic of Enlightenment: Philosophical Fragments*. Translated by Edmund Jephcott. Edited by Gunzelin Schmid Noerr. Stanford, CA: Stanford University Press, 2002.

Hourani, Albert. *Arabic Thought in the Liberal Age, 1798–1939*. New York: Cambridge University Press, 1983.

Hume, David. *A Treatise of Human Nature*. Edited by David Fate Norton and Mary J. Norton. New York: Oxford University Press, 2000.

Hunter, Ian. *Rival Enlightenments: Civil and Metaphysical Philosophy in Early Modern Germany*. New York: Cambridge University Press, 2001.

Hunter, Shireen, ed. *Islam, Europe's Second Religion: The New Social, Cultural, and Political Landscape*. Westport, CT: Praeger, 2002.

Huntington, Samuel P. *The Clash of Civilizations and the Remaking of World Order*. New York: Touchstone, 1997.

Hutchings, Kimberly. *Kant, Critique and Politics*. New York: Routledge, 1996.

Israel, Jonathan. *Radical Enlightenment: Philosophy and the Making of Modernity, 1650–1750*. New York: Oxford University Press, 2001.

————. *A Revolution of the Mind: Radical Enlightenment and the Intellectual Origins of Modern Democracy.* Princeton, NJ: Princeton University Press, 2010.

Jamal, Arif A. "Moving Out of Kazanistan: Liberal Theory and Muslim Contexts." In *Muslim Societies and the Challenge of Secularization: An Interdisciplinary Approach,* edited by Gabriele Marranci, 83–98. Dordrecht: Springer, 2010.

Juergensmeyer, Mark. *Global Rebellion: Religious Challenges to the Secular State, from Christian Militias to Al Qaeda.* Berkeley: University of California Press, 2008.

Kalin, Ibrahim. "Does Islam Need Enlightenment?" *Today's Zaman,* August 27, 2009.

Kant, Immanuel. "An Answer to the Question: What is Enlightenment?" In *Practical Philosophy,* translated and edited by Mary J. Gregor, 11–22. New York: Cambridge University Press, 1996.

————. "An Answer to the Question: What is Enlightenment?" In *Toward Perpetual Peace and Other Writings on Politics, Peace, and History,* edited by Pauline Kleingeld, 12–23. New Haven, CT: Yale University Press, 2006.

————. "Anthropology from a Pragmatic Point of View." In *Anthropology, History, and Education,* edited by Günter Zöller and Robert B. Louden, 227–429. New York: Cambridge University Press, 2007.

————. "Conjectural Beginning of Human History." In *Anthropology, History, and Education,* edited by Günter Zöller and Robert B. Louden, 176–81. New York: Cambridge University Press, 2007.

————. *Critique of the Power of Judgment.* Translated by Paul Guyer and Eric Matthews. Edited by Paul Guyer. New York: Cambridge University Press, 2000.

————. "Critique of Practical Reason." In *Practical Philosophy,* translated and edited by Mary J. Gregor, 133–272. New York: Cambridge University Press, 1996.

————. *Groundwork for the Metaphysics of Morals.* Translated and edited by Allen W. Wood. New Haven: Yale University Press, 2002.

————. "Groundwork of the Metaphysics of Morals." In *Practical Philosophy,* translated and edited by Mary J. Gregor, 37–108. New York: Cambridge University Press, 1996.

————. *Lectures on Logic.* Translated and edited by J. Michael Young. New York: Cambridge University Press, 1992.

————. "Observations on the Feeling of the Beautiful and Sublime." In *Anthropology, History, and Education,* 18–62. New York: Cambridge University Press, 2007.

———. "On the Common Saying: This May Be True in Theory, but It Does Not Hold in Practice." In *Toward Perpetual Peace and Other Writings on Politics, Peace, and History*, edited by Pauline Kleingeld, 44–66. New Haven, CT: Yale University Press, 2006.

———. "Public Declaration Concerning Fichte's *Wissenschaftslehre*, August 7, 1799." In *Correspondence*, translated and edited by Arnulf Zweig, 559–60. New York: Cambridge University Press, 1999.

———. "Religion within the Boundaries of Mere Reason." In *Religion and Rational Theology*, translated and edited by Allen W. Wood and George Di Giovanni, 39–216. New York: Cambridge University Press, 1996.

———. "Toward Perpetual Peace." In *Toward Perpetual Peace and Other Writings on Politics, Peace, and History*, edited by Pauline Kleingeld, 67–109 New Haven, CT: Yale University Press, 2006.

———. "The Metaphysics of Morals." In *Practical Philosophy*, translated and edited by Mary J. Gregor, 353–602. New York: Cambridge University Press, 1996.

Kassab, Elizabeth Suzanne. *Contemporary Arab Thought: Cultural Critique in Comparative Perspective*. New York: Columbia University Press, 2010.

Katznelson, Ira. *Desolation and Enlightenment: Political Knowledge After Total War, Totalitarianism, and the Holocaust*. New York: Columbia University Press, 2003.

Keddie, Nikki R. *An Islamic Response to Imperialism: Political and Religious Writings of Sayyid Jamal Ad-Din "Al-Afghani."* Berkeley: University of California Press, 1983.

Kelly, George Armstrong. "Veils: The Poetics of John Rawls." *Journal of the History of Ideas* 57, no. 2 (1996): 343–64.

Kerslake, Christian. "Copernican Deleuzeanism." *Radical Philosophy: A Journal of Socialist and Feminist Philosophy* 114 (2002): 32–33.

———. *Deleuze and the Unconscious*. New York: Continuum, 2007.

———. "Deleuze, Kant, and the Question of Metacritique." *Southern Journal of Philosophy* 42, no. 4 (2004): 481–508.

———. *Immanence and the Vertigo of Philosophy: From Kant to Deleuze*. Edinburgh: Edinburgh University Press, 2009.

King, Stephen. *On Writing*. New York: Scribner, 2000.

Kitcher, Patricia. "Changing the Name of the Game: Kant's Cognitivism Versus Hume's Psychologism." In *Immanuel Kant's Prolegomena to any Future Metaphysics: In Focus*, edited by Beryl Logan, 178–218. New York: Routledge, 1996.

Klosko, George. "Political Constructivism in Rawls's Political Liberalism." *The American Political Science Review* 91, no. 3 (1997): 635–46.

Korsgaard, Christine M. *The Constitution of Agency: Essays on Practical Reason and Moral Psychology*. New York: Oxford University Press, 2008.

———. *Self-Constitution: Agency, Identity, and Integrity*. New York: Oxford University Press, 2009.

———. *The Sources of Normativity*, edited by Onora O'Neill. New York: Cambridge University Press, 1996.

Krause, Sharon R. *Civil Passions: Moral Sentiment and Democratic Deliberation*. Princeton, NJ: Princeton University Press, 2008.

Kuehn, Manfred. *Scottish Common Sense in Germany, 1768–1800: A Contribution to the History of Critical Philosophy*. Kingston, QC: McGill-Queen's University Press, 1987.

Lampert, Laurence. *Leo Strauss and Nietzsche*. Chicago: University of Chicago Press, 1996.

———. *Nietzsche's Task: An Interpretation of* Beyond Good and Evil. New Haven, CT: Yale University Press, 2001.

Larmore, Charles. *The Autonomy of Morality*. New York: Cambridge University Press, 2008.

———. "Behind the Veil." *The New Republic* 238, no. 3 (2008): 43–47.

———. "Political Liberalism." *Political Theory* 18, no. 3 (1990): 339–60.

———. "Reflection and Morality." *Social Philosophy and Policy* 27, no. 2 (2010): 1–28.

Laursen, John Christian. "The Subversive Kant: The Vocabulary of 'Public' and 'Publicity.'" In *What is Enlightenment?: Eighteenth-Century Answers and Twentieth-Century Questions*, edited by James Schmidt, 253–69. Berkeley: University of California Press, 1996.

LaVaque-Manty, Mika. "Dueling for Equality: Masculine Honor and the Modern Politics of Dignity." *Political Theory* 34, no. 6 (2006): 715–40.

———. "Kant's Children," *Social Theory and Practice* 32, no. 3 (July 2006).

Lefebvre, Alexandre. *The Image of Law: Deleuze, Bergson, Spinoza*. Stanford, CA: Stanford University Press, 2008.

Lipton, Peter. "Kant on Wheels." *Social Epistemology* 17, no. 2 (2003): 215–19.

Lorenz, Konrad. "Kant's Doctrine of the *A Priori* in the Light of Contemporary Biology." In *Philosophy After Darwin: Classic and Contemporary Readings*, edited by Michael Ruse, 231–47. Princeton, NJ: Princeton University Press, 2009.

Louden, Robert B. *The World We Want: How and Why the Ideals of the Enlightenment Still Elude Us*. New York: Oxford University Press, 2007.

Lynch, Marc. *Voices of the New Arab Public: Iraq, Al-Jazeera, and Middle East Politics Today*. New York: Columbia University Press, 2006.

MacIntyre, Alasdair. *After Virtue: A Study in Moral Theory*. South Bend, IN: University of Notre Dame Press, 1984.

Mackenzie, Iain. *The Idea of Pure Critique*. New York: Continuum, 2004.

Mahmood, Saba. "Religious Reason and Secular Affect: An Incommensurable Divide?" In *Is Critique Secular?: Blasphemy, Injury, and Free Speech*, edited by Talal Asad, 64–100. Berkeley: University of California Press, 2009.

———. "Secularism, Hermeneutics, and Empire: The Politics of Islamic Reformation." *Public Culture* 18, no. 2 (2006): 323–47.

Mandaville, Peter G. *Global Political Islam*. New York: Routledge, 2007.

———. "Sufis and Salafis: The Political Discourse of Transnational Islam." In *Remaking Muslim Politics: Pluralism, Contestation, Democratization*, edited by Robert W. Hefner, 302–25. Princeton, NJ: Princeton University Press, 2005.

Mansbridge, Jane. "Using Power, Fighting Power." *Constellations: An International Journal of Critical and Democratic Theory* 1, no. 1 (1994): 53–73.

March, Andrew F. *Islam and Liberal Citizenship: The Search for an Overlapping Consensus*. New York: Oxford University Press, 2009.

———. "The Post-Legal Ethics of Tariq Ramadan: Persuasion and Performance in *Radical Reform: Islamic Ethics and Liberation*." *Middle East Law & Governance* 2, no. 2 (2010): 253–73.

———. "Reading Tariq Ramadan: Political Liberalism, Islam, and 'Overlapping Consensus.'" *Ethics & International Affairs* 21, no. 4 (2007): 399–413.

Mawdudi, Abu'l-A'la. "The Islamic Law." In *Princeton Readings in Islamist Thought: Texts and Contexts from Al-Banna to Bin Laden*, edited by Roxanne Leslie Euben and Muhammad Qasim Zaman, 79–106. Princeton, NJ: Princeton University Press, 2009.

McMahon, Melissa. "Immanuel Kant." In *Deleuze's Philosophical Lineage*, edited by Graham Jones and Jon Roffe, 87–103. Edinburgh: Edinburgh University Press, 2009.

Meillassoux, Quentin. *After Finitude: An Essay on the Necessity of Contingency*. Translated by Ray Brassier. New York: Continuum, 2008.

Mendelsohn, Daniel. "Nailed!" *New York Review of Books* 51, no. 12 (2004): 43–46.

Mengue, Philippe. "The Absent People and the Void of Democracy." *Contemporary Political Theory* 4, no. 4 (2005): 386–499.

Michalson, Gordon E. *Kant and the Problem of God*. Malden, MA: Blackwell, 1999.

Mill, John Stuart. *On Liberty*. Edited by David Bromwich. New Haven, CT: Yale University Press, 2003.

Munzel, G. Felicitas. *Kant's Conception of Moral Character: The "Critical" Link of Morality, Anthropology, and Reflective Judgment*. Chicago: University of Chicago Press, 1999.

Murdoch, Iris. *The Sovereignty of Good*. New York: Schocken Books, 1970.

Muthu, Sankar. *Enlightenment Against Empire*. Princeton, NJ: Princeton University Press, 2003.

Nietzsche, Friedrich. *The Anti-Christ, Ecce Homo, Twilight of the Idols, and Other Writings*. Translated by Judith Norman. Edited by Aaron Ridley, Judith Norman. New York: Cambridge University Press, 2005.

———. *Beyond Good and Evil*. Translated by Judith Norman, edited by Rolf-Peter Horstmann, Judith Norman. New York: Cambridge University Press, 2002.

———. *The Gay Science: With a Prelude in Rhymes and an Appendix of Songs*. Translated by Walter Kaufmann. New York: Vintage Books, 1974.

———. *On the Genealogy of Morality*. Translated by Carol Diethe. Edited by Keith Ansell-Pearson. New York: Cambridge University Press, 2007.

———. *Philosophy and Truth: Selections from Nietzsche's Notebooks of the Early 1870's*. Edited by Daniel Breazeale. Amherst, MA: Humanity Books, 1979.

———. *Untimely Meditations*. Translated by R. J. Hollingdale. Edited by Daniel Breazeale. New York: Cambridge University Press, 1997.

———. *The Will to Power*. Translated by Walter Kaufmann and R. J. Hollingdale. New York: Vintage Books, 1968.

O'Neill, Onora. "Constructivism in Rawls and Kant." In *The Cambridge Companion to Rawls*, edited by Samuel Freeman, 347–67. New York: Cambridge University Press, 2003.

———. *Towards Justice and Virtue: A Constructive Account of Practical Reasoning*. New York: Cambridge University Press, 1996.

Parr, Adrian. *The Deleuze Dictionary*. New York: Columbia University Press, 2005.

Patton, Paul. *Deleuze and the Political*. New York: Routledge, 2000.

———. *Deleuzian Concepts: Philosophy, Colonization, Politics*. Stanford, CA: Stanford University Press, 2010.

———. "Foucault and Normative Political Philosophy." In *Foucault and Philosophy*, edited by Timothy O'Leary and Christopher Falzon, 204–21. Malden, MA: Wiley-Blackwell, 2010.

———. "Redescriptive Philosophy: Deleuze and Guattari's Critical Pragmatism." In *Micropolitics of Media Culture: Reading the Rhizomes of Deleuze and Guattari*, edited by Patricia Pisters, 29–42. Amsterdam: Amsterdam University Press, 2001.

Pippin, Robert B. *The Persistence of Subjectivity: On the Kantian Aftermath*. New York: Cambridge University Press, 2005.

Pogge, Thomas. "Is Kant's *Rechtslehre* a 'Comprehensive Liberalism?'" In *Kant's Metaphysics of Morals: Interpretative Essays*, edited by Mark Timmons, 133–58. New York: Oxford University Press, 2002.

————. *John Rawls*. Translated by Michelle Kosch. New York: Oxford University Press, 2007.

Protevi, John. *Political Affect: Connecting the Social and the Somatic*. Minneapolis: University of Minnesota Press, 2009.

————. *Political Physics: Deleuze, Derrida, and the Body Politic*. New York: Athlone Press, 2001.

Putnam, Hilary. "John Rawls, 21 February 1921–24 November 2002." *Proceedings of the American Philosophical Society* 149, no. 1 (2005): 113–17.

————. "Why Reason Can't Be Naturalized: Evolutionary Epistemology." In *Philosophy After Darwin: Classic and Contemporary Readings*, edited by Michael Ruse, 217–19. Princeton, NJ: Princeton University Press, 2009.

Putnam, Robert D., David E. Campbell, and Shaylyn Romney Garrett. *American Grace: How Religion Divides and Unites Us*. New York: Simon & Schuster, 2010.

Qutb, Sayyid. *Milestones*. Cedar Rapids, IA: Mother Mosque Foundation, 1995.

Rabinow, Paul. "Foucault's Untimely Struggle Toward a Form of Spirituality." *Theory, Culture & Society* 26, no. 6 (2009): 25–44.

Radcliffe, Elizabeth. "Kantian Tunes on a Humean Instrument: Why Hume is Not Really a Skeptic about Practical Reasoning." *Canadian Journal of Philosophy* 27, no. 2 (1997): 247–70.

Ramadan, Tariq. *Aux Sources Du Renouveau Musulman: D'Al-Afghani à Hassan Al-Banna, Un Siècle De Réformisme Islamique*. Paris: Bayard éditions/Centurion, 1998.

————. *Islam, the West and the Challenges of Modernity*. Leicester, UK: The Islamic Foundation, 2001.

————. *The Quest for Meaning: Developing a Philosophy of Pluralism*. New York: Allen Lane, 2010.

————. *Radical Reform: Islamic Ethics and Liberation*. New York: Oxford University Press, 2009.

————. *To Be a European Muslim*. Markfield, UK: Islamic Foundation, 1999.

————. *Western Muslims and the Future of Islam*. New York: Oxford University Press, 2004.

Rawls, John. *A Brief Inquiry into the Meaning of Sin and Faith: With "On My Religion."* Edited by Thomas Nagel. Cambridge, MA: Harvard University Press, 2009.

————. "*Commonweal* Interview with John Rawls." In *Collected Papers*, edited by Samuel Freeman, 616–22. Cambridge, MA: Harvard University Press, 1999.

————. "The Independence of Moral Theory." In *Collected Papers*, edited by Samuel Freeman, 286–302. Cambridge, MA: Harvard University Press, 1999.

———. *Justice as Fairness: A Restatement*. Edited by Erin Kelly. Cambridge, MA: Harvard University Press, 2001.

———. "Kantian Constructivism in Moral Theory." In *Collected Papers,* edited by Samuel Freeman, 303–58. Cambridge, MA: Harvard University Press, 1999.

———. *The Law of Peoples*. Cambridge, MA: Harvard University Press, 1999.

———. *Lectures on the History of Moral Philosophy*. Edited by Barbara Herman. Cambridge, MA: Harvard University Press, 2000.

———. *Lectures on the History of Political Philosophy*. Edited by Samuel Freeman. Cambridge, MA: Harvard University Press, 2007.

———. *Political Liberalism*. New York: Columbia University Press, 2005.

———. "Themes in Kant's Moral Philosophy." In *Collected Papers*, edited by Samuel Freeman, 497–528. Cambridge, MA: Harvard University Press, 1999.

———. *A Theory of Justice*. Cambridge, MA: Harvard University Press, 1971.

———. *A Theory of Justice, Revised Edition*. Cambridge, MA: Harvard University Press, 1999.

Redfield, Marc. *The Rhetoric of Terror: Reflections on 9/11 and the War on Terror*. New York: Fordham University Press, 2009.

Reggio, David. "The Deleuzian Legacy." *History of the Human Sciences* 20, no. 1 (2007): 145–60.

Ripstein, Arthur. *Force and Freedom: Kant's Legal and Political Philosophy*. Cambridge, MA: Harvard University Press, 2009.

Rockmore, Tom. *In Kant's Wake: Philosophy in the Twentieth Century*. Malden, MA: Blackwell, 2006.

———. *Kant and Idealism*. New Haven, CT: Yale University Press, 2007.

———. *On Constructivist Epistemology*. Lanham, MD: Rowman & Littlefield, 2005.

Roffe, Jon. "David Hume." In *Deleuze's Philosophical Lineage*, edited by Graham Jones and Jon Roffe, 67–86. Edinburgh: Edinburgh University Press, 2009.

Rorty, Richard. "Kant vs. Dewey: The Current Situation of Moral Philosophy." In *Philosophy as Cultural Politics*, 183–202. New York: Cambridge University Press, 2007.

———. "The Priority of Democracy to Philosophy." In *Objectivity, Relativism, and Truth*, 175–96. New York: Cambridge University Press, 1991.

Rossi, Philip. "Kant's Philosophy of Religion." In *The Stanford Encyclopedia of Philosophy*, edited by Edward N. Zalta, 2009. http://plato.stanford.edu/entries/kant-religion/.

Rostbøll, Christian F. "Autonomy, Respect, and Arrogance in the Danish Cartoon Controversy." *Political Theory* 37, no. 5 (2009): 623–48.

Rove, Karl. *Courage and Consequence: My Life as a Conservative in the Fight*. New York: Threshold, 2010.

Ruthven, Malise. *Historical Atlas of Islam*. Cambridge, MA: Harvard University Press, 2004.

Ryan, Alan. "Intellectual Courage." *Social Research* 71, no. 1 (2004): 13–28.

Sandel, Michael J. *Liberalism and the Limits of Justice*. New York: Cambridge University Press, 1998.

Satkunanandan, Shalini Pradeepa. "The Extraordinary Categorical Imperative." *Political Theory* 39, no. 1 (2011): 234–60

Saurette, Paul. *The Kantian Imperative: Humiliation, Common Sense, Politics*. Toronto: University of Toronto Press, 2005.

Schaefer, David Lewis. *Illiberal Justice: John Rawls Vs. the American Political Tradition*. Columbia: University of Missouri Press, 2007.

Schmidt, James. "Civility, Enlightenment, and Society: Conceptual Confusions and Kantian Remedies." *American Political Science Review* 92, no. 2 (1998): 419–27.

———. "Claiming the Enlightenment for the Left." *Government & Opposition* 42, no. 4 (2007): 626–32.

———. "Inventing the Enlightenment: Anti-Jacobins, British Hegelians, and the Oxford English Dictionary." *Journal of the History of Ideas* 64, no. 3 (2003): 421–43.

———. "What Enlightenment Project?" *Political Theory* 28, no. 6 (2000): 734–57.

Schmidt, James, and Thomas E. Wartenberg. "Foucault's Enlightenment: Critique, Revolution, and the Fashioning of the Self." In *Critique and Power: Recasting the Foucault/Habermas Debate*, edited by Michael Kelly, 139–48. Cambridge, MA: MIT Press, 1994, 283–14.

Schneewind, J. B. *Essays on the History of Moral Philosophy*. New York: Oxford University Press, 2010.

———. *The Invention of Autonomy: A History of Modern Moral Philosophy*. New York: Cambridge University Press, 1998.

Schulman, Alex. *The Secular Contract: On the Politics of Enlightenment*. New York: Continuum, 2011.

Schwartzman, Micah. "The Relevance of Locke's Religious Arguments for Toleration." *Political Theory* 33, no. 5 (2005): 678–705.

Schwarzenbach, Sibyl A. "Rawls, Hegel, and Communitarianism." *Political Theory* 19, no. 4 (1991): 539–71.

Scorza, Jason A. *Strong Liberalism: Habits of Mind for Democratic Citizenship*. Hanover, NH: University Press of New England, 2008.

Shaviro, Steven. *Without Criteria: Kant, Whitehead, Deleuze, and Aesthetics*. Cambridge, MA: MIT Press, 2009.

Shell, Susan Meld. *Kant and the Limits of Autonomy*. Cambridge, MA: Harvard University Press, 2009.

Smith, Daniel W. "Deleuze and the Liberal Tradition: Normativity, Freedom, and Judgment." *Economy and Society* 32, no. 2 (2003): 299–324.

———. "Deleuze, Kant, and the Theory of Immanent Ideas." In *Deleuze and Philosophy*, edited by Constantin V. Boundas, 43–61. Edinburgh: Edinburgh University Press, 2006.

———. "Deleuze's Theory of Sensation: Overcoming the Kantian Duality." In *Deleuze: A Critical Reader*, edited by Paul Patton, 29–56. Cambridge, MA: Blackwell, 1996.

———. "Inside Out: Guattari's Anti-Oedipus Papers." *Radical Philosophy: A Journal of Socialist and Feminist Philosophy* 140 (2006): 35–39.

Sniderman, Paul M., and Louk Hagendoorn. *When Ways of Life Collide: Multiculturalism and its Discontents in the Netherlands*. Princeton, NJ: Princeton University Press, 2007.

Spinoza, Benedictus de. *Theological-Political Treatise*. Translated by Jonathan I. Israel. New York: Cambridge University Press, 2007.

Strauss, Leo. *An Introduction to Political Philosophy: Ten Essays*. Edited by Hilail Gildin. Detroit, MI: Wayne State University Press, 1989.

Strawson, P. F. *The Bounds of Sense: An Essay on Kant's* Critique of Pure Reason. London: Routledge, 1966.

Tampio, Nicholas. "Assemblages and the Multitude: Deleuze, Hardt, Negri, and the Postmodern Left." *European Journal of Political Theory* 8, no. 3 (2009): 383–400.

———. "Constructing the Space of Testimony: Tariq Ramadan's Copernican Revolution." *Political Theory* 39, no. 5 (2011): 600–29.

———. "A Defense of Political Constructivism." *Contemporary Political Theory* 11, no. 3 (2012).

———. "Multiplicity." In *Encyclopedia of Political Theory*, edited by Mark Bevir, 911–12. Thousand Oaks, CA: Sage Publications, 2010.

———. "Rawls, Constructivism, and the Tragic." *H-Net: Humanities and Social Sciences* (2011). http://www.h-net.org/reviews/showrev.php?id=33740.

———. "Redefining Kant's Legacy." *Political Theory* 34, no. 6 (2006): 807–13.

Tasioulas, John. "From Utopia to Kazanistan: John Rawls and the Law of Peoples." *Oxford Journal of Legal Studies* 22, no. 2 (2002): 367–96.

Taylor, Charles. *Sources of the Self: The Making of the Modern Identity*. Cambridge, MA: Harvard University Press, 1989.

Taylor, Robert S. "Kantian Personal Autonomy." *Political Theory* 33, no. 5 (2005): 602–28.

———. *Reconstructing Rawls: The Kantian Foundations of Justice as Fairness*. University Park: Pennsylvania State University Press, 2011.

Telhami, Shibley. "Of Power and Compassion." In *The Philosophical Challenge of September 11*, edited by Tom Rockmore, Joseph Margolis and Armen Marsoobian, 71–80. Malden, MA: Blackwell, 2005.

Thoburn, Nicholas. "Vacuoles of Noncommunication." In *Deleuze and the Contemporary World*, edited by Ian Buchanan and Adrian Parr, 42–56. Edinburgh: Edinburgh University Press, 2006.

Timmons, Mark, ed. *Kant's* Metaphysics of Morals: *Interpretative Essays*. New York: Oxford University Press, 2002.

Walton, Douglas N. *Courage: A Philosophical Investigation*. Berkeley: University of California Press, 1985.

Watt, William Montgomery. *Islamic Creeds: A Selection*. Edinburgh: Edinburgh University Press, 1994.

Weithman, Paul. "John Rawls and the Task of Political Philosophy." *Review of Politics* 71, no. 1 (2009): 113–25.

White, Stephen K. *The Ethos of a Late-Modern Citizen*. Cambridge, MA: Harvard University Press, 2009.

———. *Sustaining Affirmation: The Strengths of Weak Ontology in Political Theory*. Princeton, NJ: Princeton University Press, 2000.

Widder, Nathan. *Reflections on Time and Politics*. University Park: Pennsylvania State University Press, 2008.

Willatt, Edward. *Kant, Deleuze and Architectonics*. New York: Continuum, 2010.

Willatt, Edward and Matt Lee. *Thinking Between Deleuze and Kant: A Strange Encounter*. New York: Continuum, 2009.

Williams, James. *Gilles Deleuze's 'Difference and Repetition': A Critical Introduction and Guide*. Edinburgh: Edinburgh University Press, 2003.

———. *The Transversal Thought of Gilles Deleuze: Encounters and Influences*. Manchester, UK: Clinamen Press, 2005.

Wilson, Peter H. "Dynasty, Constitution, and Confession: The Role of Religion in the Thirty Years War." *International History Review* 30, no. 3 (2008): 473–514.

———. *The Thirty Years War: Europe's Tragedy*. Cambridge, MA: Harvard University Press, 2009.

Wolff, Robert Paul. "Hume's Theory of Mental Activity." *Philosophical Review* 69, no. 3 (1960): 289–310.

Wolin, Sheldon S. *Politics and Vision: Continuity and Innovation in Western Political Thought*. Princeton, NJ: Princeton University Press, 2004.

———. "Political Theory as a Vocation." *The American Political Science Review* 63, no. 4 (1969): 1062–82.

Wood, Allen W. *Hegel's Ethical Thought*. New York: Cambridge University Press, 1990.

———. *Kant's Ethical Thought*. New York: Cambridge University Press, 1999.

———. *Kantian Ethics*. New York: Cambridge University Press, 2008.

———. "Philosophy: Enlightenment Apology, Enlightenment Critique." In *What Is Philosophy?*, edited by C. P. Ragland and Sarah Heidt, 196–210. New Haven, CT: Yale University Press, 2001.

———. "The Supreme Principle of Morality." In *The Cambridge Companion to Kant and Modern Philosophy*, edited by Paul Guyer, 342–80. New York: Cambridge University Press, 2006.

———. "What Is Kantian Ethics?" In *Groundwork for the Metaphysics of Morals*, translated and edited by Allen W. Wood, 157–81. New Haven, CT: Yale University Press, 2002.

Wright, Lawrence. *The Looming Tower: Al-Qaeda and the Road to 9/11*. New York: Knopf, 2006.

Yovel, Yirmiahu. *Kant and the Philosophy of History*. Princeton, NJ: Princeton University Press, 1980.

Zayani, Mohamed. "The Nietzschean Temptation: Gilles Deleuze and the Exuberance of Philosophy." *Comparative Literature Studies* 36, no. 4 (1999): 320–40.

Zhang, Wei. *What Is Enlightenment: Can China Answer Kant's Question?*. Albany: State University of New York Press, 2010.

Index

Roger Berkowitz, *The Gift of Science: Leibniz and the Modern Legal Tradition*

Jean-Luc Nancy, translated by Pascale-Anne Brault and Michael Naas, *The Truth of Democracy*

Drucilla Cornell and Kenneth Michael Panfilio, *Symbolic Forms for a New Humanity: Cultural and Racial Reconfigurations of Critical Theory*

Karl Shoemaker, *Sanctuary and Crime in the Middle Ages, 400–1500*

Michael J. Monahan, *The Creolizing Subject: Race, Reason, and the Politics of Purity*

Drucilla Cornell and Nyoko Muvangua (eds.), *uBuntu and the Law: African Ideals and Postapartheid Jurisprudence*

Nicholas Tampio, *Kantian Courage: Advancing the Enlightenment in Contemporary Political Theory*

Drucilla Cornell, Stu Woolman, Sam Fuller, Jason Brickhill, Michael Bishop, and Diana Dunbar (eds.), *The Dignity Jurisprudence of the Constitutional Court of South Africa: Cases and Materials, Volumes I & II*